UNCIVIL RIGHTS

Protecting and Preserving Your Job Rights

The Better Way of Resolving Conflicts at Work

FREDERICK T. GOLDER

Lyra Enterprises, Ltd.
Marblehead, Massachusetts

Uncivil Rights: Protecting and Preserving Your Job Rights

Published by
Lyra Enterprises, Ltd.
205 Pleasant Street, Marblehead, MA 01945 USA

"This publication is designed to provide accurate and authoritative information in regard to the subject matter covered. It is sold with the understanding that the publisher is not engaged in rendering legal, accounting, or other professional service." From a Declaration of Principles jointly adopted by a Committee of the American Bar Association and a Committee of Publishers.

The stories in this book are based on true facts, but the names and factual situations have been changed to protect the privacy of the parties.

Printed in the United States of America.

Library of Congress Cataloging-in-Publication Data
Golder, Frederick T., 1943–
Uncivil Rights: Protecting and Preserving Your Job Rights/by Frederick T. Golder.—1st ed.
    p.   cm.
    Includes bibliographical references and appendices.
  1. Employment Rights—United States. 2. Employment
Discrimination—United States: 3. Employment Rights—
United States—Law and Policy. I. Title
    ISBN: 1-58425-007-0 (paperback)

1 2 3 4 5 DE 03 02 01 00 99

To my wife Caron, and
our children Rachel, David, and Naomi,
and to my students in their efforts
to promote civil rights in the workplace and to resolve
employer-employee conflicts fairly.

ALSO BY PROFESSOR FREDERICK T. GOLDER

Labor and Employment Law: Compliance and Litigation
The West Group, 1998

Legal Compliance Checkups
Clark, Boardman, Callaghan, 1998, Labor and Employment
Law sections

Federal Employment Rights: Cases and Materials
Massachusetts School of Law, 1997

Employment Discrimination: Cases and Materials
Massachusetts School of Law, 1996

State Employment Rights: Cases and Materials
Massachusetts School of Law, 1993

Counseling Organizations in Labor and Employment Law
Suffolk University Law School, 1999

CONTENTS

PART I

Why Your Job Rights Are Not Working

INTRODUCTION

"Opinion is a flitting thing,

But truth outlasts the sun-

If then we cannot own them both-

Possess the oldest one."

Emily Dickinson

Everyone should know his or her employment rights, and everyone is entitled to a fair work environment. Millions of American workers lose their jobs every year. This may come as a surprise, but in 49 states, an employer can fire you for a good reason, a bad reason, or no reason at all. It may sound un-American, but that's the law in this country; your employer can one day decide he or she no longer wants you around. Some workers will be "downsized," "laid off," or "reorganized" out of their jobs. Thousands will be fired, with or without "cause." Some workers will be forced to resign because of intolerable working conditions. If you work for someone else—and most of us do—sooner or later either you or someone you love will lose his or her job. It is important to understand your rights and to know your options.

Suing your employer is a declaration of war. What chance do you have against a powerful and well-financed adversary? Even David, when he went to battle against Goliath, had a slingshot.

There are serious problems in the workplace and in the courts, and the laws designed to protect workers are failing.

The courtroom can be a very frightening and intimidating place, particularly when you have no idea what to expect. Knowing your rights and knowing what to expect will increase your chances of surviving.

Most people think of a lawsuit as a search for the truth. In reality, it is a complex set of rules, which must be followed, and where one misstep can lead to defeat. These rules are complicated and confusing to most people, including lawyers, often making it difficult to find the truth. As a trial lawyer, I often think of these words from Dante's *Inferno* when I enter a courtroom: "Abandon all hope, ye who enter here." It is said that the law and justice are distant cousins. Frequently, they are not even related.

There are numerous minefields to cross before an employee can win his or her lawsuit. The legal system is designed so that even one misstep can prevent you from prevailing. Step on one mine, your case explodes, and you get nothing but shattered pieces. Losing your job can be devastating. Losing your case in court can be even more devastating after spending thousands of dollars you cannot afford, not to mention the emotional trauma and wasted years. There are serious problems in the workplace and in the courts, but they can be fixed, and everyone can benefit.

There are a number of ways of resolving disputes in the workplace. The most expensive, time-consuming, and least-effective method is a lawsuit. It is important for employers and employees to realize that they share mutual interests. All employers should foster an environment that respects and values their employees. The cooperation between the employer and its employees benefits the organization.

Employees are generally the most important part of any organization. Employers who recognize this will have an organization that works for everyone. Employees who are valued and respected in the organization are more likely to exert a positive effort that can only benefit the organization.

Providing a framework where both the employer and the employee win is a higher form of dispute resolution then the lawsuit where one side wins and one side loses. In reality, both sides usually lose in a lawsuit in terms of wasted time and money. Even when the employer wins a lawsuit, in addition to the high cost of litigation, key personnel are taken away from their normal jobs to deal with the preparation and defense of the lawsuit.

For many people, their job is the single most important aspect of their lives. Our job provides the means for us to obtain the necessities of life and, hopefully, some financial security. That job supports our dreams of having families, homes, education, entertainment, and hobbies. Most of us rely on the job to provide health insurance, disability coverage, and manage pension contributions for our retirement. Friends and social connections at the workplace become important to us. Our work also provides us with self-esteem and self-worth. When you meet someone for the first time, the first question you usually ask is, "What do you do?" For many of us, our job defines who we are.

Not surprisingly, then, losing our job is a devastating event in our lives. Maybe we've just started with the company, but we need the income to support our family. Maybe we have devoted fifteen or thirty years to our job, and then new management comes in and tells us that we are no longer needed.

The financial, social, and interpersonal losses might be more tangible, but the psychological impact could take the heaviest toll on you if you are not careful. Losing your job arouses feelings of helplessness, shame, guilt, anger, and a loss of identity. It can make you doubt your abilities, or lead to isolation as you avoid loved ones and friends. The stress affects both your mind and your body, making it harder to make decisions or rise above growing depression.

In my experience, the loss of a job triggers four major stages of the grieving process: shock, depression, anger, and acceptance. Tom's case comes to mind as a good example of the shock stage.* For one week after he was let go, Tom continued to go to the job site and walk around the building from eight o'clock in the morning until five o'clock at night. Then he went home to his wife and family as usual. Over the weekend, Tom was finally able to tell his wife what had happened, and together they began to deal with the reality of his lost job.

Workers usually seem to get over this shock stage fairly quickly, but then they get stuck in the second stage, depression. When Paul lost his job, he became so depressed that he rarely left his bed for the next five years. For the balance of her life, Connie was unable to bring herself to even look for another job. Many people become suicidal during this stage, especially if they are isolated or lack a support network. As a society, we need to be more sensitive to the pain that comes with the loss of a job. We support each other when a loved one dies, but often neglect work-related grief experiences.

In the third stage, the former employee is angry and wants to get even with the employer for causing such grief. In the extreme, we know that some fired workers return to their workplaces and kill their former bosses and colleagues. I had one client who had a recurring nightmare of going into work, killing all his supervisors, and then killing himself.

Fortunately, this outcome is rare. But for those individuals, who do get stuck in this anger phase, the consequences for themselves and their family can be tragic. Some develop what I call "litigation psychosis." Their whole life revolves around their lawsuit and plans to get even with their former employer and all of

---

*All names used in the cases are fictitious although each is based on real cases. When specific case law is cited, the individuals' real names are used.

the people who had anything to do with their firing. Attention is focused on the past, rather than on the present and the future. Getting stuck in the anger stage leaves you feeling bitter, helpless, and frustrated.

With time and the proper support, people can move beyond the shock, depression, and anger into the acceptance stage. Each of us has to get to the fourth stage to remain healthy and productive, and to make the decisions necessary for our own well-being. At the acceptance stage, they can move on with their lives and make a fruitful search for another job. Once settled in with the new job, many experience relief at being out of the precarious or previous hostile work environment. From this rational perspective, they can decide if they have the energy, patience, stamina, resources, and support to file a claim against their former employer.

Litigation is costly, time consuming, and, very often, disappointing. The worker needs to be emotionally prepared for this battle. The employer has to understand the ramifications of using litigation as a way of resolving workplace disputes. The employer may know the cost of defending the claim in court by looking at the monthly bills. But that is only a small part of the cost. A lawsuit may affect worker morale and decrease worker productivity. Valuable time of key personnel may be wasted in dealing with the lawsuit causing these key workers to leave. One lawsuit may spur other lawsuits by disgruntled workers. While most employers win in court, they really end up losing. The better way of resolving workplace disputes will benefit all of us.

Given that most of us would rather continue our current employment as loyal and well-compensated employees, preferably in a positive and affirming work environment, one major focus of this book will be to coach you in how to assert your rights and keep your job while doing so. If your employer makes promises and then fails to deliver, or discriminates against you in violation of the law, then this book will walk you through your options. Keep in mind that our first goal is to have you be fairly treated in your current employment situation, so a prudent employee should learn his or her rights—and how to protect those rights on a daily basis. This book will help you do just that. Then, if things start to unravel, or if you find yourself being shown the door, the book will coach you in the process of asserting your rights in an effective and timely way.

One last point before we get started: I really care about employee rights, and I want to inform you not only about your rights, but how to assert them in a timely and effective manner. This book is an educational tool, however, and is not intended to replace competent, professional legal advice. State laws and procedures differ across the country. New judicial decisions that could affect your rights are being decided every day. Also, each employment case hinges on a few major factors, such as union membership, the existence of a contract or employee handbook, other written documentation or evaluations, tenure or seniority rights, the employer's history of business practices, and how you behaved during the stress of your employment difficulties.

When something goes wrong at work, get professional help immediately! Don't wait for things to get worse. You may decide not to take action at that time, but you must provide yourself with every advantage by knowing your rights and the deadlines that could cause you to lose significant rights if you delay.

Also, it is important to know that most attorneys are not well versed in employment law. Be sure that your legal advisor specializes in this area of legal practice, preferably almost exclusively. Employment law is complicated and involves a variety of federal and state claims and agencies. One "simple" case, for example, may require a choice of filing under federal or state laws or with federal and state agencies simultaneously, plus an independent application for relief under a workers' compensation law, unemployment compensation, litigation for damage to your reputation, or for breach of contract. This book can help you find resources and to assert your rights, but please do not rely on it solely. My intent is that you can learn from other people's mistakes as I help you understand your employment rights. But don't make the big mistake of taking on your employer without competent, specialized legal guidance:

As you read this book, you may have comments or questions that come to mind. I want to hear from you. Since this is my passion, the odds are excellent that I will be updating this book in the years ahead. Learning is a lifelong process and teaching is an art, so I welcome your insights and suggestions. I cannot dispense legal advice, and I may not be able to respond personally to all of your correspondence. But I will take your ideas to heart in any future update of *Uncivil Rights*. You may write to me at: Ftgolder@aol.com

Thank you, and best wishes,
Fred Golder

CHAPTER 1

What's Wrong with Our Courts?

"It is revolting to have no better reason for a rule of law than that so it was laid down in the time of Henry IV. It is still more revolting if the grounds upon which it was laid down have vanished long since, and the rule simply persists from blind imitation of the past."

Justice Holmes

The Path of the Law, 10 *Harv.L.Rev.* 457, 469 (Jan. 8, 1897).

The quality of justice depends upon the quality of the parties involved in the **dispute*** resolution system. Whether it is the judge, the attorneys, you, jury members, mediators, arbitrators, agency personnel, and/or witnesses, justice depends on the abilities of every single individual involved in the case. Essentially, justice depends on people—and people are fallible.

THE SEARCH FOR THE TRUTH

Each of us has our own unique mental filtering system that gives us our perspective on the world. It starts with our genetic makeup and personality and is expanded by our life experiences. We grow up in families, communities, and within a geographic location that influences our value system and opinions. While many of these values and opinions may be noble and compassionate, our filtering system also may include conscious and subconscious biases and prejudices.

Our filtering system is so ingrained in us that we think everyone sees the world the same way that we see it. Unfortunately, that is not so. Many of our beliefs are so deeply held that we may think of them as facts rather than opinions. Our opinions may be based on facts, prejudice, incomplete **evidence,** no evidence, a book that influenced us, or just a feeling. The arena of employment

---

*All bold terms found throughout this book are defined in A Survivor's Guide to Legal Terms, starting on page 169.

disputes usually is cluttered with individual perspectives that consciously or unconsciously cause harm to others.

If a person believes that women belong in the home raising children, he or she may think of this as a profound good for families, individuals, and society. This belief may harm individual women job candidates by helping the employer rationalize the process of favoring a male applicant or by promoting a male employee. Similarly, our society has some long-held beliefs about the inherent inferiority of certain ethnic groups or the dangers of homosexuality. Since these beliefs are so ingrained in our society and us, we tend to look for information that confirms this information as fact. If we do encounter a person or experience that challenges our belief system, often we view that person or experience as an anomaly rather than rethink this aspect of our belief system.

In the employment arena, individuals have tremendous power over the welfare of others. Employers and their agents can hire, fire, promote, reward, excuse, harass, assure, and/or abuse each employee. While this is power enough for most of us, the bottom line is that the employer's actions affect the very quality of life for that employee and his or her family. Worries about unemployment, lack of money, lack of health insurance, plant closings, **sexual harassment, discrimination,** unfair promotions, verbal abuse, embarrassment, or health concerns have severe tangible and emotional consequences.

Overt forms of discrimination and bias are easy to see. Unconscious or subconscious biases are much harder to address. The results may be the same, but intentional bias is much harder to prove or to correct. Our legal system recognizes this complexity by permitting individuals to claim actual harm and/or a pattern of behavior that harms individuals like the aggrieved party. If an employer has few or no members of a protected group in its management ranks, yet has turned down applicants or refused promotion to current employees who are members of that protected group and believe they meet the qualifications, this information can be used against the employer.

Employment disputes are very difficult cases, since so much is riding on your specific qualifications and conduct in relation to the myriad options the employer has, such as job descriptions, qualification requirements, performance evaluations, salaries, promotions, terminations, personalities, and the **employment-at-will** doctrine. While employers like to argue that these factors are objectively determined, the reality is that most are based upon subjective values and opinions. Unchecked, this system has not worked too well. That's why the federal government and state governments have passed antidiscrimination laws over the past thirty years. It also is why labor unions and special interest law foundations have formed—to collectively combat the historically almost unchecked powers of employers.

THE PROBLEM WITH LAWYERS

Having talked about individuality and bias in relation to our flawed employment dispute system, let's look briefly at another character in the mix—lawyers. Not all lawyers are the same, and many lawyers specialize in particular areas of law. The American Bar Association has more than thirty areas of specialization for lawyers. The National Employment Lawyers Association, a national group of lawyers advocating for employee rights, recognizes more than ten categories of specialization in the employment field.

Many lawyers know very little about labor and employment law. In addition, our legal system is profoundly complex. To complicate it further, aspects of each area of law can change any day, as a legislative body or a judge makes a decision that affects employment issues. So, you want a lawyer who knows and understands the complex legal system and the specialty of employment law.

Since these cases can be very expensive and time-consuming with uncertain results, many lawyers will not take these cases without being paid as the case progresses. It is difficult to pay $150 to $300 an hour for a lawyer's time when you cannot afford to pay for groceries.

Some lawyers will take these cases on a **contingent fee** basis, which means you don't have to pay any attorney's fee unless you win. Unfortunately, finding a competent lawyer to take your case on a contingent fee basis is very difficult for a number of reasons. The lawyer may have to wait three or more years before getting paid. It is not unusual for a lawyer to invest hundreds of hours of time and lose after years of waiting because most workers lose their cases in court.

Most experienced and knowledgeable employee lawyers will only take the best cases, the ones that are likely to generate large damage awards. Lawyers may also take cases that appeal to them for a variety of reasons. I only take cases where I like the person and the person's cause.

THE PROBLEM WITH JUDGES

A judge is nothing more than a lawyer with political connections. Judges are selected or elected on the basis of these political connections, not because of their intelligence, experience, compassion, or even legal knowledge. Very few judges have any in-depth knowledge of labor and employment law because most have practiced in other areas of law, such as criminal, corporate, or domestic relations law, prior to becoming a judge.

Many judges may have little knowledge or understanding of working people. They graduated from college, went to law school, and then went to work in a large law firm. Many came from a world of money and political connections that had created its wealth and power at the expense of workers. In those large firms they most often represented the interests of the employer or corporate shareholders. All too often, then, their view of employment disputes favored the employer over the employees.

Consider, too, that a judge will have the same biases she or he held before becoming a judge. A narrow-minded, arrogant lawyer will be a narrow-minded, arrogant judge. The only difference is that she or he now has the power to make decisions that affect other people's lives. A judge has the power to make decisions, not necessarily the wisdom to decide them fairly and justly. In fact, given the requirement of close ties to political influence in order to be appointed or elected a judge, often their very selection depends upon the perception that this individual will champion the view of his or her supporters.

Many people think that the law is black and white, an absolute changed only by legislation. Such is not the case. Regardless of the guidelines of the written law, a judge holds the power to exclude evidence, grant **motions,** distinguish certain facts or issues as more or less significant, limit testimony, and convey support or disdain. In the end, a judge can avoid a decision, find fault with the employee that mitigates the employer's liability, or rule in favor of the employee. Even if you win, however, the judge can then refuse to grant you reinstatement in your job, or fail to award you significant monetary damages and legal fees or punitive damages. In addition, a case can take years to complete, can be very expensive, and can exact high emotional cost.

I once argued an **appeal** before a three-judge panel in the Federal Court of Appeals in Boston. One of the judges on that panel is now a Supreme Court Justice. The case involved a worker who was wrongfully discharged because of his age and race. None of the judges seemed to understand the nature of my arguments about age and race discrimination, and we lost. As I was walking out of the courtroom, a janitor who had been listening to my case said, "Boy that guy really got shafted, didn't he?" I thought to myself, "Why wasn't he deciding my client's case instead of those three 'learned' judges?"

Employment cases are difficult to win. Often, one individual who has lost his or her job is fighting against a large business that can afford countless legal fees. Plus, it is not hard for employers to create legitimate reasons for your termination even if those reasons were not the true basis for dismissal. It's not hard for an employer to create documentation to support its actions, and the corporate attorney will help them create excuses to justify the employer's actions.

Similarly, your colleagues may be afraid that if they offer information against the employer, they may lose their jobs. So, at your expense, they remain silent or assist with the employer's case.

In one case involving sex discrimination, for example, an employee was told what to say in her upcoming **deposition.**[1] If she made the company look good, her reward would be a promotion. Instead, she told the truth. As soon as her employer learned that she had not followed orders, she was fired. In another case, an employee was told to lie at an **arbitration** hearing. She did and within a year she received a promotion she had been trying to get for six years. Unfortunately, that's how some people get ahead in the world, and their belief system helps them rationalize such conduct.

Since many judges have never had these negative work experiences, they may not understand the problems. Similarly, they may not understand the almost insurmountable obstacles the average worker must overcome to succeed in a claim against his or her employer. Logic would suggest that if an employee is valuable and doing a good job, then an employer would have no interest in discriminating or harassing that individual. It would be nice if things were that straightforward.

Compounding all of this is the fact that judges often have an enormous workload. The faster they can get through a case and make a decision, the better—right? Plus, judges often seem to get frustrated and annoyed by the legal process and express hostility towards the attorneys and their clients. Some judges think their most important job is to manage their caseloads. The quicker they depose of a case the better. No one can argue that cases should be handled in a quick and efficient way, but never at the expense of justice. The judge's prime role is to provide a fair process where the outcome will be a just result. Any judge who does not strive to be just and fair should not be sitting as a judge. Unfortunately, a bad experience can go a long way in convincing you that litigation is not the path to humane dispute resolution.

Governors in some states appoint judges. In some states, judges are elected by popular vote of the general public, and in some states, governors appoint judges who can be removed from office by vote in a general election. The president with the advice and consent of the senate appoints federal judges. All of these are political processes and do not ensure that we will get the best judges. There is a better way.

If you want to know the best doctors, ask the doctors. If you want to know the best lawyers, ask the lawyers. I have tried hundreds of cases and have used the courts for many years. I can tell you who the best lawyers are in my state. If the lawyers who use the courts select the judges, the quality of our judges will improve dramatically. The lawyers who use the courts will want to pick only the best judges.

Just as workers have evaluations for feedback, judges need to be evaluated on an annual basis in order to get feedback to improve the quality of their judging. Educational programs should be offered to improve any shortcomings.

If the judges fail to meet certain standards, the lawyers who selected them should be allowed to remove them by voting. If a worker fails to perform to standards and is given an opportunity to improve and fails to improve, the worker may be discharged for poor performance. If a worker commits an act of misconduct, the worker can be fired. Why shouldn't the same rules apply to judges? Why should judges be selected for life regardless of their performance or conduct?

The system of selecting judges can be improved. Let's not complain about the quality of our judges. Let us work to making the selection process better.

WHY THE LAWS AREN'T WORKING

The antidiscrimination laws passed by state legislatures and the federal government have not eliminated discrimination in the work place. Few people are successful in claims brought against employers. Why aren't the laws working?

The first major civil rights law was the **Civil Rights Act of 1964.** Title VII of this act made it unlawful for employers to discriminate against people because of their race, color, sex, national origin, or religion. The act did not provide for a right to a jury trial, however, and cases were tried before judges. Almost all the judges were white males who had benefited from our discriminatory society. In 1991, the Civil Rights Act was amended to provide for jury trials.

The federal **Age Discrimination in Employment Act** (ADEA) of 1967 made it unlawful to discriminate against people forty years of age or older. It did not provide a right to a jury trial until it was amended in 1978.

Even with the rather recent right to a jury trial, individuals facing discrimination encounter other obstacles. You must find a lawyer who specializes in employment disputes and is willing to take your case for a fee you can afford. Since these cases are so time consuming and difficult to win, many lawyers will ask for substantial retainers and will not take the cases on a strict contingency basis. (If a case is taken on a contingency basis, the client does not have to pay a fee unless the client wins.)

Furthermore, most employees lose their **lawsuits.** Federal sexual harassment laws permitted only the recovery of back wages, until 1991.[2] You may have suffered egregious harassment, but filing a discrimination claim would not begin to compensate you even if you won. Certainly no mechanism existed to force the employer to behave differently and to permit you to continue in your job without the threat of further retaliation. All in all, it was easier to find another job or to quietly bear the hardship of your existing employment. Similarly, many people with disabilities had no protection against discrimination until 1992, when the **Americans with Disabilities Act** of 1990 took effect.[3]

Unfortunately, our judicial system seems designed to maintain the *status quo.* People subjected to discrimination often are people without jobs or money who are trying to fight against rich and powerful corporations with unlimited time and resources. Most state agencies that regulate these laws are severely underfunded and understaffed; so in reality they have very little impact on eliminating discrimination. A January 1999 *Boston Globe* article about the Massachusetts Commission Against Discrimination (MCAD) found that the agency was facing its worst case backlog in history, with more than 9,000 complaints going unattended.[4] Each of its 22 investigators was assigned between 200 and 400 cases per year. One prominent local attorney declared that the agency was "barely functioning." I sit on the Advisory Board to the MCAD, and I know firsthand that it is severely underfunded and understaffed.

The federal **Equal Employment Opportunity Commission** (EEOC), likewise, is severely underfunded and understaffed. The EEOC is not in a position to do very much in the way of enforcing the laws or preventing discrimination. Sometimes, the leadership of these agencies may not encourage or even allow the staff to vigorously pursue certain kinds of cases. Many experts believe that when Supreme Court Justice Clarence Thomas presided over the EEOC in the 1980s, he influenced the agency to pursue few sexual harassment cases than in its prior history. Certainly, it was under Thomas' leadership, when one of the most significant sexual harassment cases ever argued came before the United States Supreme Court, that the EEOC filed a "friend of the court" **brief** urging the Court to limit the employer's liability.[5]

What you may not realize is that in order to pursue your rights under many state and federal laws, particularly in the area of employment discrimination, you must file a claim with a state agency (like the MCAD) or the federal EEOC in a timely fashion. In theory, these agencies are intended to provide fast, low-cost, and fair resolutions for both employers and employees. In reality, unless your case has high profile qualities—you are an athlete on a major league team, for example—your case may never surface for consideration. Once the statutory time period passes, you must remove your case from the state or federal agency and file a lawsuit in court. This process is tremendously expensive and time consuming.

Court actions can take three years or longer to resolve. Cases can be delayed, appealed, retried, and appealed again. Witnesses disappear, memories fade, legal fees mount up, and many employees get worn out and financially drained until they give up.

I am painting a bleak picture, and it deserves to be portrayed as such. Our legal system is not working as well as it could, either for the employer or the employee, in terms of resolving disputes and employment discrimination. What is most difficult for me is knowing that, on the undisputed facts and law, a client should prevail in a case but that a judge and jury can decide the case contrary to the true facts, and there is very little that can be done about this injustice.

While there are other alternatives to a lawsuit, such as mediation and arbitration, these methods have their own set of problems.

Although employers win many of these lawsuits, employees win enough of these cases to cause more than 75 percent of the cases to be settled before trial. The employer is well aware of the risk of trying a case to a jury. This is why the right to a jury trial is so vital to employees. It helps level the playing field.

A better outcome would be to keep your dispute from escalating to the extreme where you are out of a job or having to endure ongoing harassment and discrimination. Part II of this book will offer you tips on preserving your job, your sanity, and your money!

CHAPTER 2

"The enslaved African race were not intended to be included, and form no part of the people who framed and adopted the Declaration of Independence. The men who framed this Declaration were great men—high in literary acquirements—high in their sense of honor, and incapable of asserting principals inconsistent with those on which they were acting. They perfectly understood the meaning of the language they used, and how it would be understood by others; and they knew that it would not in any part of the civilized world be supposed to embrace the Negro race, which, by common consent, had been excluded by civilized Governments and the family of nations, and doomed to slavery ... the unhappy black race were separated by the whites by indelible marks, and laws long before established, and were never thought of or spoken of except as property, and when the claims of the owner of the profit of the trader was supposed to need protection."

Justice Curtis,
Dred Scott v. Sanford, 19 How. 393 (1857).

HOW OUR HISTORY AFFECTS US

A brief look at American history reveals much about why the judicial system does not champion the rights of the average worker. In essence, we have had a love/hate relationship in the law, with love and support being granted to land and business owners and hate reserved for workers who were deemed unruly, unskilled, and dispensable. Whether it was Master/Servant, Master/Slave, Mill

Owner/Immigrant, or Industrialist/Union Organizers, the American legal system has favored the entitled and the influential at the expense of the disenfranchised masses of unskilled workers. For example, to fuel the early economy of this country, thousands of people from African nations were imported as slaves. These African people were bought, sold, and traded as property. The **motive** was profit. In most instances, domestic animals were treated with more concern than the African slaves. With the outcome of the Civil War, American society had to begin to confront its labor problem. The rich were getting richer, and a huge class of poor, landless workers faced appalling conditions in their workplaces. As the industrial complex expanded, children, women, and immigrants were added to the pool of exploited workers.

The *Declaration of Independence,* signed on July 4, 1776, was written by and for white men who considered women, children, immigrants, and non-whites as inferior beings in need of supervision and restraints. The statement, "... all men are created equal ..." in the Declaration referred specifically to white men who held property and thus had political and economic power. This intentionally disenfranchised the majority of the population who not only were deemed to be in need of guidance, but maybe more significantly for our purposes, were viewed as having beliefs and work habits that were hostile to the interests of their employers/owners.

An interesting constellation of social, religious, and economic theories helped to justify the absolute authority of employers. For example, Darwinian theory held that rich and powerful men were the fittest in a given society and that they had a natural or earned entitlement to their assets and authority. Similarly, the Protestant ethic inculcated in the American educational system urged girls, immigrants, and non-whites to accept their lot in life, to not covet the lifestyle of their superiors, and to work diligently no matter how menial and unrewarding their life was on this earth. Each individual's real reward would come in the next world if one was obedient, trustworthy, hardworking, and not covetous of another's wealth or power.

It is an embarrassing comment on our American social and legal history that we still are struggling to actualize the phrase "all people are created equal." It took a Civil War and the Thirteenth Amendment to the U. S. **Constitution** to put an official end to slavery, but variations of racial discrimination exist today. Women did not obtain the right to vote in federal elections until 1920. Recent labor statistics report that women earn 76 percent of what their male counterparts earn while performing the same job functions, plus women face a "glass ceiling" in terms of limited promotions to the highest levels of management and authority.* Employers have exploited even white male workers. First attempts to improve their working conditions did not come from government, but came from labor unions, which could finally leverage some collective political clout. Idealists like Samuel Gompers pressed employers and the government to improve intolerable working conditions. Finally, in 1914, the Clayton Act was passed as the first piece of federal legislation for employees. The Clayton Act mandated that workers could form labor unions. Federal and state courts resisted attempts by workers to organize for their mutual aid and protection, and frequently struck down laws that favored employees at the expense of employers. With the Great Depression of 1929, however, and its widespread unemployment, bread lines, homelessness, and poverty, laws were passed to protect workers from employer abuse.

The **Fair Labor Standards Act** ensuring minimum wages and providing for overtime pay after 48 hours (now reduced to 40 hours) and restricting work by children was not passed until 1934. The U.S. Supreme Court upheld this law in 1937. The **National Labor Relations Act** protecting the right of workers to form labor unions was not passed until 1935. The U.S. Supreme Court upheld this law in 1937. As this brief history demonstrates, although the right to work is considered one of the most fundamental a person can possess, for most of this country's history the right to work in a fair and safe environment did not exist for many Americans.

WHAT ARE YOUR RIGHTS?

The traditional common-law view of the employment relationship developed in the nineteenth century.[1] As courts began to apply **contract** rules to define the terms and conditions of the employment relationship, a presumption developed in favor of construing all contracts for employment for an indefinite period to be terminable at will.[2]

Under the so-called at-will rule, either the employer or the worker were free to terminate the employment relationship without notice and without cause.[3] Under this rule an employer could fire an at-will employee "for good cause, for no cause, or even for cause morally wrong without liability."[4]

In applying the rule, courts gave employers virtually unlimited freedom to discharge their workers. For example, courts refused to grant relief to employees terminated for serving on juries,[5] for filing a lawsuit against a business

---

* U.S. Dept. of Labor, Bureau of Labor Statistics, Report No. 928.

owned by an employer,[6] for testifying adversely to an employer's interests in an administrative proceeding,[7] and for missing work as the result of a job-related injury.[8] Furthermore, the at-will rule precluded employees from asserting any claim to job security. Consequently, one court approved the termination, one year prior to his scheduled retirement, of an employee with forty-five years of satisfactory service, holding that the at-will rule precluded the employee from asserting any claim against his employer arising from that termination.[9]

There are exceptions to this employment-at-will rule that have developed over time, and they form the basis for discussion in this book. In Part II of this book, I will discuss your remedies for violations of your rights, but in this section I would like to outline areas of the law or arguments that you can assert to overcome the employment-at-will doctrine. Three broad categories of employee rights have developed: (1) protections against some forms of discrimination, (2) protections related to constitutional rights, and (3) other protections related to fair treatment.

DISCRIMINATING EMPLOYERS

There were few exceptions to the employment-at-will doctrine in American law until the early 1960s. Then, in light of the extreme segregation of the races and related unfair labor practices, state and federal officials began to consider remedial legislation. The civil rights movement of the 1950s and 1960s created the momentum that led to the passage of Title VII of the Civil Rights Act of 1964. This legislation prohibited employment discrimination on the basis of race, color, sex, national origin, and religion. Title VII seems like a wonderful example of federal legislators responding to the phrase "all people are created equal," but this was not the situation. With the assassination of President John F. Kennedy, and President Lyndon B. Johnson's commitment to racial equality, it was clear to all that legislation prohibiting discrimination on the basis of race was likely to pass in the U.S. Congress in 1964. In a last-minute effort to defeat this act, conservative Southern congressmen inserted the category "sex" into the bill, hoping that their colleagues would defeat the legislation rather than permit equality in employment for women too. The act passed anyway. It is sobering to realize in terms of our discussions of human rights and employee entitlements that this major addition of gender-related employment protections came about as a political miscalculation and not as a public commitment to gender equity in the workplace.

Since 1964, the U.S. Congress has been willing to expand employment entitlements to some other mistreated groups. For example, The **Age Discrimination in Employment Act** (ADEA) of 1967 prohibited discrimination on the
basis of age. The Americans with Disabilities Act (ADA) of 1990 prohibited discrimination on the basis of disability. The Equal Rights Amendment of 1973,
prohibiting discrimination on the basis of sex, failed to pass. This means that
sex-related discrimination might be more effectively prohibited under most state
constitutions than under federal law. Although no federal statute currently prohibits employment discrimination based on sexual orientation, nine states, the
District of Columbia, and more than 100 cities and counties prohibit sexual-orientation discrimination.[10]

Under current federal law, the following categories of individuals are protected from discrimination:

Protected Categories	Statutory Reference
Race or color	Title VII, Civil Rights Act, 42 USC §§2000e et seq.
Sex	Title VII, Civil Rights Act, 42 USC §§2000e et seq.
National origin	Title VII, Civil Rights Act, 42 USC §§2000e et seq.
Religion	Title VII, Civil Rights Act, 42 USC §§2000e et seq.
Age	ADEA, 29 USC §§621 et seq.
Disability	ADA, 42 USC §§12101 et seq.; Rehabilitation Act, 29 USC §§701 et seq.
Citizenship	IRCA, 8 USC §§1324a et seq.
Status as a veteran	E.O. 11521, as amended; 38 USC §§4101et seq.; 38 USC §§4211 et seq.; 38 USC §§4301 et seq.

Since federal laws take precedent over state laws, each state is required to
comply with the federal mandates at a minimum. But states can go above and
beyond the minimum requirements under federal law. For example, if you face
sexual-orientation discrimination, you would go to state court if you work in one
of the ten states or the District of Columbia that protects those workers. Given
this potential for options under federal and/or state law, it is important to file
most claims simultaneously in both federal and state antidiscrimination agencies. At some point in time, you will have to decide whether to bring your case

in state or federal court. In any event, it is essential that you file in a timely fashion in order to preserve your rights.

Every lawsuit must be brought within a specified period of time. The legal term is **statute of limitations.** If a particular claim has a three-year statute of limitations, the claim must be brought within that three-year period, or the court will not even consider the merits of the claim. Some statute of limitations are as short as thirty days and some are as long as six years. It is extremely important to know the time within which you must file your lawsuit.

OTHER CHALLENGES TO UNFAIR TREATMENT

In addition to federal and state statutory remedies, there has been a growing trend in the case law to allow recovery for workers under different theories relating to fair and equitable treatment. These are exceptions to and modifications of the harsh employment-at-will doctrine. Unfairly discharged workers have successfully challenged their terminations on the following grounds:

1. **public policy;**[11]
2. **tort** claims;
3. **implied covenant of good faith and fair dealing;**[12]
4. **implied promises of long-term employment;**[13] or,
5. protection against termination except for **just cause.**[14]
6. protection due to **negligent evaluation**

Let's briefly go over these concepts so you have some idea of their significance.

WHAT ARE PUBLIC POLICY CLAIMS?

The term public policy is not easy to define but often is stated as "that principle of law which holds that no subject can lawfully do that, which has a tendency to be injurious to the public or against the public good."[15]

Employees have an interest in knowing they will not be discharged for exercising their legal rights. Employers have an interest in knowing they can run their businesses as they see fit as long as their conduct is consistent with public policy. An employee must be able to point to some clearly defined and well-established principle that is threatened by the employer's action. These principles would include terminating an employee in retaliation for performing an important and socially desirable act, exercising a statutory right, or refusing to commit an unlawful act.

The principal source of erosion of the employment-at-will doctrine involves cases where the courts have decided that termination of an at will employee violates public policy. In the area of employment rights, courts have found public policy protection against the discharge of workers in three categories of cases:

EXAMPLES OF PUBLIC POLICY CLAIMS		
Refusing to Commit an Unlawful Act	**Exercising a Legally Protected Right**	**Reporting Criminal Wrongdoing**
Refusing to commit **purjury**	Filing a claim for **workers' compensation**	**Whistleblowing**
Refusing to lie under oath	Voting for a particular candidate	Calling the IRS about your employer's false tax returns
Refusing to dump toxic waste	Serving on a jury	Reporting safety violations
Refusing to defraud a customer	Supporting a public cause	Reporting drug use at work
Refusing to provide false information to the IRS	Testifying truthfully at a trial or at an administrative hearing	Reporting serving alcohol to minors

An example of the first category is when a union business agent serving under an at-will employment agreement was discharged for refusing to give false testimony before a legislative body. The court held that a discharge for such lawful conduct violated established public policy. The court found that the employer had not acted in good faith in terminating the employment relationship.[16]

An example of the second category is when an employee was terminated after the employee filed a worker's compensation claim. The court held that this violated public policy and awarded the employee monetary damages.[17]

An example of the third category is when an airline mechanic was fired for refusing to certify a false aircraft repair form and reporting that to the Federal Aviation Administration. The court held that the employee had a claim against the airline for whistleblowing.[18]

These are just some of the examples of public policy claims. New claims are developing all the time. Under the public policy exception, an employee can recover damages from his or her employer if he or she can establish a causal link between the termination and an identifiable public policy.

WHAT ARE TORT CLAIMS?

A tort is a private or civil wrong or injury. It is a violation of a duty imposed by general law. Every tort action has three parts: (1) The existence of a legal duty from the **defendant** to the **plaintiff;** (2) A breach of that duty; (3) Damage as a proximate cause of the breach.

A simple example of a tort is an automobile accident. Each one of us has a duty to drive carefully. If we don't drive carefully and we injure someone, we can be sued for negligence.

In addition to the public policy exceptions, there are a number of other tort claims that have been used by employees to recover against their employers for wrongful discharge. If the wrongful discharge of an employee at-will amounts to an **intentional infliction of emotional distress** or outrageous conduct, then a cause of action could arise. For example, a court held in favor of a former waitress under the theory of "intentional infliction of emotional distress." The employer had developed an elaborate scheme to determine who was stealing from the restaurant and then it fired the waitress. To establish such a case, the employee has to prove that:

1. the discharge resulted from conduct that the employer knew or should have known would inflict emotional distress;
2. the discharge involved conduct that was extreme and outrageous and beyond all bounds of decency;
3. the discharge caused the plaintiff's (employee's) distress; and
4. the plaintiff's distress was severe and of a nature that no reasonable person could be expected to endure it.[19]

A number of other courts have found that certain forms of employer conduct during the employee's termination or occurring after the severance of the relationship, may also give rise to an action in tort against the employer.[20] For example, if an employee is held against his or her will and questioned extensively before the discharge, he or she may have a claim for false imprisonment. If the employer provides false and derogatory information to the discharged employee's prospective employers, a claim of **defamation** may arise. If the former employer sabotages the employee's new job opportunity, a claim of interference with a contractual relationship may prevail.

In one case, for example, an employee's supervisor falsely accused her of stealing and interrogated her for two hours before firing her. The employee was devastated, treated like a criminal, and was unable to function for a number of months. She was treated by several psychiatrists and was still undergoing therapy at the time the case went to trial. The employee sued for false imprisonment and defamation and was awarded 1.4 million dollars by a jury. In another case, the employer gave out false references to the employee's new prospective employer. The employee sued for defamation and interference with prospective contractual relations and was awarded $650,000 by a jury.

Another tort claim may be available when the termination results from employer **deceit** or **misrepresentation.** A Florida **appellate court** upheld a **verdict** in favor of a former cashier who had been discharged after being promised that her admission of misappropriation of company cash would save her job. The court concluded that the jury properly found for the plaintiff where she had sustained injury resulting from reasonable reliance upon the factual representations by the employer.[21]

A New York federal district court upheld a jury verdict in favor of a discharged employee even though the corporate employer had circulated the defamatory publication to only a few people within the corporation. The court also concluded that **punitive damages** were appropriate since the malicious or reckless publication of the defamatory statements eliminated the corporation's qualified immunity.[22]

A qualified immunity or privilege gives the employer the right to make negative statements, even if the statements are false. This qualified immunity or privilege will be lost, however, when the employer acts with **malice** toward the employee.

Malice, as defined by the law, means actual hatred or ill will. Reckless disregard occurs if the statements are made without proper attention to whether they are true or false, or if the employer repeats the statements to people who have no need to know the information. Damages can then be assessed against the employer, both for the cost of actual harm suffered and a sum of money to punish the employer for his or her malicious conduct.

Several courts have permitted at-will employees to bring common-law tort actions for interference with advantageous contractual relations, where the unjustified acts of third persons have resulted in the employee's termination. A $100,000 jury verdict was upheld in favor of an at-will employee where his supervisor had intentionally interfered with the employee's job on the basis of age.[23]

A growing number of employees are suing their employers for invasion of **privacy,** either when private information is conveyed to prospective employers, or when the termination involved an intrusive invasion of the employee's privacy. The Eleventh Federal Circuit upheld an award of damages on a related state claim for invasion of privacy because the employer engaged in sexually oriented interrogations, demands, and threats.[24]

WHAT IS GOOD FAITH AND FAIR DEALING?

Good faith and fair dealing means that parties to a contract, including employment contracts, must deal with each other fairly and honestly and must not do anything to deprive a person of the benefit of the bargain. An example of this would be an employer firing an employee to deprive the employee of a commission he or she had earned but had not yet received, so that the employer could keep the commission.

Some courts have found implied contractual covenants in the facts of the dispute, thus limiting terminations to those made in "good faith."[25] Other courts have relied on related evidence surrounding the circumstances of termination and the promises made at the inception of the employment relationship. Taken all together, the court might find an implication of a limited degree of job security due to the promises made by the employer to the employee, where normally, no such job security exists.[26] To prove lack of good faith in a termination, for example, the court might look at statements made in the hiring process assuring the employee of long-term employment, or letters indicating a long term-relationship and job security if the employee accepts the job.

WHAT ARE IMPLIED PROMISES?

An implied promise is an agreement that is not stated orally or in writing but is inferred by the parties' conduct and circumstances surrounding the relationship. For example, if your employer asks you to do some work but does not agree on an amount that you will be paid, your employer would be obligated to pay you a reasonable amount of money for your time and services. If you hire someone to paint your house, one of the unspoken understandings would be that the house be painted in a reasonable way within a reasonable amount of time.

The at-will doctrine lies in application of a legal presumption that a contract of employment for an indefinite term is terminable at will. In order to avoid application of this presumption, employees have, with increasing frequency, attempted to rely on employer representations or written personnel policies as evidence that the employment relationship should not be so readily terminable.

A legal presumption is a rule of law that judges draw a particular **inference** from a particular fact unless and until the truth of the inference is disproved by other facts.

Two theories have been used to justify judicial determination that an at-will employment relationship was, in fact, meant to last for some extended duration, rather than being terminable at-will. First, there is the doctrine of additional **consideration.**

Consideration is what forms the basis of any contract. It may consist of a promise for a promise. It may consist of a benefit to one party and a detriment to the other party. When you work for someone, the consideration you give to your employer is your labor. The consideration your employer gives to you is your wages.

Under the additional consideration concept, if a prospective employee tenders consideration greater than the promise to render services in exchange for compensation, then a court may infer that the employment contract was not terminable at will.[27] For example, in one case, a court enforced an alleged agreement for lifetime employment arising from the employee's sale of his business to the employer. The court reasoned that the additional consideration resulting from the sale distinguished the case from the normal at-will relationship and therefore enforced the agreement by the award of damages.[28] In another case, where an employee moved to a new state in reliance upon the promise of a permanent position, the court deemed the contract not to be terminable at will because the employee's relocation was evidence of the additional consideration necessary to make enforceable the promise of job security.[29] In addition, one court has found that an employee gave the additional consideration necessary to imply a contract of permanent employment where, as part of the employment arrangement, he donated valuable securities to his employer.[30] Still another court has held that an employee's refusal of other job opportunities in reliance upon the employer's representation of continued employment negated the otherwise at-will character of the employment relationship.[31]

The doctrine of additional consideration, however, has not met with universal acceptance. Some courts have remained unwilling to weigh the amount of consideration necessary to invoke the theory,[32] while other courts have found legally insufficient the facts asserted to constitute the additional consideration.[33]

A second source that **claimants** have utilized as a means of negating the effects of the at-will rule derives from written personnel policies or other employer representations which, employees have argued with mixed success, provide greater guarantees of job security than attend the normal at-will agreement.[34] For example, in a case where an employer orally represented to an employee that employment would not be terminated for any reason at all, the court relied, in part, upon these assurances as a basis for concluding that the employment relationship was not subject to the at-will rule.[35] Alternatively, where a personnel handbook established preferential recall rights for laid-off employees, the court deemed the personnel policies to constitute such an inducement to accept employment that the at-will rule was not a defense to the employer's failure to recall the individual in accord with the stated policy.[36]

Even absent specific representations concerning the length of employment, courts have implied an expectation of employment for a reasonable period of time. Thus, in one case, where an employee was terminated even prior to commencing employment, the court held that this violated his reasonable expectation and awarded damages.[37]

A majority of state courts construe employee handbooks or personnel manuals as constituting terms or conditions of employment, and an employer who terminates an employee in violation of the provisions of a handbook or manual may be subject to liability for breach of contract. An employer may not normally ignore promises made in a handbook or manual.[38]

Employers distribute handbooks and manuals to their employees to encourage employee security, satisfaction, loyalty, and a sense that employees will be treated fairly in the workplace. Courts are reluctant to allow employers to reap the benefits of employee handbooks and personnel manuals and at the same time avoid promises made that employees reasonably believed were part of their employment relationship.[39]

Employee handbooks or manuals may be construed by a court to constitute terms or conditions of employment, and an employer who terminates an employee in violation of provisions of a handbook or manual may be subject to liability for breach of contract.

How a court will construe an employee handbook depends on state law. Some states construe handbooks or manuals as providing contractual rights to employees and requiring employers to honor the provisions contained in them.[40] Some states require consideration and actual reliance or an exchange of benefits to determine whether handbooks or manuals provide contractual rights and benefits to employees.[41] Other states take a very traditional approach and utilize common-law principles of offer and acceptance and consideration.[42]

If an employee reasonably believes that the employer is offering to continue the employee's employment on terms stated in a manual, the employee's continuing to work after receipt of the manual can be construed as a unilateral acceptance of a unilateral contract, and the employer may be bound by the terms stated in the manual.[43]

An offer is the manifestation of willingness to enter into a bargain, so made as to justify another person in understanding that his assent to that bargain is invited and will conclude it.[44]

An employer that wants to modify an employee handbook so as to restore at-will status must offer additional consideration to the employees whom the handbook covers. The implied employment contract created by the handbook is subject to the principle that an agreement altering a written contract must be based on consideration. The employee's continued employment does not suffice as consideration. Some additional consideration must be provided, either a benefit to the employees, a detriment to the employer, or some bargained-for exchange must be provided.[45]

A hospital's handbook amendment that sought to establish at-will employment did not modify the valid employment contract created by the handbook's economic separation policy. The continued employment of nurses was not valid consideration for the loss of their rights under the handbook's economic separation policy.[46]

WHAT IS JUST CAUSE?

While there is no universally accepted definition of just cause, the general meaning is that a worker cannot be discharged except for a good reason, such as misconduct or poor work performance. This phrase limits the traditional employment-at-will doctrine and requires that the employer have a good reason before he or she can fire an employee.

One asset to an employee in arguing unfair termination may be the employer's written personnel manuals or other related documentation. Often these written materials state that employment is terminable only for just cause or for good cause or for cause. The concept of just cause or good cause or cause comes from labor arbitration. In one case, for example, the court held that the employer's written manual of personnel policies stated that an employee who completed a probationary period would be terminated "for just cause only."

Thus, this phrase created a legitimate expectation in the employee that employment would not be terminated in the absence of just cause.[47] In another case, the court held that an employment application containing assurances against termination without just cause induced an employee to leave his prior employment. Accordingly, this constituted part of the individual's contract for employment, and the employer could only terminate him for cause.[48]

Under California law, when an employer adopts either oral or written personnel policies designed to preclude arbitrary terminations, a long-term employee will become the beneficiary of an implied promise not to be terminated except for good and sufficient reason.[49] Similarly, a Michigan court refused to apply the at-will doctrine as the basis for upholding the termination of a probationary employee two days prior to his acquisition of union membership. In the view of the court, ruling that the employer could terminate the employee without just cause would have been unduly harsh because the terminated employee had given up substantial benefits and job security to take the new position.[50] Other courts, however, have refused to enforce an employer's oral representation not to discharge an employee except for just cause. These rulings are often based upon the finding that the employee did not give up other significant benefits to take this particular job, so the loss of this job is not unjust or unduly harsh in excess of the normal trauma of being fired.[51]

Workers should not be discharged or disciplined except for good cause. While most other countries require good cause in order to terminate employees, except for Montana, the United States does not have this requirement. There are a number of people and some prominent groups in this country that are trying to pass just cause legislation. You should work with these groups and with your state legislatures to require just cause legislation.

WHAT IS NEGLIGENT EVALUATION?

Another theory that has developed is the tort of negligent evaluation. Negligent evaluation is a breach of the duty to provide reasonable performance reviews. If an employer provides performance reviews for its employees, it has an obligation to exercise due care in making these reviews.

In a leading case, a Michigan federal district court ruled that the employer improperly discharged an employee for incompetence because the employer failed to notify the employee of perceived performance deficiencies. Such notice of deficiencies would have informed the employee of the need to correct them. The employee was awarded damages for the negligent evaluation.[52]

RIGHTS FOR PUBLIC-SECTOR EMPLOYEES

There are state and federal laws that provide special protection for public-sector employees. These are the millions of people who work for federal, state, and municipal agencies. Strong union representation has formed the negotiating basis for many of these entitlements. For example, most public-sector employees are protected from arbitrary discharges because certain procedures must be followed in order for any termination to be valid.

To determine your rights as a state or municipal worker, you would need to look at your particular state laws. If employed by the federal government, you would have to look at federal law. If you are covered by a collective-bargaining agreement, your first recourse would usually be to your union.

DEPRIVATION OF CONSTITUTIONAL RIGHTS

There is also a growing body of law in the public-sector dealing with deprivation of constitutional rights, which is giving rise to increasing employee claims of wrongful termination.[53] While there is a difference between a private-sector employer and a public-sector employer, a worker who fights either one of those employers has a formidable uphill battle.

There are state and federal constitutional rights that may protect workers from being discharged. For example, it would be a violation of your first amendment rights to free speech if you were fired from your job because you publicly complained about a safety or health issue in your town.[54]

In states with an equal rights amendment, it would be unlawful to fire you because of your sex. Some states also have constitutional protection against an invasion of privacy.

WHAT CAN YOU GET IF YOU SUE?

The type and amount of damages that a wrongfully discharged employee may recover depends substantially on the claim. In breach of contract claims, for example, the traditional purpose of damages is to provide the injured plaintiff the benefit of his or her bargain. This usually means an award of vested earnings, lost wages, and lost fringe benefits. In tort actions, generally courts award damages to compensate for employee's injuries. Often, this includes lost wages, pain and suffering, emotional distress, loss of consortium (compensation to your spouse and/or children for the disruption of their intimate relationship with you), and damages intended to punish the employer (punitive damages).

If you prevail, it is nice to know that the court may recognize that the loss of your job caused suffering to your family as well. They may be entitled to be compensated if they were originally included in your complaint against the employer.[55] Punitive damages are awarded to penalize the employer for wrongful conduct and to serve as a warning to other employers not to engage in similar outrageous or unfair conduct in the future.

Many contract cases alleging a breach of the implied covenant of good faith and fair dealing involve situations where the employer has terminated the employee in order to avoid payment of vested earnings, such as commissions.[56] In these cases, the discharged employee is entitled to "the fruits of the contract"[57] and may obtain payment of sums related to past services.[58] While no court has ordered **reinstatement** (rehiring) in a breach of contract action, at least one court has refused such a remedy only after being satisfied that monetary damages made the plaintiff whole and after concluding that the current animosity between the parties would render reinstatement unproductive.[59]

In tort actions for wrongful discharge, courts have demonstrated a much greater willingness to award **compensatory damages.**[60] In cases involving breach of public policy, intentional infliction of emotional distress, fraud, defamation, invasion of privacy, or interference with advantageous relations, a successful aggrieved employee may obtain compensation for actual damages, including loss of wages, damage to one's reputation, emotional injuries, pain and suffering, and loss of consortium.[61] Punitive damages also may be awarded when the employer's actions are deemed to be willful or reckless violations of the employee's rights.[62]

Punitive damages are awarded to punish an employer for particularly outrageous actions. Although punitive damages are not awarded often and the amounts awarded are not usually very high, in that rare case, they can be substantial.

PART II

What You Can Do

CHAPTER 3

Setting Boundaries

"Wisdom too often never comes, and so one ought not to reject it merely because it comes late."

Justice Frankfurter,

Henslee v. Union Planters Bank, 335 U.S. 595 (1949).

You have the right to be treated humanely in your workplace. You have the obligation to treat others in the workplace just as humanely as you should be treated. You have the right to a fair day's pay, and you have the obligation to provide to your employer a fair day's work.

While there are some supervisors who are abusive for a variety of reasons, there are many who will treat you respectfully if you do your job.

You can approach your job in a positive and proactive way or in a reactive way. If you approach your job with a positive attitude, you are less likely to lose that job. If you have a negative attitude about your job or the people you work with, you should either change your job or your attitude. Since each of us spends so much of our time working, it is important that the work we do is satisfying, fulfilling, and meaningful.

Supervisors are people too. They like to be around people who are pleasant, cooperative, competent, and hardworking. If you are that kind of person, you are less likely to suffer an adverse employment action and more likely to receive raises and promotions.

If you are negative and react in negative ways, you are more likely not to receive raises and promotions and more likely to lose your job.

In spite of your best efforts, there may come a time where you will sense danger to your job. At the first sign of trouble, you should get your resume up to date and discreetly look for other job opportunities. It is important to be prepared for the worst. If you maintain a positive and upbeat attitude, you may find an even better job.

DOCUMENT, DOCUMENT, DOCUMENT

At the same time, you should document everything that is happening to you. Then, if trouble does arise, you will have the tools you need to navigate and help you if you need to get professional legal advice.

Keep a diary of the events, making sure to be as specific and comprehensive as you can. In the diary, include dates, times, names of all persons present, and conversations in as much detail as possible. If you are describing an event, provide specific details. Don't say "I was sexually harassed." Tell what actually happened. Get names, addresses, and telephone numbers of employees who you think might assist you. Do this very discreetly. Do not ask them while you are still working there if they will be witnesses for you when you sue the employer. You should also include in your diary what testimony or statements they could make that would help your case.

Keep copies of any records that affect you, such as performance appraisals; memos that indicate good or poor performance; thank you notes from clients, co-workers, other managers, etc.; notes from meetings between yourself and your supervisor, etc. It makes sense to keep copies at home or some other location away from the office. Caution: Never take *any* employer records or even copies of records without permission. If you do, you will be subject to the **after-acquired evidence defense.**[1]

The basis of the after-acquired evidence defense is that after you are fired, your employer finds out something through discovery that would have justified your being fired. Taking documents or copies of documents without permission could constitute a valid basis for terminating you. Although you can't be fired twice, what the court does is stop your right to **front pay** damages and/or reinstatement and **back pay** damages to the time your employer finds out about your theft of employer documents.

USING DIPLOMACY

If a problem does arise, work with your supervisor in a positive and constructive way to find out what the problem is and how you can work with your supervisor to fix the problem. There are many problems that occur through miscommunication. Be proactive and cooperative, maintain a positive attitude, and do everything you can to work out the problem with your immediate supervisor. There may be times where you will have no choice but to go over your supervisor's head or go to an outside state or federal agency. That should be your last choice when all other steps have failed.

When you go over your supervisor's head to complain, you are likely to make a new enemy who will stop at nothing to make your life miserable and to force you out. In most instances, your employer will support the supervisor and not you.

Cooperating with state or federal agencies investigating your company may be good citizenship, but it may cost you your job. Many workers have been fired for cooperating with state or federal agencies investigating their employers. Although firing a worker for that reason is against public policy in most states, after you're fired, you have the burden of proving you were fired for a reason that was against public policy. The litigation could take three to five years of your life and the result of litigation is always uncertain. Your former employer may also prevent you from getting a job somewhere else, and you will probably never know it.

If you are contacted by a municipal, state, or federal agency concerning your employer, you should have a lawyer giving you advice. The lawyer may be able to protect you from being fired. It is much better and easier to find a way to keep your job than to fight to get it back after you've been fired.

DEFENDING YOURSELF

If your company has a formal procedure for complaining about discrimination, harassment, or some other work-related issue, you may have to follow that procedure. At this point, you should already have consulted an attorney to guide you. You can be sure that before taking any action against you, your employer has consulted their attorney.

Be aware that in some companies, as soon as you initiate the company grievance procedure, chances are the company will start a campaign to terminate you. In other companies, complaining and using the appropriate procedure may save your job. Your own knowledge of how your organization really works may help you prepare properly for the consequences of asserting your employment rights.

In any event, it is important to document everything. If you do decide to sue, having this information, in detail and in chronological order, along with the names and testimony of witnesses, can easily make the difference between winning and losing.

If you are fired without any advance knowledge or warning, which is rare, you have an obligation to look for another job. Keep a log of every job you apply for. Write down the name and address of the prospective employer; the date of your application; the job or jobs you applied for; the person or persons you spoke with, including dates; the date you were rejected; or if the job was offered, the specific offer, and why you rejected it.

If your case is well documented, you are much more likely to settle the case without a long and protracted trial. Most employment cases are settled without a long and protracted trial. I have managed to settle a large number of cases without a trial, some for hundreds of thousands of dollars, where the case was well documented and there were witnesses.

FINDING THE RIGHT LAWYER

At the first sign of trouble, you should find a lawyer who is familiar with employment law. There are many situations that require prompt action. If you don't bring your claim in a timely fashion to the right agency, you may not get to do it later. The best lawyer cannot help you if you don't file your claim in time with the right agency.

I have had more cases than I would like to count where the worker had a strong case, but did not file the claim in time or filed the case in the wrong place. In one case, the employee had written proof of age discrimination, but he filed his claim with the wrong agency. By the time he came to see me, the time for bringing the claim had long since past. A claim that might have been worth as much as a million dollars was worth nothing. Had he gone to a knowledgeable lawyer as soon as possible, he might have recovered enough money to retire early or open his own business.

A lawyer may also be able to guide you in negotiating a fair severance package or even get your job back. I have been successful in many cases negotiating severance packages for workers and even getting their jobs backs, although getting a job back is extremely rare. Most employers will not want to take a worker back where the worker has sued, but it does and can happen.

Listed in Appendix A are state and federal agencies that deal with employment discrimination.

Listed in Appendix B are organizations that may provide guidance to workers on a variety of work-related issues.

The law has become very complex, and there now are lawyers who concentrate their practices in labor and employment law. Listed in Appendix C are legal organizations and bar associations of lawyers where you may find a lawyer to help you. You should take the time and effort to find a lawyer who is knowledgeable in labor and employment law. But you also need a lawyer you can talk with; who will keep you informed and explain things to you.

In searching for a lawyer, it is important to use some discretion. It may not be a good idea to ask your company's personnel manger for a recommendation. Even asking a co-worker may be dangerous, especially if that co-worker thinks he or she could score some points by telling your boss that you're looking for a lawyer.

Even if the lawyer cannot help you keep your job, the lawyer may be able to help you negotiate a reasonable settlement, which may include a good letter of reference to help you become reemployed quickly and get on with the rest of your life. Remember, a lawsuit is not good for the employer or the worker. A lawsuit is good for the lawyers because that's how they make their money.

CHAPTER 4

Resolving Workplace Disputes

"For this plain and rational test, this court now attempts to substitute one in its nature vague and arbitrary, and tending inevitably to confusion and conflict."

Justice Daniel,

Jackson v. The Magnolia, 61 U.S. 296 (1858).

There are a number of ways to resolve workplace disputes. Most workplace conflicts, like everywhere else, occur because of a lack of understanding or poor communication. Since each of us is unique, it is inevitable that there will be differences of opinion. Such differences are not necessarily good or bad, but it is important to resolve them so the organization can achieve its goals and the employee can do his or her job effectively. The best and most effective way to resolve disputes is for the parties to work together to resolve the problem themselves.

Many companies have a formal **grievance process** for resolving employer/employee disputes. If such a process exists, this is where the employee should begin. Even if your organization does not have a formal grievance process, however, a lawsuit is not the first step in resolving disputes. Between a company's formal grievance process and a lawsuit there are other, more effective methods for resolving workplace disputes. **Negotiation** is the most efficient way because no third party is involved. Mediation is usually less efficient than negotiation, but still more efficient than arbitration. The lawsuit should always be your last option, partly because it is the most expensive and least efficient way to resolve a dispute. You'll learn why in the next chapter.

NEGOTIATION

This is the most commonly used and usually the most efficient way of resolving disputes. The parties have differences of opinion, they talk to each other, they make compromises or concessions, and they work out a resolution that satisfies their needs or interests.

A simple example might involve two co-workers in the same office. One likes a warm office. The other one likes a cool office. By talking to each other they may be able to set the temperature of the room that will satisfy both of them.

Negotiating a resolution of a workplace dispute may be more difficult when the dispute involves a supervisor and a subordinate, because there is an imbalance of power. The supervisor can set the temperature at whatever setting he or she wants. While the supervisor might not have to make any compromise, it may be in his or her best interests to moderate the temperature to satisfy the needs of the worker. Human nature being what it is, people respond in a positive way when their needs and interests are taken into consideration.

The successful negotiation will allow the parties to resolve their differences in a positive way and continue their relationship. The negotiated resolution may be oral or it may be set in writing.

MEDIATION

Mediation is a method of resolving a dispute through a disinterested third party who acts as a facilitator. Mediation is not binding on either party; is generally confidential, and is usually voluntary, i.e., both parties want to resolve their dispute but need the intervention of a third person.

Going back to the room temperature example, if the co-workers could not arrive at a negotiated resolution, they might go to an impartial third party that they mutually select.

The parties arrange a time and place to meet. The mediator will usually first meet in a joint session with both parties. Each party will tell his or her side of the dispute. The mediator may then meet with each person separately to learn more about the real needs and interests of the parties. The mediator may then bring them both back to another joint session to explore some creative ways for resolving the dispute.

The most important aspects of mediation are that it is confidential, it is voluntary, and it is not binding on the parties. If the dispute cannot be resolved, the parties are free to find some other way to resolve it.

ARBITRATION

Arbitration is a very formal process for resolving disputes. It is less formal than a lawsuit, but it does involve the use of a disinterested third person, who will listen to the parties and make a decision that will be binding on both parties. Arbitration shares many of the same difficulties encountered in a lawsuit, and adds as another problem, limited discovery. In a lawsuit, the employer is required to provide information that may be helpful. The employer usually has most of the information, and if you cannot get this information, you may have little chance of winning. Discovery is very limited in arbitration, and this gives the employer an advantage, and the worker a disadvantage.

In a true mediation, the parties resolve their own dispute. The mediator helps in that process, but the final resolution is left to the parties. They fashion their own remedies. In a true arbitration, the arbitrator listens to the parties, hears the evidence, and makes the decision for the parties.

How are arbitrators are selected? The parties to the dispute select arbitrators. There are a number of organizations such as the American Arbitration Association, state boards, and others that have lists of labor arbitrators to chose from. Unfortunately there is a conscious, subconscious, or unconscious bias that favors employers. A discharged employee will only select an arbitrator once. The employer may use the same arbitrator many times. If the arbitrator finds for the employee, will the employer be inclined to use this arbitrator in the next case? On the other hand, if the arbitrator finds for the employer, is the employer likely to use this arbitrator again? I think you get the point.

Getting back to the room temperature example, if arbitration is used, both parties will present their case as to what the proper room temperature should be. The arbitrator will listen to the parties, hear the evidence, and will then make a decision binding on both of them. It is possible that the decision made will not satisfy either party.

Since arbitration is more formal than mediation and there may be a winner and a loser, arbitration may damage an ongoing relationship. A mediated resolution, not having a winner and a loser, but two winners, may actually strengthen a relationship.

THE LAWSUIT

The most expensive and least efficient way of resolving a dispute is through a lawsuit. This is an extremely formal process than can take years. The actual as well as hidden costs should discourage most sane and rational people. A lawsuit should always be considered as a last resort when all other methods have failed or there is no other choice.

If you get fired from your job for an unlawful reason and your employer refuses to consider resolving the matter, you may not have much of a choice. Walk away and find another job somewhere else or consult with an attorney to consider filing suit.

Contrary to popular belief, lawsuits are not good for employers. In fact, employees and employers have a mutual interest in avoiding lawsuits. A lawsuit is expensive and time-consuming for both sides. Only the lawyers, not the parties, benefit from long, protracted litigation.

The employer wants capable and qualified workers. Most workers want to do their jobs to the best of their ability, be respected for their contributions to the organization, and be well compensated.

A simple illustration. A long-term employee who was about to be fired asked for a $10,000 severance payment. His employer refused. The employee brought suit for age discrimination. The employer paid more than $150,000 to defend the suit. Two of the principal officers of the company spent valuable time preparing for the lawsuit. Several key employees quit because they were upset over the unjust firing. The morale of the other workers suffered as well. The business deteriorated. The employee won his lawsuit after a five-year battle and was awarded more than $500,000. The word got out that this company had fired a loyal employee for age discrimination. Within a year after the company was forced to pay the award, the company went into bankruptcy and the owners went into personal bankruptcy, all because they refused to give the employee a $10,000 severance.

The lesson to be learned is that lawsuits can be devastating to employers as well as employees. Even when the employer wins the lawsuit, the employer may still lose in a real sense.

I had one case where all the employee wanted was a letter of apology. He had been falsely accused of stealing. The company refused to give him a letter of apology. The company spent more than $250,000 to defend the lawsuit brought by the employee. Key employees quit, and the morale of the remaining employees suffered. The company eventually won the lawsuit after more than eight years of trials and appeals, but the drain on their resources led the company to file bankruptcy.

Having tried hundreds of cases over the years, it is my experience that the employer would be much better served to resolve these workplace disputes as soon as possible, through negotiation if possible, and if not, through mediation. Does it make any sense for a company to pay a lawyer $150,000, or more, to defend a lawsuit that could be resolved in most cases for a fraction of the cost? It defies common sense that every year employers pay out millions of dollars in attorneys fees to defend lawsuits involving claims by their employees; disputes that can usually be resolved more quickly and at a significantly lower cost. There is a better way, and it involves designing and implementing fair and reasonable methods of resolving conflicts at work.

When the dispute cannot be resolved through any other means, however, the lawsuit may be your only option. The more you know about the process, the greater your chances of surviving and maybe even prevailing or at least keeping your sanity and moving on with your life.

It is important to keep in mind that while lawsuits are difficult to win and are time-consuming, more than seventy-five per cent of the employment cases are settled before trial because of the risk faced by employers in jury trials. This is why it is so vital to preserve our sacred right to jury trials in employment cases.

PART III

The Court of
Last Resort

CHAPTER 5

The High Cost of Litigation: Everyone Loses

"It is better for all the world, if instead of waiting to execute degenerate offspring for crime, or to let them starve for their imbecility, society can prevent those who are manifestly unfit from continuing their kind. The principle that sustains compulsory vaccination is broad enough to cover cutting the Fallopian tubes ... three generations of imbeciles are enough."

Justice Holmes,

Buck v. Bell, 274 U.S. 200 (1927).

In 1998, more than twenty-three thousand employment cases were filed in the federal courts. There were more than fifty thousand employment cases filed in the state courts. According to a recent study by the Rand Corporation, the average cost to defend one of these employment cases exceeds $100,000. Using these numbers, the attorneys' fees paid by employers each year exceeds fifty billion dollars. In addition to the formal cases that are filed in court, there are close to 80,000 complaints filed with the Equal Employment Opportunity Commission and the various state fair-employment agencies. Substantial sums of money are paid to defend those claims as well.

In addition to these tangible costs, there are substantial hidden costs in terms of creating poor worker morale, causing key employees to leave organizations, and the adverse effect on the public.

Since we all see the world in a unique way, conflicts and differences of opinion are inevitable. In fact, without different points of view and different perspectives, very little progress can occur in the workplace. It would not be wise to find ways of stifling conflict in the workplace. By encouraging conflicts or differences of opinion, new ways and approaches may be discovered that will improve the organization.

Public-sector employees work for municipal, state, or federal governments or governmental agencies. It is important to understand that a government exists until a new government comes in and takes over. A government has no natural life, no soul, no heart, no mind, no pity, and no remorse. You cannot kill it, you cannot wound it, and you cannot shame it.

Most private-sector employees work for corporations that are also artificial creations. It has no life, no heart, and no soul. It has no feelings, it has no loyalty, and it has no compassion. The primary purpose of the corporation is to make money.

Depending on where you live, it could take anywhere from a year to ten years to complete a typical lawsuit against your employer.

The employer may win the lawsuit but lose the war. There was a case involving an employee who worked for the company for 32 years. He started with the two owners, and they built a multi-million dollar business with more than 200 employees. When the employee turned 55, the owners decided to replace him with a much younger worker. The employee went to the owners and said he knew the handwriting was on the wall. He asked for a three-month severance package worth less than $7,500, he would sign a release, and would leave the company without any problem. The owners refused. The employee came to me. We brought an age-discrimination complaint against the company. The company paid over $150,000 to an attorney to defend the suit. After five years of litigation, a jury awarded more than $500,000 to my client. About a year after my client collected his money, the company and the two owners went into bankruptcy, all because they refused to pay a $7,500 severance package.

The only thing an employer can be sure of when defending a wrongful-discharge lawsuit is that the employer is likely to spend in excess of $150,000 in attorney's fees, significant time will be lost by employees of the employer in preparing for the case, and there may be adverse employee morale problems. Workers who perceive that the employer was unfair may leave. Workers who stay may become less motivated. Other workers may decide to bring their own lawsuits.

Where one worker is treated unfairly, it is likely that there are others. I had an age-discrimination case against a company. In my investigation, it turned out that the company had a pattern of discriminating against older workers. By the time I was done with that company, I had almost a dozen cases of age discrimination that cost the company over one million dollars.

Not only have the number of employment lawsuits risen dramatically but the average verdicts have also risen dramatically.

LRP Publications recently conducted a jury verdict research study that found the following data for employment cases:

Type of Case	Median Verdict	Mean Verdict	Percent of Awards over One Million Dollars
Discriminatory discharge	$175,000	$315,065	9%
Sexual harassment discharge	$79,750	$297,8445%	
Retaliatory discharge	$104,500	$588,144	5%
Discharge with no discrimination	$130,000	$514,660	8%
Constructive discharge involving sexual harassment	$106,250	$277,863	10%
Constructive discharge without discrimination	$200,000	$370,000	10%
Failure to hire involving discrimination	$46,012	$74,749	0%
Other discrimination	$75,000	$327,732	8%
Other sexual harassment	$79,500	$158,367	2%
Demotion and failure to promote	$115,000	$317,111	4%

The study also revealed that verdicts increased in sexual harassment cases, from a verdict median of $84,000 in 1990 to $100,100 in 1996. The verdict mean went from $252,491 in 1990 to $299,644 in 1996.

Verdicts increased in other discrimination cases, from a verdict median of $168,000 in 1990 to $299,372 in 1996. The verdict mean went from $222,058 in 1990 to $405,109 in 1996.

Punitive damages were awarded in at least 21 percent of the cases and were as high as 41 percent in cases involving retaliation.

Workers do not want to sue their employers. Most workers want to be valued and esteemed in the workplace and to do meaningful work. Workers want a fair day's pay for a fair day's work.

Most employers do want to defend lawsuits, spend hundreds of thousands of dollars in defense costs, and pay out millions of dollars in verdicts and judgments. Employers want workers to give them a fair day's work for a fair day's pay.

CHAPTER 6

What Claims Can You Make?

"The right to work for a living in the common occupations of the community is of the very essence of the personal freedom and opportunity that it was the purpose of the [Fourteenth] Amendment to secure."

Justice Hughes,

Truax v. Raich, 239 U.S. 33, 41 (1915).

The first question you must answer after you are fired from your job is do I have a claim? Unless you were terminated in violation of some federal or state law, you have no claim and no rights against your employer. The discharge may be unfair, unkind, or unjust, but if the discharge does not violate some law, you are out of luck. Unless you are a member of a union, you can be fired for good cause, bad cause, or no cause at all. If you are a member of a union, you are usually protected from arbitrary discharge. Of course, as a member of a union, you may have a number of other problems. If the government employs you, you may have certain civil service protection.

If you do have a claim, the second question is what rights and remedies do you have? Different claims give rise to different remedies. Although for some claims you can get your job back or the promotion you deserve, this seldom happens. Why is this? Use your common sense. If you sue your employer, do you think your employer will want to take you back? Even if a court orders your employer to take you back to work, how long will that last? Do you think your employer will welcome you back with open arms? Or do you think management will make your life so difficult that you will want to leave? In most cases, very few employees ever get their jobs back, and in those rare cases where they do, fewer still last there very long. Most people who win their lawsuits receive monetary damages and not the large amounts you read about in the newspaper.

The third question is where and when must you bring this claim? There are some claims that must be brought within a short period of time, some within thirty days. If the claim is not brought within the appropriate time period, you lose the right to bring that claim, even if it is a meritorious claim.

I have included a chart to give you an overview of the most common types of claims. If your facts do not fit any of the claims, you still should consult with a competent lawyer. First, I have not listed every possible claim. Second, the lawyer may be able to develop a theory of recovery for you. Third, the law is constantly changing, and by the time you read this, some recently passed statute or a newly decided case may provide a remedy for you.

FEDERAL EMPLOYMENT CLAIMS

There are over 150 federal laws dealing with employment rights. In addition, states have their own laws providing protection for employment rights. These federal claims are the more common ones.

STATE EMPLOYMENT CLAIMS

Almost all states have their own fair employment practice laws modeled after Title VII of the Civil Rights Act. However, some states do not prohibit discrimination with respect to all of the protected categories outlined in Title VII, and some states include more protected categories then Title VII, such as marital status and sexual orientation. Furthermore, some state fair employment laws prohibit discrimination on the basis of handicap and most states prohibit discrimination on the basis of age. To determine whether or not your state protects your particular claim, it is necessary to examine your state laws.

If your state does have fair-employment laws that prohibit discrimination, you may have a choice of either proceeding with a claim under the federal discrimination laws or proceeding with a claim under the state discrimination laws. Sometimes, these are referred to as fair-employment laws.

Most states also provide protection for injured workers through workers' compensation. That is, if you sustain a personal injury arising out of and in the course of your employment, you are entitled to compensation and medical benefits while you are out of work. It is necessary to look at your own state law to determine what your rights are regarding those types of claims.

FEDERAL EMPLOYMENT CLAIMS

NUM.	CLAIM	POPULAR NAME OF LAW	STATUTORY REFERENCE	REMEDIES	FORUM FOR CLAIM	WHEN CLAIM MUST BE BROUGHT
1.	Violation of **collective bargaining** rights; violation of union rights; breach of **duty of fair representation.**	National Labor Relations Act or Labor Management and Relations Act	29 U.S.C. §151 et seq.	a. Compensatory damages b. Reinstatement c. Other equitable remedies	**National Labor Relations Board** State or federal court	Within six months of unfair labor practice
2.	Failure to pay minimum wage or failure to pay time and one half for every hour over forty hours in a workweek.	Fair Labor Standards Act	29 U.S.C. §201 et. Seq.	a. Unpaid minimum wages and/or unpaid overtime b. **Liquidated damages** c. Attorney's fees d. Cost of suit	State or federal court	Within two years of the violation, or three years if a willful violation
3.	Wage discrimination based on gender.	**Equal Pay Act**	29 U.S.C. §206(d).	a. Compensatory damages b. Liquidated damages c. Attorney's fees d. Costs of suit	State or federal court	Within two years of the unlawful act, three years if a willful violation

(continued)

FEDERAL EMPLOYMENT CLAIMS

NUM.	CLAIM	POPULAR NAME OF LAW	STATUTORY REFERENCE	REMEDIES	FORUM FOR CLAIM	WHEN CLAIM MUST BE BROUGHT
4.	Discrimination on account of race, color, sex, national origin, or religion.	Title VII of the Civil Rights Act of 1964	42 U.S.C. §2000e et seq.	a. Compensatory damages b. Emotional stress damages c. Punitive damages d. Attorney's fees e. Costs of suit f. Front pay g. Reinstatement	Charge of discrimination must be first filed with the EEOC within 180 days of discriminatory act.	Within 90 days after receiving notice of right to sue letter from EEOC.
5.	Age discrimination	Age Discrimination in Employment Act	29 U.S.C., §621 et seq.	a. Liquidated damages b. Attorney's fees c. Cost of suit d. Front pay e. Reinstatement f. Other equitable relief	EEOC Within 180 days of discriminatory act.	Within two years of the discriminatory act or three years if a willful violation.

(continued)

FEDERAL EMPLOYMENT CLAIMS

NUM.	CLAIM	POPULAR NAME OF LAW	STATUTORY REFERENCE	REMEDIES	FORUM FOR CLAIM	WHEN CLAIM MUST BE BROUGHT
6.	Discrimination for failure to take a lie-detector test.	**Employee Polygraph Protection Act**	29 U.S.C., §20001 et. seq.	a. Compensatory damages b. Attorney's fees c. Cost of suit d. Reinstatement e. Promotion f. Other equitable relief	State or federal court	Within three years of the unlawful act.
7.	Loss of job from plant closing or mass layoff without adequate notice.	**Worker Adjustment and Retraining Notification Act**	29 U.S.C., §210 et. Seq.	a. Back pay b. ERISA benefits c. Attorney's fees d. Cost of suit	Federal court	Varies depending on state where violation occurs.
8.	Handicap discrimination where federal assistance or federal contract involved.	**Rehabilitation Act of 1973**	29 U.S.C., §791 et seq.	a. Compensatory damages b. Reinstatement c. Attorney's fees d. Cost of suit e. Equitable relief	State or federal court	Varies depending on state where violation occurs.
9.	Federal employees discriminated against because they assisted or complained about governmental fraud, waste, abuse, or unnecessary expense.	Whistle-Blower Protection Act of 1989	P.L. 101-12.	a. Compensatory damages b. Reinstatement c. Attorney's fees d. Other equitable relief	Merit Systems Protection Board	

(continued)

FEDERAL EMPLOYMENT CLAIMS

NUM.	CLAIM	POPULAR NAME OF LAW	STATUTORY REFERENCE	REMEDIES	FORUM FOR CLAIM	WHEN CLAIM MUST BE BROUGHT
10.	Discrimination against veterans	**Veterans' Readjustment Benefits Act**	38 U.S.C., §2000 et seq.	a. Compensatory damages b. Reinstatement c. Promotion d. Attorney's fees e. Other equitable relief		Within 30 days of the retaliatory act.
11.	Discrimination on basis of citizenship	**Immigration Reform and Control Act** of 1986	8 U.S.C., §1324a et seq.	a. Compensatory damages b. Civil penalties c. Attorney's fees d. Other equitable remedies	Special **counsel** within the Department of Justice	Within 180 days of discriminatory act.
12.	Discrimination on the basis of disability	Americans with Disabilities Act	8 U.S.C., §1324B(g) et seq.	a. Compensatory damages b. Emotional stress damages c. Punitive damages d. Attorney's fees e. Cost of suit f. Reinstatement g. Other equitable relief	EEOC	Within 180 days of discriminatory act. To court within 90 days after receiving right to sue letter from EEOC.

(continued)

FEDERAL EMPLOYMENT CLAIMS

NUM.	CLAIM	POPULAR NAME OF LAW	STATUTORY REFERENCE	REMEDIES	FORUM FOR CLAIM	WHEN CLAIM MUST BE BROUGHT
13.	Discrimination for taking medical leave of absence or to care for family member.	**Family and Medical Leave Act of 1993**	29 U.S.C., §2601 et seq.	a. Compensatory damages b. Liquidated damages c. Attorney's fees d. Cost of suit e. Reinstatement f. Other equitable relief	State or federal court	Within two years of the unlawful act or three years if a willful violation.
14.	Violation of pension benefits or other employee benefits.	**Employee Retirement Income Security Act (ERISA)**	29 U.S.C., §1132 et seq.	a. Compensatory damages b. Attorney's fees c. Cost of suit d. Other equitable relief	State or federal court	From three years to six years depending upon type of claim.
15.	Safety and health claims in the workplace.	**Occupational Safety and Health Act**	29 U.S.C., §651 et seq.	a. Reinstatement b. Compensatory damages	Secretary of Labor	Within 30 days of the unlawful act.
16.	Complaining about government fraud or waste or other whistleblowing.	Numerous federal laws including Whistle-Blower Protection Act Federal Claims Act	5 U.S.C. §2302(b) et seq. 31 USCA §3729(a).	Varies depending on federal law	Varies depending on federal law	Varies depending on federal law.

All states have unemployment compensation for workers who have lost their job through no fault of their own. While the laws are similar, there are differences, and you should look at your own state law to determine your rights and remedies under the particular law of your state.

There are also hundreds of state laws, some statutory, and some developed by common-law court decisions that create potential claims for workers. To determine what claims you may have, you have to look at your own state laws, both statutory laws and claims that have developed from the **common law** by court decision.

A number of states have held that employee handbooks and/or policies and practices made by employers constitute contractual relationships that can give rise to claims for breach of contract. Many state courts have developed claims for violation of public policy. For example, if you have complained to a state or federal agency about some problem at work, if you are terminated for that reason, that would violate public policy, and you would have a claim against your employer for a violation of public policy.

There are a number of states that have also developed a claim for what is called the breach of the covenant of good faith and fair dealing. This means that an employer cannot terminate the employment relationship unless the employer is acting in good faith. Only a few states have adopted this claim.

Many states have laws that protect your right to privacy, your right to jury duty, and your right to complain about safety or health issues. To determine whether or not you may have a claim, you have to check with your own state laws. Before proceeding, you should always consult with competent legal counsel, who is knowledgeable in labor and employment law.

The table on pages 61–66 lists some of the potential state employment claims.

STATE EMPLOYMENT CLAIMS

NUM.	NATURE OF CLAIM	LEGAL NAME OF CLAIM	WHAT YOU MUST PROVE	REMEDIES	WHERE TO BRING CLAIM	WHEN CLAIM MUST BE BROUGHT
1.	Actions that inflict severe emotional stress.	Intentional infliction of emotional distress	1. Action or conduct of employer where employer knew or should have known would inflict emotional distress. 2. Action or conduct was extreme and outrageous and beyond all bounds of decency. 3. Action or conduct caused the worker's distress. 4. Worker's distress was severe and of a nature that no reasonable person could be expected to endure it.	a. Compensatory damages b. Emotional stress damages c. Punitive damages in some states	State court	Statute of limitations varies from state to state, but most claims must be brought within three years.

(continued)

STATE EMPLOYMENT CLAIMS

NUM.	NATURE OF CLAIM	LEGAL NAME OF CLAIM	WHAT YOU MUST PROVE	REMEDIES	WHERE TO BRING CLAIM	WHEN CLAIM MUST BE BROUGHT
2.	False statements or accusations, whether oral or written.	Defamation: **libel** (written) and/or **slander** (oral)	1. False statement. 2. Employer knew statement was false or made statement in reckless disregard of whether it was true or false. 3. Made the statement maliciously. 4. Statements discredit employee in the eyes of a respectable segment of society. 5. Published to third parties. 6. Suffered damage to reputation.	a. Emotional stress damages b. Damage to loss of personal and professional reputation c. Punitive damages in some states	State court	Statute of limitations varies from state to state, but most claims must be brought within three years.
3.	False promises regarding employment.	Misrepresentation and deceit Fraud	1. A statement of fact that is false. 2. The employer intended that the statement be relied upon. 3. Reliance was reasonable. 4. Damages	a. Compensatory damages b. Emotional stress damages c. Punitive damages in some instances d. Other equitable relief	State court	Statute of limitations varies from state to state, but most claims must be brought within three years.

(continued)

STATE EMPLOYMENT CLAIMS

NUM.	NATURE OF CLAIM	LEGAL NAME OF CLAIM	WHAT YOU MUST PROVE	REMEDIES	WHERE TO BRING CLAIM	WHEN CLAIM MUST BE BROUGHT
4.	Supervisor or some other employee interferes with employment.	**Intentional interference with contractual relations**	1. The person knows you have an employment contract. 2. The person interferes with the contract by some unlawful conduct, either by improper means or some improper motive. 3. Damages	a. Compensatory damages b. Emotional stress damages c. Punitive damages in some instances	State court	Statute of limitations varies from state to state, but the most typical is three years.
5.	Not following the terms of the employment agreement or not following the policies and procedures.	Breach of contract	1. Agreement 2. Breach of the agreement. 3. Damages	a. Compensatory damages b. Emotional stress damages in some cases	State court	Statute of limitations varies from state to state, but most typical is six years.
6.	Retaliation for refusing to commit an unlawful act.	Violation of public policy	1. Termination from employment. 2. An identifiable public policy. 3. Damages	a. Compensatory damages b. Emotional stress damages c. Punitive damages in some cases d. Equitable relief in some cases	State court	Statute of limitations varies from state to state, but most typical is three years.

(continued)

STATE EMPLOYMENT CLAIMS

NUM.	NATURE OF CLAIM	LEGAL NAME OF CLAIM	WHAT YOU MUST PROVE	REMEDIES	WHERE TO BRING CLAIM	WHEN CLAIM MUST BE BROUGHT
7.	Being terminated to deprive the employee of commissions or other benefits earned, so that the employer can retain the benefits.	Breach of covenant of good faith and fair dealing	1. Commissions or other benefit already earned by employee. 2. Termination to deprive employee of commissions or benefits he earned. 3. Damages	a. Compensatory damages b. Emotional stress damages in some cases c. Punitive damages in some cases	State court	Statute of limitations varies from state to state, but most typical is six years.
8.	Cooperating with state or federal agencies in an investigation of the employer.	Violation of public policy	1. The employee cooperated in an investigation with a state or federal agency dealing with the employer. 2. The employee was terminated. 3. Damages	a. Compensatory damages b. Emotional stress damages in some cases c. Punitive damages in some cases	State court	Statute of limitations varies from state to state, but most typical would be three years.
7.	Terminated for asserting a legally guaranteed right, such as filing a claim for workers' compensation.	Violation of public policy	1. Employee asserts a legally guaranteed right, such as filing a claim for workers' compensation. 2. The employer terminates employee. 3. Damages	a. Compensatory damages b. Emotional stress damages in some cases c. Punitive damages in some cases	State court	Statute of limitations varies from state to state, but most typical is three years.

(continued)

STATE EMPLOYMENT CLAIMS

NUM.	NATURE OF CLAIM	LEGAL NAME OF CLAIM	WHAT YOU MUST PROVE	REMEDIES	WHERE TO BRING CLAIM	WHEN CLAIM MUST BE BROUGHT
8.	Terminated for doing what the law requires.	Violation of public policy	1. The employee followed the law. 2. Employee was terminated. 3. Damages	a. Compensatory damages b. Emotional stress damages in come cases c. Punitive damages in some cases	State court	Statute of limitations varies from state to state, but most typical is three years.
9.	Terminated for refusing to testify falsely at a trial or refusing to do what the law forbids.	Violation of public policy	1. The employee followed the law. 2. Employee was terminated. 3. Damages	a. Compensatory damages b. Emotional stress damages in come cases c. Punitive damages in some cases	State court	Statute of limitations varies from state to state, but most typical is three years.
10.	Refusing to provide information to employer where such request is interference with privacy.	Violation of public policy	1. Employer requested information that had substantial interference with privacy rights. 2. Employee refused to provide the information. 3. Employee terminated for damages.	a. Compensatory damages b. Emotional stress damages in some cases c. Punitive damages, in some cases	State court	Statute of limitations varies from state to state, but most typical is three years.

(continued)

STATE EMPLOYMENT CLAIMS

NUM.	NATURE OF CLAIM	LEGAL NAME OF CLAIM	WHAT YOU MUST PROVE	REMEDIES	WHERE TO BRING CLAIM	WHEN CLAIM MUST BE BROUGHT
11.	Discrimination on the basis of race, color, national origin, sex, age, religion, handicap, sexual orientation, marital status.	Violation of state employment discrimination law	1. Adverse action taken because of race, color, sex, age, or some other protected category. 2. Damages	a. Compensatory damages b. Emotional stress damages in some cases c. Punitive damages, in some cases d. Other equitable relief like reinstatement e. Attorney's fees and costs of suit	State administrative agency and/or state or federal court depending on state.	Statute of limitations varies from state to state, but most usually must first file with state administrative agency usually within six months of the discriminatory act and then a claim has to be filed in court, usually within three years.

CHAPTER 7

What You Face in Court

"One wonders whether the majority still believes that race discrimination—or more accurately, race discrimination against nonwhites—is a problem in our society, or even remembers that it ever was."

Justice Blackmun,

Wards Cove v. Antonio, 490 U.S. 642 (1989).

There are numerous minefields to cross before a claimant can win a lawsuit. The system is designed so that one misstep is enough to prevent a claimant from prevailing. Step on one mine, your case explodes, and you get nothing but shattered pieces. Losing your job can be devastating. Losing your case in court can be even more devastating after spending thousands of dollars you cannot afford, not to mention years of your life.

If you fail any one of these steps, you will probably lose your case in court.

If you do win your lawsuit, one other problem remains, collecting the judgment. In one case, the client overcame every obstacle and received a verdict in excess of one million dollars, but he never saw a penny, because the company that he sued filed bankruptcy. After almost ten years of litigation, he obtained a successful verdict, had it sustained on appeal, but when it came time to collect the money, the employer went bankrupt.

Every profession has certain inside information usually known only to the professionals involved in that trade. The legal profession has its own language and procedures that may be difficult to understand for anyone looking in from the outside. To better prepare you for your trip through the legal maze, I want to explain the language and the process your case is likely to take.

STEPS NEEDED TO WIN YOUR LAWSUIT

Step 1:   Find a competent and knowledgeable lawyer.
Step 2:   Determine ability to afford the lawyer.
Step 3:   File a timely charge of discrimination or lawsuit.
Step 4:   Court papers are properly filled out.
Step 5:   Filed with the appropriate state or federal agency and court.
Step 6:   Agency does not lose the charge.
Step 7:   Survive a motion to dismiss.
Step 8:   Survive summary judgment.
Step 9:   Have witnesses present in court when the case is tried.
Step 10: Have credible and believable witnesses.
Step 11: Have the employer's witnesses tell the truth.
Step 12: Have a knowledgeable and compassionate judge.
Step 13: Have a fair and impartial jury.
Step 14: Have evidence admitted and understood by the jury.
Step 15: Have **prejudicial evidence** excluded.
Step 16: Have clear and fair jury instructions.
Step 17: Have a fair panel of judges on the appellate court.

Assume you have found an attorney to represent you at a price you can afford. Assume you have managed to file a timely charge with the right agencies, and they have not misplaced your charge. Now comes the hard part.

The lawyer first must draft and file a complaint in an appropriate court. The employer will then hire a lawyer to file an answer to your complaint. The employer's lawyer may also try to bring a counterclaim against you. If at all possible, the employer's lawyer will also file a motion to dismiss to get the court to dismiss as much of your complaint as possible.

WHAT IS A MOTION TO DISMISS?

A **motion to dismiss** is a procedure used by employers to get as much of your case thrown out of court as possible. The motion to dismiss is usually filed shortly after you have filed your complaint in court. What the motion to dismiss is saying to the court is that even if everything that is said in the complaint is true, that you have no claim.

Why would a lawyer file a complaint that he or she knows the court will dismiss? There are many complaints or claims that are not so clear cut. For example, I had a case where my client was fired for refusing to file a fraudulent tax return for his company. At that time, there was no law that protected him. Even though he was an employee-at-will and could be fired at any time for any reason, we argued that there should be an exception in his case and that it should be against public policy to fire someone for refusing to do something illegal. In other words, an employee should not have to chose between keeping his job or violating the law. At the time, the court was not prepared to accept my argument, and the case was dismissed. However, several years later (too late for this client) the court changed its thinking and established a common law claim for employees discharged in violation of public policy.

There are also new laws that need interpretation. Competent and conscientious lawyers will always try to push to expand workers' rights and provide as many remedies as possible for their clients.

At one time it was lawful to segregate races. At one time consumers had no protection against defective products. At one time workers had few rights. Through the efforts of courageous and dedicated lawyers like Justice Thurgood Marshall, Ralph Nader, Nadine Strossen, Paul Tobias, and others, who have devoted their lives and careers to helping others, segregation is unlawful, products are safer, consumers have rights against manufacturers of defective products, our civil rights are being protected, and our job rights are expanding.

Some lawyers will only bring claims that will survive a motion to dismiss. Other lawyers will try to push the envelope and raise as many claims as possible. Your lawyer really has at least two responsibilities: (1) to represent your interests zealously and diligently; and (2) to explain what is happening at each step of the process.

A court will dismiss claims for a number of reasons.

The reason given most often to dismiss a case is the failure to state a legally recognized claim. These may be cases where the lawyer is trying to expand the law, and the courts have not yet accepted the new legal theories.

When a motion to dismiss is filed, your lawyer will have an opportunity to file an opposition that states a reason why the claim should not be dismissed. The court will normally hold a hearing where you can be present to listen to the

REASONS FOR DISMISSING CLAIMS	
Legal Term	**Plain English**
12(b)(1) Lack of **jurisdiction** over the subject matter.	Court has no power to hear the claim.
12(b)(2) Lack of jurisdiction over the person.	Court has no power over the person you sued.
12(b)(3) Improper venue.	Suit was brought in the wrong court.
12(b)(4) Insufficiency of process.	Defendant was not properly notified of the suit.
12(b)(5) Insufficiency of service of process.	The process server did not follow the proper procedure in notifying the defendant.
12(b)(6) Failure to state a claim upon which relief may be granted.	No legal claim was set forth in the complaint filed in court.
12(b)(7) Failure to join an indispensable party.	Lawsuit failed to name a person who should be part of the lawsuit.
12(b)(8) Misnomer of a party.	Wrong legal name was used in the lawsuit.
12(b)(9) Pendency of a prior action.	The same lawsuit was filed earlier in another court.

lawyers state their reasons or arguments why the claims should or should not be dismissed. The judge may rule on the spot, but is more likely to take the matter under advisement and write a decision that states the reasons for dismissing some or all of the claims or reasons for denying the motion to dismiss.

The employer wants to dismiss as many claims as possible and avoid having a jury consider those claims and award monetary damages. If there are claims left after the motion to dismiss is decided by the court, the next process is called the **discovery process.**

WHAT IS THE DISCOVERY PROCESS?

After a lawsuit is filed, there is a period where both sides try to discover as much evidence as they can. The employer is entitled to find out everything you know about the case before the trial. The employer can also learn who your witnesses will be and what written evidence you have.

The employer's attorney will ask you a series of questions in writing. The formal name for this discovery procedure of asking questions in writing is called

Interrogatories. The employer's attorney will ask you to produce all the documents you have. The formal name for this discovery procedure is referred to as a Request for **Production of Documents.**

If you do not answer all the questions you are asked or provide all the documents requested, your case could be dismissed. In one case of race discrimination, the employer's lawyer requested to see the employee's grades in college. At first, she refused on the basis that her grades had nothing to do with the case. Eventually, she was forced to produce her grades. However, the court dismissed her case because she had taken too long to turn over the grades. Although she had a valid claim and her grades were totally irrelevant to her case, she lost on a discovery technicality.

In another case, the employer's lawyer sought medical records of the employee from the beginning of his life. Although these records had nothing to do with the case, the court allowed this discovery, most likely because the judge never reviewed the papers.

In another case, the employer's lawyer obtained the employee's financial records, his wife's financial records, and other information that had nothing to do with the case.

In another case, a court allowed an employer's motion to take a mental examination of the employee's four-year-old daughter, even though this had nothing to do with the case.

A judge has almost unlimited discretion to allow discovery that is irrelevant or to refuse discovery that is relevant. When the case gets to the court in which appeals are heard, a discovery decision made by a trial judge during the trial will seldom be reversed on appeal, even though the decision affected the outcome. The typical response made by the appeals court is that the trial judge's decision was not an abuse of discretion or that it did not affect the outcome.

In addition to Interrogatories and Requests for Production of Documents, the employer's attorney will usually take your **deposition** and the depositions of all of your witnesses. A deposition is an examination taken under oath. You are required to answer all of the questions asked by the employer's attorney. The testimony is transcribed by a court reporter who takes down everything that is said. Some depositions can last for several days, and they can be very expensive. Furthermore, the depositions can be very intrusive, and very personal questions can be asked. While you have the right to take depositions of the employer's witnesses, the cost involved may limit you from taking too many depositions of their witnesses. Each deposition can cost as much as eight or nine hundred dollars. In one case a client was willing to settle her case for twenty thousand dollars. The employer's attorney took thirty depositions and incurred costs and legal fees of close to ninety thousand dollars. The employer spared no expense to win.

Another discovery device used is called a **Demand for Admission of Facts.** A series of facts will be sent to you, and you have to either admit or deny each fact. Any facts not denied are admitted as true and can be used against you.

The discovery process usually takes many months, sometimes years. The employer often will not fully answer the Interrogatories and will not turn over all of the documents your lawyer has requested. The employer has no incentive to provide the information. You are asking the employer to give you the ammunition you need to win your lawsuit. Another quiz. What do you think the employer will do with documents in their possession that will help prove your case? What are the chances you will ever see those documents? Need a hint?

When the employer does not fully answer the questions or does not turn over all the documents, additional legal documents will then have to be filed, such as a motion to compel further answers to Interrogatories and a motion to compel the production of documents. Legal papers will have to be filed and presented to a judge who will then decide what information the employer has to disclose. This increases the costs and further delays the resolution of the case. Remember, delay aids the employer, not the employee. Corporations, governmental bodies, and other organizations have unlimited lifespans, unlike people. As an example, I had a very good case against a company, but the company was able to delay the case until my client died of a heart attack. Then they settled quickly with his widow for a fraction of the case's value. It is also important to remember that the longer the case takes the more billable hours for the employer's lawyer.

Another quiz. Will the lawyer representing the employer have an incentive to speed up the process, limit the paper work, and limit the hours? This calls for a yes or no answer. Hint: Think about those billable hours.

One way of limiting discovery abuse might be to have the employer pay double the attorney's fees to the employee for any discovery disputes. Another method might be to have members of the bar sit as discovery mediators to resolve discovery issues.

The judge's decision on these discovery issues can affect the outcome of the case, and the decision of the judge on these discovery issues is very seldom reversed on appeal. In one case, an employer laid off a long-term employee allegedly for economic reasons claiming that she was the least effective employee. The real reason was that she had complained to a federal agency about illegal activities of the employer. We tried to get the personnel records of the ten employees retained who had less time with the employer to show that their on-the-job records were much worse. This would have been strong evidence that the reason given by the employer was not true, and if the jury found the explanation given by the employer was false, they would have found in favor of the employee. Unfortunately, the court refused, even though there was no valid legal reason. The employee was forced to try her case without this essential and relevant evidence. She lost, and on appeal, the appeals court said that it was not an abuse of the trial judge's discretion and did not affect the outcome.

After discovery has been completed, the employer's lawyer will again try to get as much of your case dismissed as possible, using a procedure called a **Motion for Summary Judgment.**

WHAT IS A MOTION FOR SUMMARY JUDGMENT?

In simple terms, a Motion for Summary Judgment tells the judge that you don't have enough evidence to prove your case. It is not enough that you believe you were wrongly treated, you have to have evidence to prove it. If you don't have enough evidence to prove your case, the court does not want the jury to even consider your case, so the court will grant summary judgment to the employer, and you will lose your constitutional right to have a jury decide your case.

This is one the most critical stages of the litigation. If the judge grants summary judgment in favor of the employer, your case is over, and you lose without a trial. Summary judgments can be used in any civil case but is a device used by most employers' lawyers in employment cases to prevent claimants from getting jury trials. Most judges do not favor the workers and too many cases are dismissed at the summary judgment stage.

Summary judgment should rarely be granted in employment cases because the motive of the employer is almost always a disputed issue of fact. Summary judgment is not supposed to be granted where there are any material issues of fact in dispute.

At the summary judgment stage, the employer's attorneys will prepare **affidavits,** which are sworn statements made under oath, that the employer's reason for firing you was made for some legitimate business reasons. The employer's attorneys will prepare and present to the judge a legal memorandum of law in support of this Motion for Summary Judgment. Although the claimant's attorney will have the opportunity to file affidavits and legal memoranda in opposition to this Motion for Summary Judgment, it is may be difficult to win for a variety of reasons. The employer usually has all the evidence and knows the truth, but will withhold critical evidence in many cases. The judges find that granting summary judgment eases their case loads. It takes a lot less time to decide a Motion for Summary Judgment then it does to have a trial.

Furthermore, if you give employers enough time with their lawyers, they can always come up with a good reason for discharging an employee. They may even be able to produce evidence in support of their explanations, although producing evidence is not required in many courts. The federal courts do *not* require employers to produce any evidence to support their explanations. To obtain summary judgment, all the employer has to do is give an explanation, almost any explanation, even an explanation that is incredible.

In one case, a black employee had worked for a company for seventeen years and had put in for a promotion. Instead of considering him for the promotion, the company hired a new person who had never before worked for the company. The company's explanation was that the white person selected was better qualified. Since the black employee could not prove this was a false reason to cover up a discriminatory reason, summary judgment was granted for the company.

While many cases are decided in favor of the employers at the summary judgment stage, many of them survive. It is very difficult to prove the negative. If the employer says someone was selected over you because he or she was better qualified, how can you prove that is a false reason? The employer will almost always state a legitimate business reason for its decision that will be difficult to disprove.

The court does not consider what you believe, only what you can prove. You may believe you have been discriminated against, but you have the burden of producing evidence to prove that. Since most employers do not go around admitting to discrimination, proving discrimination is very difficult.

Direct evidence is that rare instance when the employer admits he or she has discriminated. For example, if an employer refuses to hire you because you are black or a woman and tells you that is why you are not being hired, that is direct evidence of discrimination. I have yet to have an admission like that in any of the hundreds and hundreds of cases, and I have handled over the years.

Since most claimants do not have direct evidence of discrimination, the court does allow **circumstantial evidence** to be used. Circumstantial evidence is when you are able to draw reasonable inferences from other facts. For example, if an employer has never hired a black person to a position, that might constitute some circumstantial evidence of discrimination.

If you have no direct or circumstantial evidence, you may still go forward, but it is very difficult. You have to be able to show that you were in a protected class, i.e., you were black, a woman, over forty, a handicapped person, or some other protected category; that you were qualified for the position; that in spite of your qualifications, you were not selected; and that the employer continued to seek applicants with similar qualifications for the position. When you have proved all of these elements, the employer then must state a legitimate business reason for not selecting you. The employer will almost always state a legitimate business reason. An often-used excuse will be that the other person selected was better qualified. Unless you can prove that is false, the employer will win the lawsuit.

If a judge grants summary judgment, that is the end of the case for that judge. If the judge denies summary judgment, it means there will be a trial. It also means much more work for the judge. Do you think the judge might have some incentive to grant summary judgment? Of course, if summary judgment is granted, the case is over for you, and you don't get your day in court. All you are left with is an appeal to an appellate court, consisting of another panel of judges with an incentive to affirm the summary judgment. If the appellate court reverses the summary judgment, the case goes back to the trial court for a trial. What incentive do you think the appellate courts have to reverse a decision of one of their colleagues and send the case back to the trial court where it will take up more time?

When considering a motion for summary judgment, the judge will often conduct a hearing in court and allow the lawyers to make oral arguments where you can be present. A judge will seldom allow or deny a motion for summary judgment at this hearing, but will take it under advisement before making a decision. The decision could be made in a day or could take months depending on the particular judge and the caseload. Taking a case under advisement simply means the judge wants to read the papers submitted more carefully, do some legal research, or has made a decision and does not want to offend the losing side.

Since a good deal of energy is spent by employers' lawyers trying to win these motions for summary judgment, the good news is that when the employer loses this motion, they are much more interested in settling the case, because this means there will be a trial.

As a matter of practice, employers bring motions for summary judgment in almost every case. There is very little risk to the employer. If the employer wins the motion, the case is over, subject to an appeal. If the employer loses the motion, the case continues. Summary judgment should be used infrequently in employment cases. To discourage the use of summary judgment in employment cases, a rule could be made that if the employer loses the motion that the employee be reinstated to his or her job pending the outcome of the trial.

If you do survive the summary judgment stage, you must then prepare for the trial phase, a process with its own set of difficulties. Although most cases settle after summary judgment motions have been denied, significant time must be spent getting ready for trial just in case settlement cannot be made.

WHAT CAN YOU EXPECT AT TRIAL?

From the time you started your lawsuit until the actual start of the trial, you may have lost contact with **key witnesses;** some may be unavailable when the case goes to trial. It is not unusual for a case to take from three to five years to come to trial from the time you first filed your lawsuit. In one case, a client had to wait more than ten years for her day in court. At least she did make it to trial, something most clients never do.

In another case, a key witness had moved across the country. The client could not afford to pay the witness's travel expenses. Without the key witness, he lost his case. Some witnesses may change their testimony at trial to protect their jobs; witnesses may lie under oath. The trial judge may keep out valuable evidence or let in prejudicial evidence.

If you decide to try the case in a state court, you may not get a jury trial. Although jury trials are allowed in most other civil cases, many state laws do not allow jury trials in discrimination cases. If you decide to try the case in a federal court, you will get a jury trial, but it is more likely that the federal judge will grant Summary Judgment, and you will not get any trial. State court judges are less likely to grant Summary Judgment, so, although you have a better chance of getting a trial, you may not get a jury trial.

Even though you are assigned a trial date, you may appear in court with your witnesses as many as ten times before your trial actually begins. Your lawyer has to **subpoena** your witnesses to court each time the case is called for trial. At an average cost of fifty dollars per witness subpoena, the expenses add up quickly. If you have ten witnesses, it can cost you five hundred dollars each time you go to court.

Since the claimant presents his or her case first, the witnesses have to be available each time the case is called for trial. The employer, on the other hand, calls witnesses to testify only after the claimant has finished his or her case. This means the employer usually has to subpoena their witnesses only once. If witnesses are unavailable at the time of trial, the court can refuse to continue the case and force you to try the case without these crucial witnesses. Even though you may have shown up seven times with your witnesses, the trial begins only when the court is ready, not when you are ready.

Furthermore, you face additional obstacles. You need a knowledgeable and compassionate trial judge to help level the playing field. Judges are not selected on the basis of their competency, they are usually selected on the basis of their political connections, and they come with all their biases and prejudices. If the judge is a racist or a sexist before becoming a judge, he will now be a racist or sexist with power. A judge is given the power to decide legal issues, but a judge does not necessarily have the wisdom to decide the issues fairly, justly, and impartially. If your trial judge is employer-oriented, you are not likely to win. The judge determines what evidence the jury is *allowed* to hear and see. The trial judge has a great deal of discretion in admitting or excluding evidence. If the judge keeps out important information, the jury is likely to find against you. The trial judge can let in highly prejudicial evidence, which would also increase your chances of losing.

For example, in one case involving age discrimination, two other former employees, who were also terminated because of their age, were flown in from other states at considerable expense. The judge refused to allow them to testify, even though their evidence was relevant and important to the case.

In another case involving race discrimination, the trial judge allowed into evidence, over objection, evidence that the employee had accidentally shot his son. The shooting incident occurred seven years after the employee was fired from his job and had nothing to do with the case. The employer's attorney was trying to paint a picture of the employee as a raving black lunatic who was gun happy, and the judge let him. Who would want to work with someone like that? If the trial judge displays hostility toward you, either verbally or through body language, the jury will pick that up and will be more likely to find against you.

SELECTING THE JURY

The trial begins with the selection of the jury. In Massachusetts, everyone between the ages of 18 and 70 who is listed as a resident can be called to sit as a juror. As a potential juror, you receive notice for jury duty in the mail to come to a particular court on a particular day. If you are summoned (called to serve as a juror) and do not show up, you can be arrested and brought before the court.

The jurors are brought into a waiting room to wait until they are called into a courtroom to be selected. Most courthouses have several courtrooms where trials are conducted. The jurors are given some instructions about jury service.

The judge will then have a court officer bring forty or more of these prospective jurors into the courtroom to have the lawyers select fourteen of these people to sit as jurors in the case. The lawyers usually have very little information about these prospective jurors, and whether to exclude them from sitting as jurors. Each side is usually able to prevent up to six persons in some states from the jury pool. Many of the jurors will have excuses or reasons why they cannot sit as jurors, and will be excused by the trial judge. The process of picking a jury can take an hour or more, or even days. After the jury is selected, the lawyers will then make their opening statements.

TRYING THE CASE

After the jury has been selected, the trial proceeds with an **opening statement** by each of the lawyers. An opening statement is an opportunity to tell the jury what the case is all about and to persuade them on what they should decide.

The lawyers then have witnesses testify to tell their stories and introduce documents and any other evidence to prove their case. Depending on the number of witnesses and exhibits, trials can take an hour, weeks, or on rare occasions, months. The lawyer who brings the lawsuit goes first. He or she calls witnesses one at a time and asks questions about the case. The other lawyer can cross-examine each witness to try and point out discrepancies or bias on the part of the witness to discredit the witness. The lawyers may make objections to questions or other evidence, and the trial judge has to rule on whether to let the jury hear certain evidence or not.

After your lawyer has finished questioning all your witnesses and introducing all the exhibits, your lawyer will say "**I rest.**" That simply means he or she is done. The employer's lawyer will then usually move for a **directed verdict,** which is when the judge, not the jury, decides the outcome of the trial.

After your lawyer is done, if the judge does not think you presented enough evidence, he can grant what is called a directed verdict in favor of the employer.

WHAT IS A DIRECTED VERDICT?

At the close of presentation of your evidence, the employer will usually file a Motion for a Directed Verdict. This motion is the employer's way of telling the judge that you have not produced enough evidence for a jury to rule in your favor. A judge has the power to disregard the jury's decision. If the jury decides in your favor, the judge can reverse the jury verdict and find in favor of the employer, if he or she does not think you have presented enough evidence. In one case, a jury awarded the employee $250,000. The trial judge directed the verdict in favor of the employer, and the client wound up getting nothing after two appeals. We had fought for more than six years, and the client got nothing, even though the jury found in his favor. The jurors had given up five days to hear the case, and they had no way of knowing that the employee never saw a dime of the money they awarded to him. Ironically, that case established new law that helped others, but not my client.

If the judge denies the motion for a directed verdict, the employer's lawyer then has his or her witnesses testify, and your lawyer cross-examines them to try to discredit their testimony. After all of the witnesses have testified and all of the evidence has been introduced, the lawyers then make **closing arguments.**

WHAT ARE CLOSING ARGUMENTS?

A closing argument is made after the trial is over, but before the jury is sent out to decide the case. Each lawyer has an opportunity to explain to the jury why he or she should decide the case for his or her client. In some states, the employer's lawyer goes first and will usually tell the jury that the employer did nothing wrong and will emphasize any evidence that was heard that shows the employer was right and the employee was wrong. In other states, the employee's lawyer goes first and after the employer's lawyer makes a closing argument, the employee's lawyer will have a chance to make a rebuttal.

In some states, the employee's lawyer will argue last and explain why what the employer did to you was wrong and to award monetary damages to pay you for what you lost.

After the closing arguments are made, the judge has to tell the jury what the law is. The judge explains the law to the jurors by what are called **jury instructions.**

WHAT ARE JURY INSTRUCTIONS?

After the lawyers have made their closing arguments, the judge is required to tell the jury what the law is. This formal legal process is called **charging the jury** or giving the jury instructions. The trial judge has a great deal of discretion in providing instructions to the jury. Much depends on the wording of the jury instructions. If the jury instructions are confusing or misleading, the jury is likely to find against the employee. The judge, who may know very little about employment law, is in a bad position to explain this law to jurors with no legal background.

Although most judges will allow the lawyers to assist in drafting jury instructions, the final decision as to what jury instructions will be given to the jurors is up to the trial judge.

After the judge reads these jury instructions to the jurors, the jurors are then sent into a room with all of the exhibits that were introduced during the trial to decide the case.

WHAT IS THE JURY'S ROLE?

The people on the jury carry their own biases and prejudices, and you never know what persuades them. A trial is not about the truth; it is what the jury *perceives* the truth to be. Sometimes the truth and the perception of the truth coincide but often they do not. If you are telling the truth, but the jury disbelieves you, you will lose the case. If you happen to be black, and there is an all-white jury, you are less likely to win. A jury can disbelieve the truth and believe a lie. Never underestimate a juror with a hidden agenda.

Most jurors do not want to be wasting their time listening to your case. Jurors are not in court because they want to be there. They are forced to be there and usually resent being there. Since you as the plaintiff brought them there, do you think they may have some resentment toward you? Jurors think plaintiffs and their lawyers are greedy and that if they find against the employer, the cost of the service or product will go up, and it will cost them more money. Jurors are people, and like the rest of us, they are motivated by their own self interest and their own biases and prejudices. Put yourself in the juror's place. Would you rather be listening to some stranger's case or doing something you enjoy doing?

In one case we learned during the trial that one of the jurors had worked for the son-in-law of the owner of the company. Although we tried to get the juror removed because of the likelihood of bias, the judge refused and allowed the juror to decide the case with the other jurors. The other jurors did not know this. Can you guess how this case was decided? If you thought that was a serious error by the court, guess again. An appeals court found nothing wrong with allowing the juror to sit. The appeals court found no abuse of discretion.

WHAT ABOUT APPEALS?

If you win, you can expect that the employer will appeal to an appellate court. This is a court consisting of three or more different judges who read what happened in the trial court and decide whether the trial judge applied the law correctly.

When the trial is over, the side that loses, if they want to appeal, have to order and pay for the **trial transcript** or the appeal cannot go forward. A trial transcript from a trial lasting several days can cost at least one thousand dollars or more. Longer trials generate trial transcripts costing thousands of dollars. It can take many months for these trial transcripts to be written.

After the trial transcript is completed, the losing side has to submit the trial transcript and then enter the case in the appeals court and pay a filing fee. The losing party then prepares and files what is called a **brief** and a **record appendix.** The brief is the lawyer's arguments or reasons why the trial judge was wrong and why the decision should be reversed. The record appendix consists of all of the necessary **pleadings** and exhibits. The side that won in the trial court then files a brief setting forth arguments and reasons why the trial judge was right and why the decision should stand.

After all the necessary papers are filed with the appeals court, the parties then wait for a date for hearing of the appeal by the judges. Judges do not hear all cases. Many cases are decided on the papers submitted. It can take years for a decision because of the backlog.

I had a case that started in 1980, went to a first trial in 1985, an appeal in 1987, a second trial in 1991, a second appeal in 1994, and a third appeal to the Supreme Court in 1995. The case was finally decided in 1996.

Even if you win at the trial level, you may lose the appeal and wind up getting nothing. In many cases, employees who received jury verdicts in their favor, have had them reversed on appeal because of some obscure legal principle.

The appeals court consists of judges with their own filtering systems. The appeals court decision can distort the facts, include facts that did not exist in the original case, or ignore significant facts that do exist, to make the case come out the way they want, not necessarily the way it *should* come out. In addition, when the appellate court is reviewing a decision of another judge, the appellate court is likely to find a way to affirm that decision.

PART IV

**True Horror
Stories**

CHAPTER 8

Supreme Court Failures

"I like my privacy as well as the next one, but I am nevertheless compelled to admit the government has a right to invade it unless prohibited by some specific Constitutional provision."

Justice Black,

Griswald v. Connecticut, 381 U.S. 479 (1965).

The Supreme Court of the United States is made up of nine people appointed by the President. They are not necessarily the most outstanding lawyers, but they have strong political connections. Until recently, all of the judges selected were white males. Justice Thurgood Marshall was the first African-American appointed to the Court, and Justice Sandra Day O'Connor was the first female appointed.

While the Supreme Court is the highest court in the land, it does not always dispense true justice, as the following cases will show.

DRED SCOTT

Africans, imported to this country more than three hundred years ago as slaves to support the economy, were considered sub-human by the white ruling class. These Africans were bred like animals to serve their master's purposes. They were bought, sold, and traded like property.

Dred Scott was born a slave to parents brought over from Africa as slaves. His master brought Scott into a free territory that did not recognize slavery. Scott married a slave and had children. When, Scott's owner tried to reclaim him, Scott and his family resisted. The case went all the way to the Supreme Court of the United States, and the Supreme Court held that, "The descendants of Africans who were imported into this country and sold as slaves were not included nor intended to be included under the word *citizens* in the Constitution, and could not claim any of the rights and privileges provided for citizens of the United States; that at the time of the adoption of the Constitution they were 'considered as a subordinate and inferior class of beings, who had been subjugated by the dominant race, and, whether emancipated or not, yet remained subject to their authority, and had no rights or privileges but such as those who held the power and the government might to chose to grant them." [1]

MYRA BRADWELL

Throughout this country's history, women have been treated unequally and unfairly. Ironically, the only society where women were treated more favorably than men was the mythical Amazon society.

Myra Bradwell was a married woman, a citizen of the United States, and a resident of the State of Illinois. She was qualified with respect to her character and achievements to be admitted as an attorney in Illinois but was denied admission to the bar in 1873 for the sole reason that she was a married woman. Myra took her case to the Supreme Court.

The Supreme Court had to decide whether a married woman, being a citizen of the United States, a resident of Illinois, and possessing the necessary qualifications, could be denied admission to the bar and the right to practice as an attorney in the State of Illinois. With only one dissenting vote, the Supreme Court held that:

> There are privileges and immunities belonging to citizens of the United States, in that relation and character, and that is these and these alone, which a state is forbidden to abridge. But the right to admission to practice in the courts of a state is not one of them. This right in no sense depends on citizenship of the United States. It has not, as far as we know, ever been made in any state or in any case to depend on citizenship at all. Certainly many prominent and distinguished lawyers have been admitted to practice, both in the state and federal courts, who are not citizens of the United States or of any state. [2]

The Supreme Court excluded Myra from practicing law. It was not until 1920 that women were given the right to vote. Gradually and slowly, states recognized a woman's right to practice law. However, there were few women lawyers until the 1970s. Among those early women lawyers most were expected to type and perform other secretarial duties for the real lawyers—the men.

HOMER PLESSEY

Legal slavery was finally abolished by the Thirteenth Amendment to the Constitution, only after a civil war that divided a nation at the cost of thousands of lives. Although legal slavery was officially abolished by the Thirteenth Amendment, African Americans continued to be discriminated against just because of the color of their skin. People of color were given sub-standard education, sub-standard living accommodations, and unequal employment opportunities. People of color were relegated to the lowest rungs of the political and economic ladder. Although slavery was abolished de jure (by law), it continued to exist de facto (in fact). States in the South enacted Jim Crow laws, which sanctioned the segregation of races. Signs that read Colored Only and White Only separated the races in public bathrooms, hotels, restaurants, at water fountains, and just about everywhere else.

Thomas D. Rice wrote a song and dance called "Jim Crow" in 1832, and he would dress up with a black face and black hands, mimicking the African slaves. The term Jim Crow came to refer to these segregation laws. This discrimination occurred in every aspect of a black person's life, including public transportation.

Some years after slavery was legally abolished, a young man named Homer Plessey bought a ticket to ride in the first-class section of a train in the state of Louisiana. At the time, Louisiana had a Jim Crow state law that stated:

"All railway companies carrying passengers in their coaches . . . shall provide equal but separate accommodations for the white and colored races," and "that the officers of such passenger trains shall have power and are hereby required to assign each passenger to the coach or compartment used for the race to which such passenger belongs; any passenger insisting on going into a coach or compartment to which by race he does not belong, shall be liable to a fine of $25 or in lieu thereof to imprisonment for a period of not more than twenty days."

Plessey got on the train and took a vacant seat in the first-class section reserved for whites. When he refused to obey the conductor's order to leave that section and move to the section reserved for "persons of the colored race, he was forcibly ejected with the aid of a police officer, and imprisoned." Homer challenged the constitutionality of this Louisiana law and brought his case to the

Supreme Court. In spite of the fact that Homer was seven-eighths white and only one-eighth Negro, the Supreme Court held that separate but equal facilities were constitutionally permissible. "We consider the underlying fallacy of the plaintiff's argument to consist in the assumption that the enforced separation of the two races stamps the colored race with a badge of inferiority . . . If one race be inferior to the other socially, the Constitution of the United States cannot put them on the same plane."[3] The Supreme Court found nothing wrong with racial segregation in 1896.

Racial segregation was the law of the land until 1954, when, the Supreme Court finally reversed the decision in *Plessey.* Unfortunately, unequal treatment of the races continues to exist.

It took the Supreme Court fifty-eight years to recognize its mistake, and even after reversing its position on in *Plessey,* segregation of the races continues to exist.

CHAPTER 9

Race Discrimination

"A statute which implies merely a legal distinction between the white and colored races-a distinction which is founded in the color of the two races, and which must always exist so long as white men are distinguished from the other race by color-has no tendency to destroy the legal equality of the two races, or re-establish a state of involuntary servitude ... The enforced separation of the two races [does not] stamp the colored race with a badge of inferiority ... If one race be inferior to the other socially, the Constitution of the United States can not put them upon the same plane."

Justice Brown,

Plessy v. Ferguson, 153 U.S. 537 (1896).

MICHAEL
"Justice is color blind or do they mean blind to color"

Michael started working in the Malden school system in August 1969, as a physical education teacher. In March 1970, the principal told Michael that if Michael voluntarily resigned, that the principal would give Michael excellent recommendations to obtain a job somewhere else. Michael was never told why the principal wanted him to resign.

Shortly after that incident, the same principal called Michael into his office and told Michael how popular Michael was with the students, and that the principal was impressed with the rapport Michael had with the students, and that it was unusual in view of the fact that Michael was black. At that same meeting, Michael was told by the principal that there was no racism in Malden. The day after that meeting, there were signs all over the locker room stating, "We hate niggers," "Niggers go back to Africa," "KKK," and other racial statements. No action was ever taken against anybody because of the signs, nor did they even conduct an investigation.

One of the senior teachers would refer to Michael as "boy." Because of continuous racial slurs, insults, and harassment by the staff at the school, Michael attempted to seek employment at other schools. When Michael complained about the racial harassment, slurs, and insults, he was told there was nothing that could be done. He was told that it was just a personality clash. Although Michael continued to ask for support concerning the unprofessional conduct by the other staff members, his complaints were consistently ignored.

When Michael found it necessary to discipline students for causing disruption in his classes, the white students who caused disruption in the classes were never suspended, and only on the rarest occasions were any disciplinary actions taken against any of them. However, on one occasion, when Michael stated that a black student had been unruly in his class, the black student was immediately suspended from school.

Although Michael had run track in high school and college, he was intentionally past over for the position of track coach in favor of a white instructor who had no background in track whatsoever. Certain members of the school administration would check on Michael's whereabouts by coming over to his gym classes. This was never done with the other gym teachers, who were white. Michael was consistently harassed by one of the other teachers concerning the size of Michael's penis. As a result of all of these actions by the administrators, staff, and teachers at the school, Michael filed a claim for race discrimination in 1974, with the Massachusetts Commission Against Discrimination and the Equal Employment Opportunity Commission.

After the complaints were filed, the racial harassment became even worse. Michael was arbitrarily removed from a principal's screening committee because he was black. The reason given to him was it would be reverse discrimination if he were left on. Another teacher filed a complaint against Michael, and Michael was not given a fair hearing concerning that complaint. Michael was denied keys to the gym for over a year, while all the white instructors had keys. Michael would sometimes have to stand out in the cold for as long as an hour before a janitor would come to open the door to let him in.

Shortly after Michael filed his charges of discrimination, the school committee brought charges against Michael to discharge him for conduct unbecoming a teacher. The school committee listed eighteen reasons for discharging Michael. A hearing of the charges was conducted in Michael's absence without giving Michael the opportunity to be represented by counsel and to call and examine witnesses on his own behalf. The primary basis for the charges against Michael was that Michael allegedly assaulted a white female teacher. Although ten to fifteen percent of the student body was black, out of four hundred teachers in the system, Michael was the only black schoolteacher. There were no black administrators. There were a couple of black custodians.

After Michael was discharged by the all-white school committee for conduct unbecoming a teacher, Michael brought suit in the state superior court on November 12, 1980, alleging in the complaint that he was discharged because of his race and in retaliation for having complained about race discrimination in the past. After extensive discovery, the case was tried to a jury in April 1987. The case was tried to an all-white jury. Michael objected to the all-white jury and objected to the fact that the only black juror was excluded by the attorney for the school committee, without any given reason.

Counsel for the defendants, over objection, was allowed to introduce into evidence highly inflammatory information that was not relevant to the issues. Michael had accidentally shot his son while cleaning his rifle. This incident occurred years after Michael had been discharged by the school committee and had nothing to do with the case, but the trial judge allowed it into evidence.

The trial judge also excluded evidence that should have been admitted and allowed other evidence in that should have been excluded. The trial judge also interrupted Michael's counsel and displayed body language that clearly favored the school committee over Michael. The school committee was allowed to paint a picture of Michael as an unstable black militant, who was gun happy. Certainly, no one you would want teaching your children.

After hours of deliberations, the jury found in favor of the school committee. Michael filed a motion for new trial based upon clear errors of law and based upon newly discovered evidence of discrimination by the school committee. While the motion for a new trial was pending, the parties entered into settlement negotiations and settled the case on August 19, 1988. As part of the settlement, the school committee wanted Michael to sign a clause that he and his wife would not seek or accept employment with the Malden school committee, the Malden school department or the City of Malden in the future, and that unless invited to do so in writing by an official of the Malden school committee, the Malden school department or the City of Malden, would refrain from visiting or contacting any office or facility of the Malden school committee, the Malden school department, or the City of Malden. The clause would prevent Michael and his family from using the school system for his children, would prevent him from traveling in the City of Malden for any reason, use the library, or visit any of the municipal offices unless invited to do so. Michael refused to sign the settlement agreement with that clause in it. The defendants refused to remove the clause. The clause was clearly unconscionable and unconstitutional. Michael appealed the case to the appellate court, and although the three-judge panel expressed outrage with the clause in the settlement agreement, they affirmed the lower court's decision dismissing the case.

As a result of being terminated from his position as a teacher, Michael was emotionally devastated and has been unable to find any work in his profession. He has been unemployed since 1980. Any prospective employer would have to ask about his last employment. He would have to tell them that he was removed as a teacher for conduct unbecoming a teacher. He would have to tell them that he brought a lawsuit for race discrimination against his former employer. Unfortunately for Michael, he had two strikes against him in his search for a job-one, he was black, and two, he was over the age of fifty. The third strike against Michael was the stated reason for his termination—conduct unbecoming a teacher. Given those facts, Michael will never work anywhere as a teacher.

After more than thirteen years of litigation, Michael was not able to vindicate any of his rights. However, the attorney representing the school committee earned in excess of three hundred thousand dollars in legal fees.

THE LESSON TO BE LEARNED

A biased judge can affect the outcome of a case even where there is substantial evidence of race discrimination.

CAROLE
"Pictures in black and white"

Carole began working for Quick Photo Laboratories on July 22, 1969. Over the years, she applied for a number of promotional opportunities but was rejected for each and every one.

On March 11, 1986, a job was posted for a manual technical operator, grade step 17. Carole bid on this promotion and had an excellent recommendation from her immediate supervisor. Her supervisor had held the position and was about to retire, and considered Carole the best-qualified person to take that position. On October 21, 1986, Carole learned that the promotion was going to a white male who had less time with the company and who was not as well qualified. Carole had two strikes against her, she was black, and she was a woman. The person who made the selection was a white male.

In explaining why Carole did not get the job, Quick Photo's attorneys stated that Carole was not the best-qualified person for the job in view of the persons responsible for filling the job. They stated that the candidate chosen possessed the skills required for a successful performance as a manual technical aid to a greater degree than Carole did. They also stated that the white male had greater leadership skills and experience, more advanced technical knowledge with respect to product assembly, and greater report writing experience, in the view of the persons whom made the choice. They also stated that he had experience troubleshooting and repairing Quick Photo's product at a higher level than Carole did, and that significantly greater "lead, direct, and assign" experience than Carole did. Carole filed a lawsuit against Quick Photo Laboratories in the federal district court claiming that she was denied the promotional opportunity because of her race. Quick Photo maintained throughout the course of discovery that Carole was not selected because the white male was better qualified.

Just prior to the trial, Carole filed a **motion in limine** to prevent Quick Photo from introducing into evidence at the trial, any explanation of why Carole was not promoted other than the explanation already provided in the pleadings. A motion in limine is a device that is used to prevent surprises at trial. In other words, Quick Photo had maintained throughout the litigation that Carole did not get the job because she was not as well-qualified as the white male. The trial judge, who was visiting from Louisiana, denied the motion in limine and allowed the attorney for Quick Photo to introduce new evidence at the trial.

At the trial, I argued that employers are very good at covering up forbidden motives and that they often consult with their lawyers and devise boilerplate explanations for their discriminatory actions. Employers can also distort the evidence, destroy documents, and create documents that did not exist for the sole purpose of defeating these claims. During a break in the trial, counsel for Quick Photo spent thirty minutes telling me how insulted he was that I accused him of fabricating evidence. He was indignant. How could I dare to impugn his integrity?

Shortly after this tirade, when the trial resumed, this lawyer introduced into evidence, over my objection that no one at Quick Photo had ever been promoted from a level 9 to a level 17. Carole had no opportunity to challenge that evidence, since the evidence had never come up before the trial and it was a complete surprise.

The trial judge also excluded from evidence a letter signed by the chairman of the board just prior to Carole's bid for a promotion, which stated "during the past few years we haven't pursued these issues (race and gender) with the vigor they deserve . . . I have personally witnessed a level of concern and frustration with sexual and racial prejudice that exceeds what I thought existed at Quick Photo." This letter was prepared shortly after Carole had filed her lawsuit.

The trial judge also gave jury instructions that were incorrect. Although a request was made to provide the correct jury instructions, the trial judge declined to provide the proper jury instructions. The trial judge submitted jury instructions that were too complex.

At the time the decision was made not to promote Carole to the position, the decision-maker, in assessing Carole's qualifications at the time the decision was made, stated in a written document that "Carole is a key person in mechanical assembly. Her product knowledge and outstanding production abilities are paramount in terms of our success. Excellent training skills rates her serious consideration for the promotion to level 17." Nowhere in any of the exhibits or documents created by Quick Photo at the time the decision was made, was there anything about Carole *not* being promotable to a level 17 from a level 9 position.

The evidence presented at the trial that employees could not be promoted from a level 9 position to a level 17 position was false testimony. After the trial, Carole was able to learn that at least five employees were promoted four or more steps during one promotion. All of the employees who were promoted four or more steps were white. One white male was promoted from a level 7 to a level 17 position at one of the facilities. Another white male employee was promoted from a level 9 position to a level 18 position. Another white male employee was promoted four or five steps at one of the other facilities. Another white male was promoted four or five steps at one of the other facilities.

Unfortunately, Quick Photo was able to manufacture a nonexistent reason and was able to use it to defeat Carole's claim of race discrimination.

Carole still works for Quick Photo, but because she filed this lawsuit, she will always remain in a level 9 position. When she retires, her retirement benefits will be significantly less than they should have been.

THE LESSON TO BE LEARNED

An incompetent judge can affect the outcome of a case even where there is substantial evidence of race discrimination.

LOUISE
"For want of a witness the truth was lost"

Although Louise came from a very poor socio-economic background, she was a very bright student. She went to Dartmouth College on a full scholarship and graduated magna cum laude. She then went to Yale Law School on a full scholarship and graduated with honors. She then came to Chicago to work for legal aid representing the poor and disadvantaged in that city. On October 26, 1988, she went to a local law school to use their library. While reading a law book at one of the tables, she was approached by James G., who identified himself as a security guard. James G. asked Louise if she was a law student at the law school. Louise told him she was not a law student but she was a lawyer and showed James G. her file identification card. After Louise showed James G. her bar identification card, James G. asked Louise to produce something with picture identification on it.

A law student sitting nearby then said "I've been here several times and you have never asked me for any identification." James G. then told the law student to mind his own business. Louise showed James G. her Illinois driver's license. James G. then told Louise that if she did not like the policies of the law school, she could leave. Louise told James G. that she had no problems with the law school policies, but she did not like the way she was being treated. James G. then ordered Louise to leave the law school. Louise told James G. that she had done nothing wrong, and that she wanted to finish her legal research project. At this point, James G. told Louise that if Louise did not leave, that they were going to call the police.

Louise then got up and read a copy of the law school rules and regulations, which stated that the law school library was open to "members of the Illinois Bar, and that one could be admitted to use the law library by showing a bar identification card." After reading that, Louise came back into the law school library to complete her legal research project.

At this point, Brian M. came over to Louise and ordered her to leave the law school premises. Brian M. identified himself as the chief of security for the law school. Louise told Brian M. that she had done nothing wrong, and that she would like to be left alone in order to finish her legal research project. Brian M. then grabbed a law book out of Louise's hands, slammed Louise's briefcase shut, and threatened to call the police and have Louise arrested, unless Louise left the premises. Louise then reached for a law book on the shelf next to the table, at which point, Brian M. slapped Louise's hand away from the bookshelf. At this point a person came over, identified himself as a professor and the director of the library, and invited Louise upstairs to discuss the problem. The law professor told Louise that it would be better if Louise left the library because of the situation, and that Louise could come back some other time when tempers had cooled off. He also told Louise that there was a public library just down the street, and that anybody could use it. Louise then told the law professor that she was so upset, that she could not concentrate anymore anyway, and that if she could just go back and copy some cases and some statutes, she would then leave the library. The law professor told Louise that that would be fine with him. Louise then went back downstairs to the law school library and started copying some of the statutes. About ten minutes later, the law professor went over to Louise and told Louise that the police had arrived and told Louise that security had called the police after speaking with the dean of the law school. Unfortunately, the security guard did not talk to the law professor, who had given Louise permission to copy the statutes and the cases. Six police officers then came over to Louise, told Louise that she was trespassing, and ordered her out of the building. Louise was outraged and totally humiliated and decided that she was not going to let the law school get away with it.

In case you were wondering, Louise was the only African-American using the law school library that day. Very few law students who attended the law school were African-Americans.

Louise brought suit in the federal district court claiming that she was a victim of race discrimination, and that her civil rights had been violated. She also brought a claim against Brian M. for assault and battery, and brought claims against the law school, James G., and Brian M. for intentional infliction of emotional distress.

During the jury impanelment, there were several prospective jurors, who were white, and who were part of a reverse discrimination class-action lawsuit, claiming that they were denied promotional opportunities and that blacks with less seniority were promoted over them. The trial judge allowed those jurors to be part of the jury panel. When a prospective black juror indicated that it might be difficult for her to render an impartial verdict, she was immediately excused.

At the trial, the trial judge excluded important and significant evidence. By the time the case came to trial, the white law student who witnessed the events had moved out of state and could not be located. However, before he moved away, he had his deposition taken, where he testified under oath as to all of the events, which he observed regarding the incident. Louise attempted to introduce the deposition transcript into evidence. The trial judge excluded the deposition transcript on the ground that no effort was made to call the witness to testify at the trial. Therefore, the jury did not have this important and relevant information.

In spite of the fact that the jury did not have all of the relevant information, in spite of the fact that most of the jurors were somewhat biased against African-Americans, in spite of the fact that the trial judge went out of his way to make favorable rulings for the law school and unfavorable rulings for Louise on the evidence, the jury was unable render a decision after deliberating for three days. This is very unusual in civil cases. Unknown to Louise at the time, the trial judge had an affiliation with the law school.

The trial judge then ordered the jury to go back again and reach a verdict. The trial judge told them that they would have to deliberate until they reached a verdict. The jurors were not aware that if they could not reach a verdict then the trial judge would have to declare a mistrial and that there would be a new trial by another jury and probably another trial judge.

In civil cases, it is not necessary for the jury to be unanimous. It only requires ten out of twelve jurors. After deliberating for another four hours, the jury came back with their verdict. The jury found in favor of the law school and the security guards. The trial judge thanked the jurors for their fine service, and as he was talking to them, one of the jurors wanted to tell the judge that the verdict was coerced by some of the stronger members of the jury. The trial judge left the courtroom and refused to consider any of the issues raised by any of the jurors with respect to the improprieties that occurred in the jury room during jury deliberations.

To add insult to injury, the lawyers for the law school filed an application for costs, and presented the application for costs to the trial judge without notifying Louise of the hearing. One of the costs included was the cost of the deposition of the white law student who did not testify at the trial, and whose deposition was not allowed into evidence.

Louise is now practicing law in Massachusetts representing other victims of discrimination.

THE LESSON TO BE LEARNED

A black plaintiff has little chance of winning without a white witness.

JASON
"Let's see what we can cook up"

Jason was a French-speaking black man who was born in the West Indies on September 25, 1950. He attended high school in France and graduated from a culinary arts college in Geneva, Switzerland, in 1972.

He came over to this country in 1975, and was initially hired by the Western Food Corporation on December 10, 1976, as an executive chef to work in a food service facility located at a bank in Boston. Jason remained in that position for over eleven years and did an outstanding job. In April 1988, Western lost that food service contract to another company. Jason and some other employees were laid off. Jason sought other similar employment with Western, but was told that there were no executive chef positions available. The food service company that took over the food services for the bank offered Jason a position there as executive chef. Jason accepted the position.

Six weeks later, Western, needing a French-speaking executive chef for its food-service contract with a local university, contacted Jason at the bank in Boston. Western offered Jason the position as executive chef at the local university. Jason accepted this position and was re-employed by Western on June 1, 1988. Jason supervised about twenty-three other employees. Jason was the only black executive chef employed by the Western Company. In April 1989, Mr. James became Jason's immediate supervisor. Although Jason was the executive chef, Mr. James would seldom speak with Jason, but would usually speak with Jason's subordinate, who was white. Mr. James would frequently have lunch with Jason's subordinate, but never had lunch and never socialized with Jason.

On May 16, 1989, Mr. Joseph, another one of Jason's supervisors, informed Jason that because problems had occurred at the university, that Jason would have to be terminated, be assigned to a job in another location with a reduction in pay, or be placed on unemployment.

When Jason asked why he was being terminated, he was first told that he was being terminated for serving contaminated fish. He was later told that he was terminated for providing incorrect information. He later learned that the university wanted him removed from the facility because he allegedly provided false information.

The story provided by the university and Western was that contaminated fish was served to twenty members of the faculty, and they got sick from eating this contaminated fish. Jason was not the person who received the fish from the supplies, was not the person who stored the fish, was not the person who cooked the fish, and was not the person who served the fish. The person who received the fish was white. The person who stored the fish was white. The person who cooked the fish was white. The person who served the fish was white. No disciplinary action of any kind was taken against any of the white employees involved in the so-called incident.

Jason cut a piece of the so-called contaminated fish and put it in the freezer so that it could be analyzed and tested.

Although the university claimed that twenty faculty members who ate the fish got sick, the fish was never tested, and no determination was ever made that the fish in fact was contaminated. Furthermore, before anything is served, Western employees are required to taste all of the food, which is served. None of the employees who ate the so-called contaminated fish got sick from eating it.

Jason filed a charge of discrimination with the Massachusetts Commission Against Discrimination on May 25, 1989, alleging discrimination on the basis of race, color, and national origin. A suit was instituted in the state superior court. The case was scheduled to start on a Monday. The Friday before the case was to be tried, Western and Jason entered into a settlement agreement. Jason had a home in Wellesley with his wife and three children and one of the most important parts of the settlement agreement was that within two years, Western would find Jason a comparable position as executive chef within a fifty mile radius of his home in Wellesley.

The settlement letter of September 26, 1990, set out the terms of the settlement agreement:

1. Effective October 15, 1990, Western will re-employ Jason as an executive chef at the facility in Monsey, New York.
2. Western agreed to pay Jason $50,000.00 for his lost wages.
3. Jason would accept the first available executive chef or comparable position with Western at no less than the salary he was receiving within fifty miles of Wellesley.
4. Western had two years to find Jason a suitable position within fifty miles of Wellesley.

In spite of the fact that the settlement agreement called for Western to re-employ Jason on October 15, 1990, as executive chef at the Monsey, New York facility, when Jason appeared at the facility, he was told there was no executive chef position available. Western then sent Jason to a number of different locations, and at each location, he was told that there was no work available for him.

Western then sent Jason settlement papers that differed significantly from the September 26, 1990, settlement letter. The September 26, 1990, letter agreed to re-employ Jason as executive chef at Monsey, New York. The new settlement papers received on October 22, 1990, stated that Western could re-employ Jason effective October 15, 1990, as an executive chef at Monsey, New York, or *other interim assignment.* Jason refused to sign the settlement.

On November 19, 1990, Western sent Jason a telegram stating it was withdrawing its settlement agreement of September 26, 1990, because of a changed financial condition facing Western and "Your client's failure to execute the settlement papers."

On December 14, 1990, Western presented Jason with their "new" settlement offer. Western offered Jason either a full-time position as an executive chef at the University of Alabama, or he could resign and receive an enhanced cash settlement. Jason refused to accept this new offer and insisted that Western comply with the terms of the original September 26, 1990, settlement agreement.

On January 3, 1991, Jason advised Western that he considered them to be in breach of the September 26, 1990, settlement agreement. On January 4, 1991, Western wrote Jason and advised him that since he had refused to accept the University of Alabama position offered on December 14, 1990, and since no other position was available within Western, that Jason would be fired by Western effective January 7, 1991.

Jason then filed a second charge of discrimination with the Massachusetts Commission Against Discrimination claiming that he was a victim of race, color, national origin discrimination, and also that this new action by Western was in retaliation for the previous lawsuit and the previous charge filed by Jason.

On May 5, 1991, Jason filed a second lawsuit. During the second lawsuit, Jason discovered that there were suitable and available executive chef positions within a fifty mile radius of his home in Wellesley, Massachusetts, and that these executive chef positions were given to white persons.

On April 10, 1992, Western filed a motion for summary judgment as to all of the claims. Summary judgment is a device used quite frequently by employers to prevent employees from getting a jury trial. The essence of a motion for summary judgment is that taking all of the facts in favor of Jason and taking all reasonable inferences in favor of Jason, that the employer is still entitled to judgment as a matter of law.

The superior court judge after reviewing affidavits, various documents, and legal memoranda, concluded that there was no genuine dispute and granted summary judgment against Jason. Jason never had his day in court.

It is clear that Jason was a victim of race discrimination. Western offered Jason a nonexistent job. Western agreed to give Jason a job as executive chef and agreed to assign him to an executive chef position within a fifty-mile radius of his home in Wellesley, Massachusetts, when one became available. Western reneged on its settlement agreement and then insisted that Jason either accept a position in Alabama at the University, or be terminated. Jason had roots in Wellesley, Massachusetts. He owned a home there. His wife and three children were well established in the community.

Jason, an executive chef, who was well educated and well trained as an executive chef and had worked for many years with an unblemished record, lost his job with Western because of the color of his skin. The white man who actually prepared, cooked, and served the so-called contaminated fish was promoted.

Jason is now driving a cab and doing whatever odd jobs he can to save his home and keep his family together.

THE LESSON TO BE LEARNED

A black plaintiff has little chance of winning with an all-white judge and jury.

CHAPTER 10

Sex Discrimination

"That woman's physical structure and the performance of maternal functions place her at a disadvantage in the struggle for subsistence is obvious. This is especially true when the burdens of motherhood are upon her. Even when they are not, by abundant testimony of the medical fraternity, continuance for a long time on her feet at work, repeating this from day to day, tends to injurious effects upon the body, and as healthy mothers are essential to vigorous offspring, the physical well being of woman becomes an object of public interest and care in order to preserve the strength and vigor of the race ... History discloses the fact that woman has always been dependent upon man. He establishes control at the outset by superior physical strength, and this control in various forms, with diminishing intensity, has continued to the present ... The two sexes differ in structure of body, in the functions to be performed by each, and the amount of physical strength, in the capacity for long-continued labor, particularly when done standing, the influence of vigorous health upon the future well-being of the race, the self-reliance which enables one to assert full rights, and in the capacity to maintain the struggle for subsistence."

Justice Brewer,

Muller v. Oregon, 208 U.S. 412 (1908).

JULIA
"An attempted rape is only making a pass if you're the one making the pass"

Julia was very bright and very ambitious, but it was difficult in the sixties for a woman to achieve much, especially in academe. However, in spite of those obstacles, Julia was able to earn a Ph.D. in Education, and was able to find a job teaching at the college level. Until 1972, it was legal for colleges and universities to discriminate against women, and they did. In 1972, Title VII of the Civil Rights Act of 1964, was amended to protect employees at colleges and universities from discrimination. As a result of the 1972 amendment, private colleges and universities began actively recruiting women to comply with the new law.

Julia was recruited by a well-known eastern university to teach as an associate professor in the department of sociology in the spring of 1972. The chairman of the Sociology Department told her, that if she published a book, she would be granted tenure. Although she did publish a book, she was denied tenure.

When Julia was denied tenure in 1974, she filed a charge of sex discrimination with the Equal Employment Opportunity Commission. She presented evidence that in her first semester of teaching, she was given a larger teaching load than either of the male professors hired at the same time, and another male professor hired the following year. The larger student teaching load was reflected in both the number of students and the course preparations. During her first semester, she was teaching nineteen percent of the students enrolled in sociology courses, even though there were four other full-time and two other part-time faculty in the sociology department, all male. Julia was hired to teach in a new and controversial subject, female studies. She had to prepare her own course material, since the courses had never been taught at the university. When Julia was hired, she was told that she would receive compensatory time or money to continue to engage in projects, which she had been committed, before she was hired. Although compensatory time had been given to the male professors, it was not given to her.

Unlike more established areas of sociology, female and minority studies required more individual counseling time with students. Furthermore, it was more difficult in procuring material and preparing research and lectures because the area was a new and growing one. There were no females on any of the boards, which reviewed and denied her tenure application. The conditions surrounding the decision making on her tenure application differed considerably from those utilized when a male colleague was granted tenure in the sociology department two years earlier.

The university claimed that she was denied tenure because her teaching performance was unsatisfactory. The university relied on unverified student evaluations to make that determination. On October 18, 1974, the six male members of the sociology department voted six to zero to deny her tenure. One of the members who voted against Julia was not even present at the meeting at which her case was discussed. He submitted his vote by mail *prior to* the meeting.

Before the October 11, 1974, meeting, the professor who voted against Julia's tenure in absentia stated in a memo dated October 8, 1974, to the chairman of the sociology department, "The reaction to Julia is surprisingly negative. While I didn't keep count, it seems that at least half of these students were negative."

By October 11, 1974, Julia had taught courses to more than two hundred and fifty students. From that group of more than two hundred and fifty students, eighteen letters were received and used to determine her teaching effectiveness. Of those eighteen letters, nine of them were primarily positive, four were characterized by the university as mixed, and five were characterized as negative. One of the letters considered negative contained somewhat of a disclaimer and stated that: "I think that a professor cannot be judged on the basis of his/her performance during a first semester here. I looked back on my first semester at the university with horror. The uncertainties both personally and academically were paralyzing. I have heard very fine things about Professor Julia from students in later courses." One of the other negative letters stated, "I bluffed my way through the mid-term and the final."

Julia did not know that she had the right to limit the number of students in her classes. This accounts for one of the principal problems one student had who gave Julia a negative evaluation. That student stated that, "The first day of class we were welcomed in and we were told that this was a much larger class than she expected. The whole idea of limited classes is to limit the number of people in it. It seems that everyone who wanted to talk to her about being let in without being accepted by the process was accepted into the class. I admit it was gracious of her, but it made things rough for us. The class was large. It had to be broken down into smaller discussion sessions."

Another one of the letters characterized as negative states in part that, "I feel that she has had many significant experiences as a woman and a sociologist, and she has a unique ability to remember and relate them . . . her ability to communicate knowledge and information successfully is directly related and limited by her inability to promote interaction and discussion. This is not to say that fruitful and meaningful discussion did not occur in both courses that I have taken with her . . . but it appears to occur in spite of her, not because of her."

These few negative student evaluations should have been contrasted with the overwhelming majority of students who had positive comments to make concerning Julia's teaching. For example, one of the letters stated that, "As a teacher, Julia was most effective. Lectures were presented in a manner to keep the students' attention. Lectures were always quite informative and stimulating. Julia was also most helpful in answering any questions from students either within the classroom or in her office. Professor Julia, it seems, had a general concern for the students, and this is a rare quality found in a university professor . . . I feel that Professor Julia was most successful and I'm looking forward to another course with her in the near future."

Another letter stated in part that, "She has been a most concerned, conscientious professor to which I am most grateful. I have been in three of her courses, all of which provided a worthwhile educational experience . . . Dr. Julia has a wealth of information to share with her classes and does so in a very rational way . . . She is always organized in thought and is as accurately prepared for class as any other professor at the university. One of her best attributes is her flexibility and understanding of class assignments . . . Her positive and amiable attitude have demonstrated to me how much she alone has improved the status of the university's sociology department . . . Since I will not be here when the question of tenure comes up for Dr. Julia, I hope you will not hesitate in any way, manner, or form to keep her on as one of the best professors the university has . . .

Another letter stated in part that, "The battles were many but I have never seen such a constant high class attendance rate or a higher degree of participation in the class in my four years at the university. The classes were a lively educational experience with everyone involved. This was unlike most of my college courses in which the rooms were filled with letter writers and clock watchers. Professor Julia presented material which was always relevant, up-to-date, and usually controversial . . . Seminar on the Family was an exciting course for me. Its overall organization was an exciting course for me. Its overall organization was tight, but each class session was spontaneous, sometimes digressing, but usually interesting . . . She is a good teacher because she not only has the knowledge, but also the rare ability to communicate that knowledge in an interesting and thought-provoking way . . . Although I do not personally believe in the tenure system, I do believe that as long as we have the system, not to give tenure to a teacher, a person like Julia would certainly be a mistake."

Julia was not allowed any concrete information on the student evaluations of her teaching, which was allegedly the reason for their decision to deny her tenure. The university claimed that the student evaluations were negative, or that some of them were "strongly negative" which "out weighed" the positive evaluations. Julia never had the opportunity to review these evaluations at the time the decision was made.

According to the department and university procedures, a faculty member's contribution to the larger community should be considered. While her contributions to the larger community were considerable, there was no consideration given to those contributions, although they were considered for the males.

A male professor hired at the same rank and responsibility level as Julia was hired at a salary of $2,500 more than Julia, with no explanation.

Although Julia was hired to teach social psychology as well as female studies, she had only been given such a course to teach once. Although Julia was a registered psychologist with many publications in the field of psychology, the psychology department disqualified her course in social psychology for psychology majors. The psychology department then hired a male, part-time, at a rank lower than Julia, to teach the psychology majors. A male colleague in the sociology department had taught a course in Social Psychology and the psychology students were able to use the course toward their majors.

The male department chairman and one of the other male colleagues had subjected Julia to public outbursts and derogatory shouting in front of students. This seriously undermined her teaching effectiveness. The male professors did not behave this way to one another. One of the male professors of the sociology department started soliciting applicants for Julia's position before her tenure application had even been considered.

While the Equal Employment Opportunity Commission seldom finds discrimination (Discrimination is found in only about 5 percent of the cases), in this case, the Equal Employment Opportunity Commission found discrimination.

Julia was hired as an associate professor of sociology in May 1972, for the period from September 1972 through June 1975. She was not offered reappointment. She was denied tenure on October 18, 1974. Julia tried to settle the case with the university, but the university refused to offer anything significant in the way of settlement. Julia brought her suit in the Federal District Court for the District of Massachusetts in 1980.

Since there was no right to a jury trial for claims under Title VII, the case was tried before a trial judge without a jury, and after a five-day trial with numerous exhibits and several witnesses, the court found in Julia's favor.

The university then appealed the decision to the United States Court of Appeals for the First Circuit and on May 8, 1987, and in spite of the decision of the District Court, reversed the decision of the district court judge and ordered a new trial before a different federal judge.

The Equal Employment Opportunity Commission had found probable cause that there was sex discrimination in 1979. The case was first tried in 1986, and the first judge found sex discrimination. The case was then remanded for a new trial before a different federal judge in 1991. The second trial was also held without a jury, but this federal judge excluded significant portions of evidence. Furthermore, for no apparent reason, this judge refused to allow any evidence of sexual harassment. This judge also refused to allow expert testimony that the evaluation process was invalid and could easily be used to cover up discriminatory motives.

It may have been of some significance that the second federal judge was a former law professor and may have been involved in some tenure decisions at his school where they may have considered women for tenure. Maybe a woman applicant claimed she was a victim of sex discrimination. The personal bias and prejudices of the trial judge has a significant impact on the result.

After hearing all of the evidence, the second district court judge concluded that the evidence did not "support a finding of gender discrimination in this case."

The judge further held that "the most powerful testimony offered by plaintiff was her recollection of a comment by Professor Graybar, a colleague in the sociology department and one of the department members who voted not to recommend tenure in her case. According to plaintiff, Graybar had told her 'That's no way to get tenure around here' the day after she had rebuffed a pass that he made at her. Even if I were to credit this statement as direct evidence of an improper motivation on the part of Graybar in a tenure vote made two years later, I could not find an improper motive on the part of one member of a six-member department would constitute direct evidence of an improper motive, on the part of the sociology department as a whole, in its unanimous vote to deny tenure. Moreover, the recommendation of the sociology department was only the first stage of a tenure review process that included unanimous concurrence by the committee on personnel, the president, the board of trustees, and the faculty review committee.

The so-called pass referred to by the judge in his decision involved a situation where Graybar had grabbed at Julia's breasts, and other parts of her body. Graybar also tried to force his way into Julia's home. The so-called pass was in reality an attempted rape.

Keep in mind that the only basis for determining that Julia was a poor teacher was based upon the unverified student evaluations. Out of the more than two hundred students taught by Julia, only five chose to write negative evaluations, and even the five negative evaluations when looked at carefully, are not as negative as they first appear.

The first judge found "strong evidence of a pervasively sexist attitude on the part of the male members of the sociology department" and "that the department of sociology was generally permeated with sex discrimination of which the plaintiff was in fact a victim." The second judge found no sex discrimination. What was the difference in the two trials? Only the judge—the decision-maker. The laws are only as good as the people who enforce them.

Julia appealed this second Decision to the First Circuit Court of Appeals. The Court of Appeals rendered its decision on June 11, 1992, affirming the decision of the second judge. Julia then filed an appeal to the Supreme Court of the United States. In March 1993, the Supreme Court declined to consider Julia's appeal, putting a special exclamation on Julia's case. The Supreme Court does not have to consider every case. It hears very few cases.

Julia had to go through almost twenty years of court proceedings, two trials in the federal district court before two different federal judges, two appeals to the United States Court of Appeals for the First Circuit, and one appeal to the Supreme Court. The law firms representing the university earned in excess of five hundred thousand dollars in legal fees. Julia to this day has not been able to find a teaching position at another college or university in spite of all her efforts, and given her age, she probably never will.

THE LESSON TO BE LEARNED

Cases can last a long time, and the case is never over until the last appeal.

ESTHER
"What do you expect working at a man's job"

Esther began working for the Concrete Manufacturing Company in 1970. She was one of the few women who worked for Concrete. Over the years she was subjected to sexual harassment and sex discrimination. Although she complained from time to time, no one took her complaints seriously. She always performed her work in a competent and professional manner and her supervisors never rated her less than effective in terms of her productivity, nor did they ever make any complaint about the quality of her work. During the course of her employment with Concrete, Esther received a number of raises and promotions.

Early in 1987, Kevin Moore became her supervisor. It was his responsibility to give out job assignments and review the work of the people under his supervision. When he would give Esther instructions about a job assignment, his instructions were normally given orally, and were confusing, contradictory, and inconsistent, while the other male employees in the department received detailed written instructions. There were also times when Kevin would assign Esther to work for employees who were in a lower job classification than Esther. Kevin never did this with the male employees. Kevin also gave Esther work that was more fitting for someone in a lower job classification. Kevin gave Esther job assignments that were menial, while the male employees were given job assignments referred to as "nice," "beautiful," or "special." Although Esther had been hired to do specialty work, Kevin rarely assigned her such work, in spite of her continued requests.

Kevin would also demean and discredit Esther in front of her male co-workers.

On April 1, 1988, Kevin tried to get Esther to falsify her time cards. When she refused, he shouted at her that she was no help to the department. Later that same day, he threw a rotten hard-boiled egg at her. Still later that day, while holding a project that Esther had just completed, Kevin asked in front of her male coworkers, "which cow did this job?"

During the course of her employment at Concrete, Esther was the subject of a number of sexist or sexual comments. For example, in 1974, she was denied a promotion, when she asked why, her supervisor told her it was because she did not have four children and a mortgage to support. Another one of her male coworkers told her that a woman belongs at home with children. Two other male employees graphically described a pornographic movie in front of Esther and another female employee. On one occasion, Kevin walked down an aisle near Esther's desk and asked, "does anybody screw?"

Esther complained orally and in writing about her treatment by Kevin and others to higher-level management at Concrete. In spite of her complaints, nothing was ever done.

On July 11, 1988, Esther was laid off while male employees with less seniority were retained.

Esther brought suit in a state superior court on April 18, 1989, against Concrete Manufacturing Corporation and against Kevin, her supervisor for sexual harassment and sex discrimination in violation of state law.

As is the custom in these cases, Concrete's lawyers filed a motion for summary judgment, claiming that there were no material issues of fact in dispute, and that Concrete and Kevin were entitled to judgment as a matter of law.

Counsel for Concrete and Kevin claimed that Esther was laid off for economic reasons, and that the reasons they retained a younger male were because he was better qualified. He claimed that the male employee who was retained was better qualified to work the automated equipment.

The employees in Esther's department used different automated equipment to perform some of their work. Concrete thought it was important for people to be trained on the different types of machines. Esther had requested training on the various equipment, but Concrete always found some reason not to give her the training she requested. She requested training in computer graphics, but Concrete denied her that training. She expressed a desire to work on the block machine, but she was only given an opportunity to do that once. Esther repeatedly requested training on the department's single graphics machine, but she was told that she could not get training on the machine because the department was too busy. Training on that machine would have taken only about four hours, and for a year prior to her discharge, the department was not busy at all.

Vincent F., the younger male with less seniority than Esther who was retained, was trained on the graphics machine *against his wishes.* Furthermore, he did not operate the other automated equipment in the department. Vincent liked to sit, relax, talk, laugh, or walk around, while Esther was busy at work. When Kevin gave Vincent an assignment, it was generally a special or nice package, while Esther was given menial assignments. When a reduction in force was required, employees were always laid off in order of their seniority. Until the situation with Esther, Concrete had never laid off an employee out of seniority.

A judge granted Concrete's motion for summary judgment on December 7, 1989, granting judgment in favor of Concrete and Kevin and never giving Esther an opportunity to try her case in front of a jury.

If the trial judge grants summary judgment, that is the end of the case and that is the end of his or her involvement in the case. If the judge denies summary judgment, this means that the judge will have to go through a long and protracted trial in some cases. The judge who is paid by the state does not get paid any more or less for the trials he or she conducts. The object of the game is to try and dispose of as many cases as possible in as short a time as possible. Trying cases on the merits takes much more time than disposing of them by summary judgment.

Esther appealed the case to the state appellate court on April 17, 1990. The appellate court reversed the granting of summary judgment and remanded the case for trial holding that there were material issues of fact in dispute. Counsel for Concrete filed an application for further appellate review to the Supreme Judicial Court, the highest appellate court in the state. Although the Supreme Judicial Court held that it was clear that Concrete had produced evidence that it had legitimate, non-discriminatory reasons for laying off Esther, Concrete had, in fact, produced no evidence that it had "legitimate, nondiscriminatory reasons for laying off Esther."

It is important to understand that you are not supposed to determine credibility issues at the summary judgment stage. Credibility is a question for the fact-finder to determine.

Esther asserted that the reasons given by Concrete were pretextual. Esther testified that she was an "excellent," worker, that she was deliberately denied training on automated equipment, and that she was the victim of several incidents of sexual harassment. The Supreme Judicial Court made findings of fact when they decided that Concrete had made a good faith judgment in comparing employees, and in deciding that Esther was less qualified for the job then those who were retained.

Whether an employer's action is discriminatory or based on a "good faith business judgment," should be a question of fact as to the employer's motive and intent. The Supreme Judicial Court decided the issue of credibility in favor of Concrete and found, as a matter of law, that the reason stated by Concrete was credible.

Concrete was able to manufacture a reason for their decision, was able to disregard Esther's seniority, ignore a qualified older female employee, and was allowed to escape a trial.

Unfortunately for Esther, given her age, she has only been able to obtain temporary jobs. There have been several advertisements in the newspaper for job openings at Concrete, but Esther will not be recalled to any of those openings.

THE LESSON TO BE LEARNED

A court can disregard facts and find what it wants to find.

CHAPTER 11

Age Discrimination

"It is the very essence of age discrimination for an older employee to be fired because the employer believes that the productivity and competence decline with age."

Justice O'Connor,

Hazen Paper Co. v. Biggins, 507 U.S. 604 (1993).

BEVERLY
"Just because they call you an old broad doesn't mean they discriminated against you because you're an older women"

Beverly divorced her abusive husband when she was in her forties and raised her two children by herself. On June 21, 1971, she went to work as a resident manager for the Norwell office of Temporary Services, Inc. Although she was fifty-one years of age at the time, she was very young looking and looked closer to forty. During her employment with Temporary Services, Beverly worked under the direct supervision of Sam Donaldson, who was the regional manager of Temporary Services.

Beverly held the position of resident branch manager from 1971 through 1979. On January 1, 1980, Sam had seven branch officers under his direct supervision. At that time, all of the resident branch managers were female, and Beverly was the oldest one of them. The next oldest resident branch manager was forty-one.

Beverly's Norwell branch office was very successful. In 1978, the Norwell resident branch office had two full-time employees, and for the last five months of that year, had a third full-time employee. In 1979, the Norwell office had three full-time employees and one part-time employee. From 1971 through 1978, Beverly did at least as good a job for Temporary Services as any of the other resident branch managers. Beverly was able to accomplish more with fewer staff because she and her personnel worked nights and most weekends, including Sundays. She was able to more than triple the business within several years in spite of the initial negative attitudes that customers had toward Temporary Services.

Beverly's confidential performance evaluation dated December 15, 1978, clearly showed that as of that date, that Beverly had a good overall evaluation. The confidential performance evaluation dated September 25, 1979, which was the last performance evaluation received by Beverly before her demotion, showed that her overall performance was good with the exception of the implementation of a special program, known as SSII. The only problem stated in the evaluation was that Beverly required further training and experience in her present position, which related solely to the SSII training program. Beverly eventually received a certification from Temporary Services that she successfully completed the SSII program.

Beverly sustained severe personal injuries including a fractured nose and a severe concussion, which arose out of and in the course of her employment on February 2, 1979, when she fell down a flight of stairs. These injuries caused problems with her memory and problems with retention of information. However, by the late fall of 1979, these problems with memory and retention of information had substantially improved. This was probably one of the main reasons Beverly had any trouble completing the SSII program successfully, since the program required memory and retention of information.

Helen Richards was also an employee of Temporary Services, and worked under the supervision of Donaldson. On December 11, 1974, she was a sixty-two-year-old female employee. She filed a charge of discrimination with the Massachusetts Commission Against Discrimination alleging that she was terminated from her position as resident branch manager of Temporary Services, because of her age. On August 10, 1977, the Massachusetts Commission Against Discrimination issued a Probable Cause finding concluding that, "In view of the complainant's excellent work performance during her employment from 1967 to 1974, all of which has been documented, there is sufficient evidence to conclude that age was a factor in the termination of the complainant's employment." The findings also stated, "The respondent likewise terminated four other female employees age forty or over, all of whom were replaced by much younger persons, which supports the complainant's allegation that her age was a factor in her termination."

Paula Prince was also an employee of temporary services. She resigned her position as resident branch manager because of age discrimination and harassment. Her immediate supervisor told her that Temporary Services had a practice of creating difficult work environments for older employees to encourage them to resign their positions. No female employee of Temporary Services in Massachusetts had ever lasted ten years with them to qualify for their pension benefits. Beverly came the closest of any of the female employees in Massachusetts to receiving pension benefits.

Karen Annese was a former employee of Temporary Services and worked in the Boston office under the direct supervision of Donaldson. In the spring of 1979, Donaldson asked Annese to obtain the list of Beverly's Norwell branch and compare last year's fifty top customers with the current year. He asked only for the listing of customers who had decreased their use of Temporary Services. He did not ask for a list of the customers who had increased their use of Temporary Services. Donaldson did not ask this information of any of his other resident branch managers under his direct supervision. Donaldson only wanted to see decreases and not increases. The narrative report prepared by Donaldson in October 1979, and submitted with the 1980 budget, referred to Beverly as his "oldest manager."

The actual figures revealed that in 1978, the Norwell office under Beverly's supervision had gross receipts of more than $750,000. In 1979, under Beverly's supervision, the Norwell office was able to improve its performance and had gross receipts in excess of $900,000.

In 1978, the Norwell office had 406 customers. That same year, the Norwell office, under Beverly's supervision, was able to bill out 159,234 hours. Only Boston and Natick did better that year in terms of hours and Boston had eight full-time employees and one part-time employee and Natick had five full-time employees and one part-time employee in comparison to Norwell, which had three full-time employees.

In 1979, the Norwell office increased the number of customers to 439. That same year, the office had 158,143 hours billed out. There was only one area where the Norwell office went down in any respect (use of clerk-typists), and even in that regard it was insignificant. The overall earnings for 1979 were $167,280.45 more than they were for 1978.

Carol Smith was the resident branch manager for the Temporary Services Cambridge office during the period 1978–1981, and was considered the best branch manager by Donaldson. In 1978, the Cambridge office, with five full-time employees and two part-time employees had totaled fewer hours than the Norwell office.

On January 2, 1980, Beverly was demoted from resident branch manager to lead supervisor without any reason or explanation. Her salary was frozen at her 1979 level. Her new job had fewer responsibilities than her former job of resident branch manager. Beverly was replaced with a much younger female, someone well under the age of forty, and someone not as well qualified as Beverly.

After Beverly was replaced as resident branch manager, her desk, chair, and telephone were taken away for a period of at least eight weeks. There were many occasions when Donaldson would meet with Beverly and talk to her in a loud and abusive manner, something that he did not do with the other resident branch managers. These confrontations with Donaldson caused Beverly severe emotional stress. At the time of her demotion in 1980, all of the other resident branch managers were under the age of forty, except for Beverly.

The stress of being demoted and the derogatory treatment by Donaldson caused Beverly such emotional stress, that she was advised by her doctor to resign her position from Temporary Services for health reasons. On the advice of her doctor, Beverly resigned her position from Temporary Services in April 1980, and brought suit in a state superior court. Temporary Services hired one of the largest law firms in the country to defend the lawsuit. Unfortunately, the case dragged on for years with defense counsel filing numerous dilatory pleadings. Beverly was subjected to an intense deposition examination that lasted for three days.

After Beverly filed her lawsuit for age and sex discrimination, Donaldson claimed for the first time that Beverly was demoted for failing to master the SSII program. In fact, prior to her demotion to lead supervisor, Beverly had passed the test and received a certification that she completed the SSII program successfully.

The day the case was scheduled for trial the trial judge granted defense counsel's motion to strike the jury claim, even though Beverly had a right to a jury trial. The trial judge ignored significant portions of evidence introduced by Beverly, including evidence of similar treatment of other older Temporary Services' employees. The trial judge also excluded relevant evidence.

The undisputed evidence at the trial showed that Beverly was the oldest resident branch manager. The resident branch manager position was the highest position held by any woman in Massachusetts. No female employee working for Temporary Services in Massachusetts had ever received a pension. With less staff than the other branches, Beverly was able to do more business for Temporary Services. Her evaluations clearly showed that her performance was good, if not excellent. Her last evaluation prior to her demotion was good. A former Temporary Services' employee testified that she too was the victim of age discrimination, and that the Massachusetts Commission Against Discrimination found that "age was a factor in the determination" and that "Temporary Services likewise terminated four other female employees over the age of forty, all of whom were replaced by much younger persons . . ." Another Temporary Services employee testified that she was harassed and discriminated against because of her age.

Beverly's supervisor asked a Temporary Services employee to find out all of the negative things she could find out about Beverly for 1979. In a narrative report, which the company reluctantly turned over only after Beverly's attorney learned of the document from the employee who actually typed it, it stated that Beverly was the oldest branch manager and something had to be done about her. Just by a fluke, Beverly met this former secretary while she was out shopping. The former secretary asked Beverly how things were going with her lawsuit against Temporary Services. Beverly told the former secretary that things were not going well because it was so difficult getting evidence. The former secretary then said that she hoped Beverly would win her lawsuit, because there was no question in her mind that it was because of Beverly's age, and the former secretary then told Beverly about what Donaldson had told her to do, and also that she had personally typed the report in 1979, referring to Beverly as the "oldest manager." The only reason she did not tell Beverly at the time was that she was afraid of losing her job.

At the trial, Donaldson testified that he did not know that Beverly was over the age of forty. Donaldson testified that Beverly was demoted for poor performance in 1979. However, according to the documentary evidence, Beverly's branch office went up in every category but one, and the one category-total hours-she went down less than one percent, and even there, her hours were much better than all of Temporary's other comparably sized branch offices.

There were no written warnings of any kind prior to Beverly's demotion. During the trial, Donaldson testified that after an incident, which occurred during a sales call at General Hospital, he decided that he would have to replace Beverly as resident branch manager at Norwell. He further testified that this incident occurred in the summer of 1979, and that his decision to remove Beverly was also made in the summer of 1979, right after that sales call. The interesting part was that Beverly obtained an order from the General Hospital the very next day. Donaldson first told Beverly that he was going to remove her as resident branch manager on December 11, 1979, at least four months *after* the so-called incident. Donaldson lists that incident as the only incident that occurred prior to making his decision to remove her as resident branch manager.

At the trial, there was testimony from other Temporary Services employees that Donaldson had referred to Beverly as the "old broad" on a number of occasions behind Beverly's back. The company maintained that Beverly resigned voluntarily after she was demoted for poor performance. After a five-day jury waived trial, the trial judge issued an eleven-page decision dismissing all of Beverly's claims. The trial judge decided that there was no evidence to substantiate Beverly's claim that she was discriminated against because of her age. The trial judge found that Beverly's resignation in April 1980 was completely voluntary, and that her demotion three months before was based on poor performance, not age. The trial judge also said that, "Donaldson's references to woman as 'broads' and to older woman as 'old broads' does not mean that he disfavored older female employees."

After more than ten years of litigation, Beverly lost her lawsuit. Shortly after the trial judge decided the case against Beverly's age discrimination claims, Donaldson was himself discharged from Temporary Services. He brought an age discrimination case against Temporary Services, and within six months, settled his lawsuit with Temporary Services for a substantial sum of money.

Donaldson has retired to Florida, a fairly wealthy man. Beverly was unable to find another job, was denied unemployment benefits, and was forced to go into business for herself. Her business is trying to place older workers in jobs. Unfortunately, she has not been very successful.

THE LESSON TO BE LEARNED

When the judge has a bias against you, your only chance is to have a jury.

CRAIG
"Truth is in the eye of the beholder"

Craig began his employment with the Brake Company in February 1961. During his employment, Craig assumed jobs of greater responsibility. He started out as a packer, progressed to a cutter, then to a grinder, then to an assistant foreman. In his various supervisory positions, he would supervise between twenty and forty employees. In 1987, there was a change in ownership of the Brake Company. Immediately before this change of ownership in 1987, Craig was a supervisor in charge of an entire building and all three shifts.

With the new ownership in October 1987, a new plant manager, Frank Roscoe, was selected, and became Craig's immediate supervisor. During the time Craig worked under Roscoe's supervision, Roscoe would make discriminatory remarks and would say that Craig looked like an ape or a monkey. He would also point to a black doll he kept on his desk and tell the other employees that the black doll was Craig. Craig was a black man over the age of forty.

In March 1988, Craig was injured in a car accident. The injuries he sustained in that accident interfered with his ability to lift, bend, and climb. Shortly after the accident, Craig returned to work and continued in his supervisory capacity.

In October 1988, Craig was involved in another serious automobile accident. As a result of this automobile accident, Craig was unable to return to work until November 1989. When Craig notified the personnel department of the Brake Company that he was ready to return to work, he was told that there were no jobs available. Two or three days later he learned that there were in fact positions available. He was told that since he was out of work for more than a year, that he would have to file a new employment application.

In December of 1990, Craig submitted a new employment application for one of the supervisory positions. He had an interview with management, who told him that there would be three supervisory positions available. He was told that he was the type of person that they wanted on their team. Several weeks after interviewing for a supervisory position, Craig was notified by letter that he would not be rehired.

On April 1, 1990, Craig filed a charge of discrimination with the Massachusetts Commission Against Discrimination and the Equal Employment Opportunity Commission claiming that he was discriminated against in his employment because of his race, age, and handicaps. Craig learned that there were three openings and that each of the openings were filled by younger, white, non-handicapped persons, who had never before been employed by the Brake Company. The Massachusetts Commission Against Discrimination and the Equal Employment Opportunity Commission were unable to do anything regarding his charge.

Craig brought suit in a federal district court claiming that he was a victim of race, age, and disability discrimination. The Brake Company admitted that there were several openings for which Craig was qualified, and that some of these openings were filled with younger, white, non-handicapped persons. After some discovery, the Brake Company filed a motion for summary judgment, claiming that there were no material issues of fact in dispute and that the Brake Company was entitled to judgment as a matter of law, and that Craig was not entitled to a jury trial to determine whether or not he was a victim of discrimination.

At the time of the new ownership, there were three black supervisors. Shortly after the new change in ownership, one of the black supervisors was demoted and replaced by a white supervisor. After Craig's automobile accident, Amos, the only remaining black supervisor, left the Brake Company. Amos was sixty-four years old and had been with the Brake Company even longer than Craig. Amos was planning to retire in 1990, and did retire in 1990. Amos submitted an affidavit on Craig's behalf in which he stated that he had worked with Craig for many years, as Craig's supervisor and as a coworker. Amos stated in his affidavit that he considered Craig to be one of the best supervisors that he had worked with at the Brake Company, and that Craig was an excellent worker and was well qualified for the various positions he held with the Brake Company. He also stated in his affidavit that after Roscoe became the new plant manager, there were numerous openings for workers, and of all of these openings, not one black person was hired for any position, nor did they hire any new black supervisors. He also stated that there were at least four supervisory positions that became available after Craig had requested to return to work as a supervisor, and that younger white persons with no handicaps filled every supervisory position.

Craig's original lawsuit was filed on May 29, 1990. On October 12, 1993, the judge granted the motion for summary judgment and entered judgment for the Brake Company against Craig.

Craig never had his day in court, nor did he ever have the opportunity of having a jury decide his fate. Instead, a white male judge decided Craig's fate for him.

The law firm, who represented the Brake Company, earned in excess of $150,000 in fees. Craig, on the other hand, has been unable to find a suitable job since 1988 to support his wife and children, and has been only able to find temporary jobs to the present time.

THE LESSON TO BE LEARNED

Stay out of the federal court, particularly if you are black, handicapped, and over the age of forty.

CHAPTER 12

Disability Discrimination

"Congress extended coverage ... to those individuals who are simply regarded as having an impairment ... Such an impairment might not diminish a person's physical or mental capabilities, but could nevertheless substantially limit that person's ability to work as a result of the negative reactions of others to the impairment."

Justice Brennan,

School Board of Nassau County v. Arline, 480 U.S. 273 (1987).

JONATHAN
"When the fruit is used up, throw away the peal."

Jonathan began working as an analytical chemist at Mass Abrasives in September 1955, where he was involved in research and development. In 1960, Jonathan was promoted to senior chemist, and in 1972, to chief chemist. While employed by Mass Abrasives, Jonathan developed three chemical patents that are still in use by Mass Abrasives and have generated millions of dollars in profits for the firm.

During his employment with Mass Abrasives, Jonathan was exposed to a number of different hazardous chemicals. Jonathan was also routinely exposed to loud noises in the work place. As a result, he began to develop Meniere's disease, tinitus (a ringing in the ears), and vertigo. His medical problems escalated further in 1981, and he requested a transfer to an area where he would not be subjected to such exposures. Whenever Jonathan was exposed to the hazardous chemicals, his symptoms would increase dramatically. As a result, he would require several long medical leaves of absence. When he felt better, he would return to work. Since he returned to the same chemical environment, his symptoms would soon reappear.

Mass Abrasives denied Jonathan's request for a transfer and insisted that the only place he could work was in the chemical laboratory. For almost a year, Jonathan continued to work in the chemical laboratory as long as he could tolerate it, then take a medical leave of absence when his condition warranted it. He would return to work each time he recovered sufficiently, and the cycle would begin again.

Finally, Mass Abrasives told Jonathan that he was taking an excessive amount of time off and that if he did not correct the problem, they would have to terminate him for excessive absenteeism. The doctors treating Jonathan said the only thing that could be done for his medical conditions was to keep him out of the hazardous environment. Jonathan continuously asked to be transferred out of the hazardous environment in the chemical laboratory, and Mass Abrasives continued to refuse to allow him a transfer.

Jonathan met with the general manager of Mass Abrasives on December 16, 1982 to discuss Jonathan's medical problems. The general manager told Jonathan that if he missed any more days from work, Mass Abrasives would have to discharge him for excessive absenteeism. On December 20, 1982 Jonathan was discharged by Mass Abrasives for excessive absenteeism.

At the time, there was no private statutory right of action for disability discrimination. Jonathan brought suit in the state superior court for age discrimination under state and federal law and for disability discrimination under a common law theory. The employer used the **removal** procedure to bring the case to a federal district court on the basis of **diversity jurisdiction,** since Mass Abrasives was not a Massachusetts corporation.

Employers generally like to remove cases to the federal court whenever they can, because the federal courts are generally more conservative and much more likely to grant summary judgment than state courts. In this case, the federal district court judge granted summary judgment.

Jonathan had given more than twenty-seven years of his life to Mass Abrasives. He developed three chemical patents that are still in use and that have made millions of dollars for Mass Abrasives. But Jonathan is out of work and has been unable to find another job in his field. Given his age and medical conditions, he probably never will. The law firm that represented Mass Abrasives earned more $150,000 in legal fees defending the suit.

Had Mass Abrasives provided Jonathan with a reasonable work environment, they would have avoided a costly lawsuit, saved a valuable, long-term employee, and prevented a good and decent man from having to suffer a difficult future.

| THE LESSON TO BE LEARNED

| Stay out of federal court, particularly if you have a disability.

MARION
"When you're in real trouble, you can always pray."

Marion was born into a dysfunctional family. She was born out of wedlock, and while she was growing up, her family was on welfare, her father was an alcoholic who abused his wife and his children and was gone for long periods of time. Marion was following the same pattern. She had a child born out of wedlock when she was just fifteen. In spite of that tragic beginning, Marion somehow was able to overcome those disadvantages to some extent. The man with whom she bore her child was abusive to her, and although they married, she soon separated from him and raised her child on her own. She managed to find a small, unknown religious organization known as the Oblivion Church. Her involvement with the Oblivion Church changed her life. For the first time in her life, she was working at something she loved, and she managed to send her daughter to college.

Marion's daughter wanted to go into social work and help disadvantaged families, and to prevent people like her mother from suffering through poverty. Unfortunately, tragedy struck Marion again when a drunk driver killed her only daughter. Marion was able to overcome this greatest tragedy in her life because of her involvement in the Oblivion Church. She began her employment with the Oblivion Church in January 1974, and continued to work at a variety of positions raising substantial funds for the organization.

Sometime in 1987, and continuing through 1980, Marion witnessed the sexual harassment of one of the employees at the Oblivion Church, a woman by the name of Linda. Marion complained to management within the Oblivion Church, the harassment continued.

When Linda was complaining about the sex harassment, Marion's supervisor told Marion that he wanted Marion to make up some negative information about Linda and then use that as an excuse for terminating Linda's employment. At first, fearing for her own job, Marion cooperated and tried to force Linda to resign. When Marion confronted Linda, Linda became extremely upset, broke down and cried. At that point, remembering her own daughter, she could not bear to see Linda suffer, and Marion broke down and refused to cooperate. Because of that, Marion was demoted and her pay was reduced.

Believing that she had no choice, Marion filed a charge of retaliation discrimination with the state Fair Employment Agency. After she filed the charge of discrimination, she was terminated from her employment with the Oblivion Church.

She brought a lawsuit against the Oblivion Church in 1991, claiming that she was a victim of retaliation discrimination.

Although the Oblivion Church offered no explanation for their decision to demote Marion and then to suspend her without pay, after a thirteen-day trial the jury found that Marion was not a victim of discrimination. One of the main reasons the Oblivion Church prevailed in this case was that the trial judge allowed the Oblivion Church to introduce evidence that was not the basis for the employment decisions.

When an employer has clearly made a discriminatory decision, they almost always concoct some rational explanation and present that as the basis for their decision, even though originally, it had nothing to do with the decision to demote and ultimately to discharge the person. Unfortunately, this method used by most employers is usually successful. Furthermore, it is difficult for many jurors to find against a religious organization.

Marion, who had worked so hard all her life to get off welfare is now back on welfare, as a result of what happened to her at the Oblivion Church, and at her age and with her background and experience, it is unlikely that she will ever return to the workforce.

THE LESSON TO BE LEARNED

Even if you have a meritorious case and a fair judge, you can still lose.

CHAPTER 13

Religious/National Origin Discrimination

"Under the tortured meaning now attributed to the word 'labor dispute' no employer-merchant, manufacturer, builder, cobbler, house keeper or what not-who prefers helpers of one color or class can find adequate safeguard against intolerable violations of his freedom if members of some other class, religion, race or color demand that he give them precedence."

Justice McReynolds,

New Negro Alliance v. Sanitary Grocery Co., 303 U.S. 552 (1938).

JOEL
"Never underestimate a judge with an agenda"

Joel was born on June 27, 1928, in Czechoslovakia where he attended public and Hebrew schools on a daily basis. He and his family were Orthodox Jews. In 1944, he and other members of his family were placed in a ghetto. Soon after, they were transported to a concentration camp in Auschwitz by cattle train. On the day of their arrival at Auschwitz, both of his parents and four of his siblings were gassed by the Nazis. By some miracle, Joel survived the concentration camps and was liberated on May 8, 1945, at sixteen with no family, no money, no home, and no place to go.

Upon his liberation, Joel was sent to England, where he learned of some distant relatives in South America. He managed to make his way there, went to school there, and subsequently taught history and religion in the Spanish language in the countries of Paraguay and Brazil.

By 1954, Joel had saved enough money to enroll at Columbia University in New York. While attending Columbia University, Joel continued to teach in order to support himself. Because of his financial condition, Joel was unable to complete his degree at Columbia University until 1963. Joel then attended New York University and received a master's degree in education in 1968.

Over the years, Joel taught at Hebrew University in Jerusalem, Hunter College in New York, City College in New York, and in a number of other schools in New Jersey and California.

In 1976, Joel applied and was hired for a part-time teaching position in a public high school to teach two classes in first-year Hebrew. Joel continued teaching Hebrew through the 1977–1978 school year. In the 1978–1979 school year, Joel taught three Hebrew classes and one social studies class. In the 1979–1980 school year, Joel taught three Hebrew classes. The social studies class that Joel taught for the 1978–1979 school year was assigned to a younger, nontenured, non-Jewish teacher, who was not as well qualified as Joel and who was not even certified to teach social studies. Although Joel was told that the social studies class was assigned to a more senior teacher, it was, in fact, assigned to a less senior teacher.

By 1979, Joel had become a tenured teacher in the school system. At the same time Joel began his employment in the school system, Stacey Esposito was hired as a part-time teacher to teach two Italian classes. Esposito was a Vassar graduate. She received a Master's degree in European studies from Harvard University in their extension program, while teaching in the school system. Esposito was certified to teach Italian, Spanish, French, and Latin. Esposito was much younger than Joel and was Roman Catholic. This was her very first teaching position. At one point, the school committee voted not to rehire Esposito or renew her contract because of her poor teaching evaluations.

Joel received his actual certification to teach Spanish on February 20, 1980, but Joel was certifiable to teach Spanish since 1978 and could have received his certification at any time after 1978, if he had applied for it.

Robert Edwards, the chair of the language department, recommended that Joel be assigned to teach Spanish classes, but his recommendation was not followed, and no explanation was ever provided. The Spanish classes were assigned to Esposito.

On April 15, 1980, Joel was notified that his position with the school system would be terminated at the end of the 1979–1980 school year, as part of a reduction in force caused by a declining enrollment in Hebrew classes. Students were discouraged from taking Hebrew classes by the school administration. Students were told that Hebrew was going to be eliminated as a foreign language.

Joel was certified to teach Spanish and social studies, and the school offered Spanish classes and social studies classes that Joel could have taught. Yet, without explanation, Joel was not assigned to teach these classes.

Joel practiced traditional Orthodox Judaism, the strictest branch of Judaism requiring him to observe many holy days. None of the other Jewish teachers in the school system practiced Orthodox Judaism. The chair of the school committee practiced Reformed Judaism, a less strict branch and, in talking about Joel, described him as being "too Jewish."

Instead of assigning classes to Joel, younger, non-Jewish teachers were assigned to teach Spanish classes and social studies classes. At the beginning of the 1980–1981, school year, Esposito was teaching Spanish and French on a part-time basis, when a high school Spanish teacher was promoted to assistant principal. Instead of recalling Joel to teach the five Spanish classes at the high school, Esposito, who had been teaching Spanish and French classes at the junior high school for two or three weeks, was moved to the high school to teach the most advanced Spanish classes, leaving the combined Spanish and French classes open at the junior high school level. Joel filed a grievance, and the arbitrator ruled that Joel's recall rights had been violated and that Joel should have been recalled.

The first time Esposito had ever taught Spanish was in this school system, and the first Spanish classes that she ever taught were during the 1979–1980, school year. In spite of this and her previous negative teaching evaluations, the school committee determined that Esposito was the appropriate choice to fill the high school vacancy and teach advanced Spanish classes.

The principal of the high school, Ralph Banks, told Joel that Joel's chances of being assigned to teach Spanish classes were not good because Joel had taken off so many days for Jewish holidays. He also told Joel that when Hebrew classes go, Joel would also go, even though Joel was certified to teach Spanish and social studies. Joel was considered by the administration as the Hebrew teacher, not as a teacher.

In discussing Joel, the superintendent of schools stated, "He took off seven days of Jewish holidays. Why was it necessary for him to take off seven days? We bent over backwards to accommodate him, yet he took off these days." Joel took these days off without pay.

A review of the written evaluations of Esposito and Joel clearly showed that Joel was the better qualified teacher.

Joel first went to a local Jewish organization for help. The chair of the school committee, also Jewish, but a reformed Jew, was able to convince a Jewish organization to send a letter absolving the school committee of any religious discrimination. While there were a number of Jewish teachers and administrators in the school system, only Joel practiced traditional Orthodox Judaism.

According to the school committee chairman, Joel was "too Jewish." What is "too Jewish?" Should a teacher lose a position for being "too Jewish?" How about for being "too Catholic?" "Too female?" "Too Spanish?" "Too black?"

Joel brought suit in a state court against the school committee in 1980 for age, and religious discrimination. Joel claimed that he should have been assigned to teach Spanish in the high school instead of Esposito. At the very least, he should have been assigned some of the Spanish classes to teach.

The case was first tried before a jury in 1985. The judge forced Joel to try his case in one day, even though, because of the number of witnesses, it was not possible. As a result of time pressures, the testimony of his witnesses was shortened. The judge interrupted the proceedings frequently, making it impossible for Joel to get a fair trial. At 4:30 P.M., realizing that the case could not be finished in one day, the judge adjourned the case to the following day. The next day, the judge refused to let Joel call back earlier witnesses to complete their testimony. The judge gave the school committee all the time it needed to present their defense, even though the school committee had no defense. When the testimony was completed, the judge gave incorrect and incomplete instructions to the jury. The jury was so confused; it found the school committee not guilty.

Unlike a criminal case, in a civil case, a jury finds either for the plaintiff Joel and awards monetary damages or finds *for* the defendant school committee.

After the jury's verdict that found for the school committee, Joel moved for a new trial because of the legal errors committed by the judge. In a *very rare* instance, the judge granted Joel a new trial.

Joel tried his case a second time in 1989, before a different judge, but this judge refused to allow Joel a jury trial, and Joel was forced to try the case in front of this judge. This judge, before becoming a judge, was a member of a school committee and was clearly sympathetic to the financial problems of the defendant school committee.

At the trial, evidence was presented that Joel was a better qualified teacher than Esposito. He had more seniority. Joel had been hired on September 1, 1976, part time, to teach Hebrew. Esposito had been hired on September 6, 1976, part time, to teach Italian. Joel had more than twenty years of teaching experience; the teaching position was Esposito's first teaching position. Joel taught a social studies class for the 1978–1979 school year. Although the following year a social studies class became available, it was not assigned to Joel, but to a non-tenured, non-certified, non-Jewish teacher who was younger than Joel. In spite of the fact that there were social studies and Spanish openings, Joel was laid off in 1980. From 1980 to the time of the second trial, Spanish and social studies classes were available, but instead of recalling Joel to teach, the school committee hired new teachers, who were younger and who were not Orthodox Jews.

Mr. Sandman, the chair of the school committee at the time, testified at the trial. He never provided an explanation of why Spanish classes were not assigned to Joel, nor did he ever explain why Joel was not given social studies classes to teach, nor did he ever explain why Joel was not recalled to teach when classes became available.

Mr. Roberts, who was head of the language department at the time, testified that Joel was qualified to teach Spanish, and that in his opinion, Joel was better qualified than Esposito.

Mr. Peters, the principal of the high school at the time of the trial, was the only other person to testify for the school committee. He also provided no explanation of why Joel was not assigned to teach Spanish classes or social studies classes.

After a two-day trial, the judge rendered his decision on June 30, 1989. Regardless of the fact that there was no evidence to support the decision, the judge found that the school committee's decision to select Esposito over Joel to teach Spanish classes was based on the breadth of her foreign language capabilities and her past performance. The judge never addressed the issue of why Joel was not considered to teach social studies classes that were available. The judge found that, when the issue of Joel's religious holidays was raised, the superintendent of schools said, "He took off seven days of Jewish holidays. Why was it necessary for him to take off seven days? We bent over backwards to accommodate him, yet he took off those days." In spite of that evidence, the judge stated in his decision: "I find that the superintendent's remarks and his handling of the matter of the holidays required by Joel's religious persuasions were not motivated in any way by his intention to discriminate against Joel but rather by a sense of frustration that would be experienced by someone running a school system in which an individual, for whatever the reason, required special treatment."

The judge then relied on a letter from a Jewish organization that stated there was not enough evidence of discrimination for them to do anything. This type of evidence is called **hearsay.** Such documents are generally not admitted into evidence, because they are considered to be unreliable and based on unsubstantiated opinions rather than facts. Hearsay evidence is not subject to being cross-examined; it is not possible to cross-examine a piece of paper. However, not only did the judge allow this letter into evidence, he relied on it as part of his decision that there was no discrimination.

In spite of the fact that the school committee gave no lawful reason for their treatment of Joel, the judge found that Joel's religious beliefs were not a factor in the school committee's treatment of Joel. The judge based his decision on the fact that Joel taught Hebrew for four years at the high school where many Jewish teachers taught and where a Jew chaired the school committee.

The only reason Joel taught Hebrew at the high school was that parents petitioned for the course. There was a rule at high school that if enough parents petitioned for a particular course, it had to be given. Hebrew was taught at high school because parents had petitioned for the course, not because the administration or the school committee wanted it taught. More importantly, Joel was the only teacher in the school system that practiced Orthodox Judaism; a fact that was lost on this non-Jewish judge. It was not that Joel was Jewish-he was "too Jewish," meaning that he was an Orthodox Jew.

Although the judge found that Joel was a better-qualified teacher than Esposito, he found that the school committee could save money by keeping Esposito instead of Joel, since his salary was higher than hers. Even though the school committee never raised that as a reason, the judge found that this was a justifiable reason.

Since years of teaching is directly related to salary and age, salary is not a factor a school committee can take into consideration when deciding to lay off teachers for economic reasons. That is probably why the school committee did not raise Joel's higher salary as a defense. Unfortunately, this judge did not know the law.

Joel appealed this decision to an appellate court. The appellate court affirmed the trial judge's decision without explanation. A further appeal was taken, but this higher appellate court refused to consider the appeal, allowing the flawed previous decision to stand.

Joel survived the Holocaust but could not survive our judicial system. He is still unemployed, and at his age, it is unlikely that he will ever be employed as a teacher again.

In Joel's case he was able to prove that he was an Orthodox Jew, he was qualified, he was not assigned Spanish classes, and that a non-Jewish person was selected. Joel even proved that the younger non-Jewish person was not as well qualified. The school committee offered no explanation. Joel should have won his case, but he lost.

With his hidden agenda, the judge wrote a decision to support his beliefs. Decide what you want and then attempt to justify or rationalize the result.

| THE LESSON TO BE LEARNED

> Even if you have a clear-cut case of discrimination, even if you prove your case in court, you can still lose.

DANIEL
"Don't you know enough to leave when you're not wanted?"

Daniel was born in Egypt on January 28, 1947. He moved to this country in 1970, to take a managerial position with Marvel Motel Corporation.

In 1988, after he was laid off, and after Marvel failed to recall him to a position for which he was qualified, Daniel filed an employment discrimination claim against Marvel. Daniel entered into a settlement agreement with Marvel on October 7, 1989. As part of the settlement agreement, Daniel was reinstated to a position with Marvel on November 1, 1989.

In November 1989, Daniel had returned to work with Marvel at a temporary grade fifty position working out of his home in Massachusetts. He worked in that position for approximately nine months. He was next assigned to the position of general manager of the dietary and nutrition department at an account in Garden City, New Jersey. This was also a grade fifty position. Daniel began that position in April 1990, and was told that it would be a permanent position.

Relying upon that, Daniel purchased a house in Garden City, and moved his family there during the last week of July 1990. He was in that position for only five months, when he was told that he would have to be relocated to New York City. In December 1980, Daniel was assigned to a lower graded position, a grade forty-eight, in New York City, a much more expensive place to live. It was a very difficult assignment. The purpose of this difficult assignment was to force Daniel to quit. His salary was frozen at grade forty-eight, while other similarly situated employees were given salary increases. Daniel was told that if he did not accept the lower-graded position he would have to be laid off.

Although the second level supervisor continued to try to force Daniel to quit, Daniel refused. Daniel was told that his life was going to be made miserable, and that he was going to be watched every single hour. The second level supervisor also told Daniel's immediate supervisor that if he observed any problems that Daniel was having, that he should start disciplinary actions immediately so that

Daniel could be fired. The second level supervisor told Daniel's immediate supervisor that it was up to him to get rid of Daniel. The second level supervisor told Daniel's immediate supervisor that he should look only at things Daniel did wrong and not at any thing that Daniel did right. The second level supervisor tried to discredit Daniel's performance whenever he could.

Other management personnel also tried to force Daniel to quit. When Daniel's travel and hotel expenses for traveling to work were discontinued, there was a question whether Daniel would arrive on time because of his complicated travel arrangements. Daniel's immediate supervisor was told that if Daniel did not put in at least an eight-hour day, that he was to immediately begin disciplinary procedures to discharge Daniel.

The second level supervisor also forced Daniel's immediate supervisor to give Daniel a written warning for wearing a sweatshirt to a food show. On May 3, 1991, Daniel joined a truck driver to observe a route. One of Daniel's responsibilities was to take food in and out of the truck. Afterwards, Daniel was going to go to a food show at one of the hotels to observe some new equipment. Because he was in the truck, Daniel wore a sweatshirt. The food show was a public show and business attire was not required.

The next day Daniel was written up for wearing inappropriate clothing. No one else in the history of the company had ever received a written warning for wearing improper clothing. Six months after Daniel received the written warning, it was finally rescinded. Daniel's relocation assistance was taken away from him, even though he had been promised this assistance.

There were at least four grade forty-nine positions that were available, but instead of giving one of those positions to Daniel, they were given to younger, non-Arabic employees who had not filed discrimination charges and who had less time with the company.

When Daniel was removed from the Garden City account, he was told that it was at the request of the client. Daniel later found out that the client had not requested his removal. Being removed from the client created a severe hardship for Daniel because he had purchased a home in Garden City anticipating a long career there.

Daniel finally brought a second lawsuit against Marvel Motel Corporation. After discovery and depositions, Marvel moved for summary judgment claiming that there were no issues of material fact but only questions of law to be determined, and that the defendant Marvel Motel Corporation was entitled to judgment as a matter of law.

The trial judge, who was formerly a partner in a prominent Boston law firm who represented employers in employment discrimination cases, rendered his decision granting summary judgment in favor of the defendant Marvel Motel Corporation.

In his decision, the judge stated that, "The timing is close enough to make a **prima facie case** of retaliation." The judge also stated that, "I draw the harshest possible conclusions in respect of Mr. Peter's treatment of the plaintiff and, to a lesser degree, Mr. William's apparent willingness to play very close to the book on the question of whether or not the plaintiff is meeting various job responsibilities, including showing up for a full eight-hour day. It is my conclusion that Mr. Peters is acting in an overbearing and arbitrary fashion. But, unless that overbearing and arbitrary fashion is in some way shown to support a pretext for retaliation, it does not itself establish a claim." The judge further stated in his decision that, "There is a certain degree of arbitrariness on the part of his current principal supervisor, Mr. Peters, but that is not enough, in my mind, to establish retaliation discrimination and certainly not race discrimination."

This was in spite of the fact that Daniel's immediate supervisor found Daniel's job performance to be very good, that he met his immediate supervisor's expectations, and that on a scale of 1 to 10 (10 being the best), Daniel's performance was rated between 8.5 to 9. After filing his first claim against Marvel in 1989, Daniel was demoted to a grade forty-eight position doing primarily custodial work. When his traveling and living expenses were taken away, Daniel was forced to commute three and one-half hours each way, each day. That situation continues to exist to the present time. It is very likely that Daniel, who was and is an excellent performer for Marvel, will soon be forced out.

THE LESSON TO BE LEARNED

Even if you have a clear-cut case of discrimination, even if you prove your case in court, you can still lose.

CHAPTER 14

Sexual Orientation Discrimination

"We can have intellectual individualism and the rich cultural diversities that we owe to exceptional minds only at the price of occasional eccentricity and abnormal attitudes. When they are so harmless to others or to the state as those we deal with here, the price is not too great. But freedom to differ is not limited to things that do not matter much. That would be a mere shadow of freedom. The test of its substance is the right to differ as to things that touch the heart of the existing order."

Justice Jackson,

West Virginia State Board of Education v. Barnette, 319 U.S. 624 (1943).

Until recently there was no protection for discrimination on the basis of sexual orientation. Even now, it is lawful to discriminate against gays, lesbians, and bisexuals in most states. There is no federal protection, except under very limited circumstances.

SAMUEL
"Why tell the truth when lying is so much more creative?"

Samuel was a dedicated English teacher. He began teaching in 1970. In September 1974, he became a full-time teacher in the English Department at East Chelsea High School. He was so well thought of by his supervisor that he was recommended for double salary increases, which is only recommended for the most highly valued teachers. After four years, he became a tenured teacher at East Chelsea High School.

When certain members of the administration found out Samuel was gay, they began to harass him, intimidate him, and treat him differently than the other teachers. As a result of this harassment, Samuel suffered severe emotional distress, which resulted in seven nervous breakdowns; two of these resulted in hospitalizations.

While he was out on a medical leave of absence, the superintendent of the school system recommended that Samuel be reduced from a full-time teacher to teaching one class in 1982. When Samuel returned to teaching in 1982, he had one class assigned to him. Samuel continued to teach one English class from 1982 through 1988, although there were at least thirteen opportunities to give him additional English classes to teach. Instead of assigning him to a full-time position, younger, "straight," non-handicapped, non-tenured teachers were selected.

As a result of being demoted from a full-time teacher, Samuel filed a charge of discrimination. After the charge of discrimination was filed, the administration at East Chelsea High School continued to make Samuel's life difficult. In 1984, Samuel filed a lawsuit in the state superior court charging the high school with age and handicap discrimination in violation of state law. There was no law against discrimination on the basis of sexual orientation at the time. Samuel's claim of handicap discrimination involved a claim that his history of mental problems constituted a handicap within the meaning of state law. In fact, having a history of mental problems is considered a handicap under state law.

On October 3, 1988, the Department Chair of the English Department, Peter Johnson, took Samuel into his office and told Samuel that he had to write two observation reports on Samuel. Mr. Johnson told Samuel that he could write them up anyway he wanted, and that the evaluations could be good evaluations or bad evaluations. Mr. Johnson told Samuel that it was completely up to him. Mr. Johnson then told Samuel, "If you want the evaluations to be good, we could go into the back room, you can pull your pants down, lean over, and I'll f___ you in the ass, and then you'll always have good evaluations from me." Samuel refused. Samuel was told by the superintendent that if he ever filed any more grievances or complaints about the way he was being treated, that he would be terminated as a teacher. Mr. Johnson gave Samuel a bad evaluation. When Samuel complained, he was placed on indefinite leave and his teaching responsibilities were taken away from him.

On January 10, 1989, the superintendent wrote Samuel a letter telling Samuel that they planned to terminate him because of the incident with Mr.

Johnson. As a result, Samuel filed another charge of discrimination on January 23, 1989, claiming age discrimination, handicap discrimination, and retaliation. Samuel filed a second lawsuit when he was terminated.

The reason the school committee had removed Samuel as a full-time English teacher in 1982 was because of so-called "significant differences." Samuel had seniority over ten younger "straight" teachers. These ten teachers also did not have any handicaps, nor did they have any history of any mental problems, as Samuel did. At the time, there was a clause in the collective bargaining agreement that allowed the school committee to reduce in force a teacher out of seniority, only if there were "significant differences" between the teacher with more seniority and the teacher with less seniority. While the superintendent claimed there were significant differences between Samuel's evaluations and the least senior member of the English Department, an examination of the evaluations of all of the English teachers revealed that there were no significant differences between any of the teachers.

It was therefore necessary for the school committee to create some confusion to provide them with a better chance of prevailing at a trial. The lawyers representing the school committee took every conceivable negative aspect of Samuel's teaching over his many years of teaching, and then created a three hundred page document and used that document in 1989 as a basis to take away the one class that Samuel was teaching. Although all the reasons stated for removing him as a teacher for his one class in 1989, were not raised in 1982, as the basis for reducing him from a full-time teacher, they used all of those reasons for removing him as a teacher in 1989.

The trial was conducted over a thirteen-day period and the school committee painted a vivid picture of Samuel as someone financially dishonest because of a 1977 incident, academically dishonest because of some grading errors as a homosexual, and finally, as emotionally unbalanced and unstable. The picture the school committee painted was of a dishonest, sexually deviant unbalanced person. The jurors must have been asking themselves, "Would we want to have a teacher like that teaching our children?"

There were two jurors that kept asking the same question during jury deliberations, which was "I have looked at the evaluations, and I don't see any significant differences between the evaluations If there are no significant differences between the evaluations, then the school committee was wrong in reducing Samuel out of seniority." One of the jurors kept convincing the other jurors to "read between the lines." She also told the jurors that she worked as a personnel manager for a corporation, and that if somebody in her company complained, they would find a way to get rid of him. Unknown to me at the time, this juror was a personnel manager for a corporation I had sued in the past and one I was going to be suing in the very near future. This information did not come to light until after the trial was over. One of the two jurors who wanted to find in favor of Samuel came to us after the trial and informed us of all of the things that went on in the jury room during jury deliberations, and she revealed the bias and prejudice of the juror who was the personnel manager for a corporation I had sued in the past.

Although we filed a motion for new trial, and although the juror signed an affidavit as to the improprieties that occurred in the jury room, the trial court refused to grant a new trial, refused to reconsider any of the rulings he made, and allowed the jury verdict to stand.

The litigation consumed almost ten years of Samuel's life. During that period of time, he attempted suicide twice. The law firm representing the school committee earned almost a million dollars in fees. Samuel is still unemployed and deeply depressed.

THE LESSON TO BE LEARNED

Even if you have clear evidence of discrimination, you have no chance when you have a biased juror.

JUDY
"Oral promises aren't worth the paper they're written on"

Judy was employed for more than twenty years with a clothing manufacturer in Chicago. In August 1977, when Judy was 57 years old, she had a conversation with a Frank Ellis, who was then the president of Moon Coat Company, a manufacturer of raincoats. Ellis wanted Judy to move to Massachusetts and become the Director of Manufacturing for his operation. Judy told Ellis that she was reluctant to relocate to Massachusetts, unless she was assured of having the job in Massachusetts for life. Ellis told Judy that if Judy wanted the job of director of manufacturing for Moon, that Judy could have the job "for life."

Relying on Ellis' promise, Judy sold her home in Chicago, uprooted her girlfriend Lisa, and moved to Massachusetts to work for the Moon Company. Judy was made director of manufacturing, was paid a salary of $35,000 per year, received double life insurance, received medical coverage, received a stock option plan, and received other company benefits. Judy's prime motivating factor in coming to work for Moon was that she would have a job with Moon for life, or when Judy decided she wanted to retire.

Judy started working for Moon on August 22, 1977. As part of the incentive to keep Judy working at Moon, Ellis agreed to pay Judy a bonus of $5,000 for each full year that Judy worked for Moon. Unfortunately, soon after Judy began working at Moon, Ellis died, and John Sampson took over as president of Moon and within weeks of the change, on August 19, 1978, Judy was informed by some of her co-workers that Judy was going to be fired by Sampson. When Judy confronted Sampson, Sampson told her, "Why would we want to fire you, you have done such a good job for us." About a week after that conversation, Sampson called Judy into the office and said to Judy, "I don't think we need you anymore. We can get along without you." Judy had received no written or oral warnings of any kind prior to her being discharged. Needless to say, Judy never received the $5,000 bonus for staying almost a full year. Judy was discharged just prior to the first full year.

Oh, one other fact I forgot to mention. Judy was a lesbian. This did not bother Ellis, but it did bother Sampson, the new man in charge.

Judy was so emotionally distraught, that for an entire week, she never told her significant other. She would get up in the morning as if she were going to work, would go to the company, walk around the building for the entire day, and then would go home when she normally would as if she was working. Finally, after a week of going to the company and standing outside for eight hours a day, once in the rain, Judy finally told her companion.

Following her discharge from Moon, Judy tried to get employment at a number of different places. On October 19, 1978, one company told her that they were going to hire her but first had to check with her prior employer. After contacting Sampson, Judy was then told there was no job available. In January 1979, Judy sought employment at another company. They also told her that they had to check with her prior employer. After checking with Sampson, Judy was told there was no job available. In March 1979, Judy contacted another employer in Los Angeles, California. She was also told that before she could get the job that they would have to check with her prior employer. That was the last Judy ever heard about that job offer.

During her entire employment with Moon, Judy never received an oral or written warning from anyone concerning any of her work performance. During her employment with Moon, she improved productivity, she improved the quality of the garments being manufactured, and was also able to stop a high turnover rate of employees at the plant. Judy was replaced with a "straight" male, whose qualifications were not as good as Judy's. Judy believed that she was terminated because Sampson hated lesbians and gays. However, there was no law against discriminating against lesbians. She could therefore not bring a claim for discrimination on the basis of sexual orientation.

Prior to coming to work for Moon, Judy had been employed in the garment industry for almost forty years, and held a similar position with a company in Chicago for twenty years.

By the time Judy had sought counsel regarding her claims against Moon, more than six months had passed. In order to bring a claim for age discrimination with the Massachusetts Commission Against Discrimination and the Equal Employment Opportunity Commission, one must bring the charge within six months, or the claims are barred by the statute of limitations. This means that even if you have a meritorious claim, if you do not bring the claim within six months, you lose the right to bring it at a later time. Since the law did not protect Judy from discrimination on the basis of her sexual orientation, she did not even think of any other basis, such as age.

Since Judy could not bring a claim for age discrimination or sexual orientation discrimination under state or federal law, she brought her claim against Moon for breach of an employment contract, since the contract she made with Ellis was a contract "for life." Where there is a contract for life, a person can normally not be discharged unless there is good cause. Judy brought suit in the state superior court alleging a breach of the employment contract.

The defendants filed a motion for a directed verdict. A motion for a directed verdict is a procedural device that asks the trial judge to direct the verdict in favor of the employer. A directed verdict is like summary judgment. The judge decides the case, not the jury. A direct verdict is only supposed to be granted by a judge if there are no issues of fact in dispute, but only questions of law. All doubts are supposed to be resolved in favor of the non-moving party, in this case, Judy. If the court had allowed the motion, that would have ended the case. The trial judge initially denied the motion for a directed verdict and allowed the case to go forward. On the second day of the trial, the trial judge allowed the motion for a directed verdict, dismissed the case, and entered a judgment for the defendants. The judge did this without hearing all of the evidence. The case was appealed to the appeals court and on July 7, 1987, the appeals court affirmed the decision dismissing the case.

It is interesting to note that the appeals court agreed that one could bring a claim for breach of employment contract under a common law theory, but that

Judy had only decided to bring her claim under a common law theory after a change in the law, and that since this was a surprise to the defendants, that the superior court was correct in dismissing the case. The fact is that there was no surprise to the defendants. The appeals court simply ignored the facts to reach their decision. Unfortunately, this is common. If the facts of a case do not allow a court to decide a case the way it wants, the court will simply ignore those facts to reach the conclusion it wants.

Following the trial, Judy moved out of the state, and to this day, has been unable to find a suitable position in the garment industry. A woman who was once the director of manufacturing for multi-million dollar international companies now works in a supermarket part-time bagging groceries.

THE LESSON TO BE LEARNED

A judge has the power to effect the outcome of every case, to ignore the facts, and to ignore the law.

CHAPTER 15

"It is part of every man's civil rights that he be left at liberty to refuse business with any person whomsoever, whether the refusal rests upon reason, or is the result of whim, caprice, prejudice or malice."

Justice Harlan,

Adair v. United States, 208 U.S. 161 (1908).

LEONARD
"Honesty will get you fired"

Leonard began his employment with Allied Car Leasing in July 1982, as vice president of finance. Leonard was a certified public accountant. At the time he was hired, Leonard told the president of Allied that he wanted the job at Allied to be the last job before his retirement. The president of the company at that time was John Bean. Bean agreed that Leonard could have the job, as vice president of finance until Leonard was ready to retire.

During the course of his employment with Allied, Leonard received a number of raises. Abraham, the owner of Allied, would constantly criticize and humiliate Leonard because Leonard refused to do a number of things, which Leonard believed to be illegal, unethical, and immoral.

Abraham demanded that Leonard adjust figures when they reported Allied's revenue to the insurance company so as to effect a lower cost for insurance premiums. Abraham did not want Leonard to report revenue earned on renting or leasing automobiles. Leonard believed that not to report those earnings would not only be a violation of his professional ethics as a certified public accountant, but that he would be violating the law and committing a fraud on the insurance company.

There were also people included on the payroll of Allied that performed no work for Allied. Leonard objected that this practice also was a violation of law.

Abraham also made payments from Allied's funds for personal expenses. Leonard also refused to be involved in that practice since that too was a violation of the law. Abraham also demanded that Leonard register automobiles in the state of Maine rather than in the state of Massachusetts in order to save fees that were required in Massachusetts. This was also a violation of law.

Whenever financing arrangements were made, the signature of the customer was required on the credit statements. Instead of obtaining the signature of the customers, Abraham would have employees of Allied forge the customer's signatures. This caused a great deal of friction between Abraham and Leonard, because Leonard refused to be a party to anything that was illegal. Abraham also pressured Leonard to file fraudulent insurance claims by inflating the value and the cost for repairs to the automobiles.

As a result of all of these illegal activities, and as a result of the work pressures, Leonard began to develop some physical problems related to this stress. Unknown to Leonard at the time, Abraham had a conversation with John Bean. During that conversation, Abraham told Bean that he was going to make life so miserable for Leonard, that he would force Leonard to quit, and if he did not quit, he would fire him. On June 5, 1985, Leonard was fired from his job without any oral or written warnings of any kind.

After his discharge, Leonard filed for unemployment compensation. At the hearing for unemployment compensation, Abraham convinced Bean to lie and testify that Leonard had voluntarily left, and that he was not fired or forced out as Leonard testified. As a result of John Bean's testimony, and the testimony of other employees of Allied, Leonard was denied unemployment compensation benefits, and the hearing officer found that Leonard had voluntarily resigned.

Leonard brought suit in the state superior court on February 26, 1986, alleging that he had been discharged because he refused to perform illegal acts as requested by Abraham. While the suit was pending, Abraham fired Bean as president of Allied. Bean then testified at a deposition that he had been forced to lie at the unemployment compensation hearing, and that Abraham told him what to say. Bean also testified in the deposition that Abraham was going to try to force Leonard out, and that if he could not force Leonard out, that he would fire him. Bean further testified that Abraham tried to force Leonard to commit illegal acts, and that Leonard refused to engage in any illegal acts.

In spite of that deposition testimony, Allied moved for summary judgment based upon the findings of the unemployment compensation hearing that held Leonard had voluntarily resigned. The state superior court judge granted summary judgment on the basis that the decision of the unemployment compensation hearing that Leonard voluntarily resigned was **res judicata,** and that Leonard could therefore not bring his claim in court. Res judicata is an affirmative defense used to dismiss claims that have been decided previously. Since the unemployment compensation hearing held before the trial determined that Leonard voluntarily resigned, Leonard could not assert that he was forced out in his state court lawsuit. The superior court judge granted summary judgment for Allied on August 28, 1989. Leonard filed an appeal with the appellate court and the appellate court affirmed the decision of the superior court, dismissing Leonard's claims. Allied is still in business, is still committing illegal activities, and is making millions of dollars for its owner. Leonard has been unable to find a permanent position in accounting and now works part time for a small company as a bookkeeper.

THE LESSON TO BE LEARNED

A judge can disregard the facts and find what he or she wants to find.

NICOLE
"Safety first, job lost"

Nicole began her employment with the defendant Cartone on November 6, 1972. She was hired as a general assembler and worked in the G-5 Department wiring gyroscopes, which were part of the guidance system for missiles sold to the federal government.

In May of 1985, she successfully bid for the position of expediter on the second shift. Her hours on the second shift were from 4:00 P.M. to 12:30 A.M. During the entire time period she held the position of expediter, she was the only expediter on the second shift. As the expediter, Nicole delivered inventory from one department to another, refilled chemical containers, logged-in materials to the storage department, and delivered requested material from storage to the appropriate departments. A substantial portion of her time as an expediter did not involve the daily lifting and movement of materials that weighed between twenty and fifty pounds. On September 6, 1985, Nicole wrote a letter to President Reagan, in which she explained that while working on the space shuttle program, she discovered problems with the gyroscopes produced by Cartone that could endanger the space shuttle. Her letter was forwarded to NASA. A NASA representative responded by a letter dated November 22, 1985, stating that NASA was interested in the productivity and quality of performance of employers involved in the NASA programs. The letter further stated that NASA would conduct an investigation concerning Nicole's allegations.

A NASA representative met with the vice president of Cartone and with Nicole. At this meeting, Nicole gave the NASA representative a list of problems with the shuttle gyroscopes. She also demonstrated the problems for him with actual gyroscopes produced by Cartone. In spite of the evidence she provided, NASA found nothing wrong. Right after Nicole had complained about the safety of Cartone's products, she began experiencing an overload of work. Prior to writing to the president, and prior to the investigation by NASA, she never had any problems completing any of her assignments. Afterwards, however, work that was not completed on the first shift was left for her to do. Shelves would be filled with undelivered materials left over from the first shift. She had to deliver the materials if the work on Cartone's products was going to be done. At the same time, she also had to perform her regular duties. This work overload got progressively worse, yet they did not hire a second expediter for the second shift.

Nicole complained to her supervisor and to her union about this work overload, since it was very stressful, but no one was taking any action to alleviate the severe overloading of work. Nicole was constantly trying to get the day shift expediters to perform their jobs, so that she would not have the extra work left over from them. The second shift supervisors would complain to Nicole that they could not get anything moved on the first shift so they would page Nicole to get her to obtain the necessary materials so they could start their work. This work overload continued until Cartone decided to demote Nicole.

In the 1970s, Nicole was under the care and treatment of several doctors for lower-back problems. In early 1986, Nicole experienced a problem with her neck and shoulder that required her to seek the care and treatment of a chiropractor. In March 1986, her chiropractor gave her a letter to give to Cartone. In that letter, the chiropractor stated that Nicole should not lift in excess of 20 pounds until her problems had been totally corrected. Cartone then put Nicole on a 20-pound weight restriction. Even though she was put on this weight restriction, Nicole continued to lift more than twenty pounds, even in front of her supervisor, who made no objection.

In May 1988, Nicole suffered a lower-back problem that caused her to be out of work from the end of May 1988, until June 13, 1988. On June 10, 1988, Nicole went to see Dr. Crane, Cartone's in-house doctor, about returning to work. Prior to speaking to him, a company nurse had informed Nicole that Nicole did not have a weight restriction on her ability to work. Nicole gave Dr. Crane a note from one of her doctors, an orthopedic surgeon, stating that Nicole could return to work on June 13, 1988. The note stated the reason for Nicole's absence, but did not place any restrictions on her ability to work. Dr. Crane asked Nicole if she could lift twenty pounds comfortably, and Nicole told him she could. Dr. Crane did not examine Nicole or check her back in any way. In spite of those facts, he placed her on a 20-pound weight restriction.

Nicole returned to work on June 13, 1988, and continued to lift more than twenty pounds with her supervisor's knowledge. On July 26, 1988, Nicole was informed that she was being demoted because of this weight restriction. She told Cartone that she had been lifting more than 20 pounds all along and that her doctor had not placed any restrictions on her ability to work. Nevertheless, she was demoted to the position of general assembler in the clean room on the second shift. Her former job was taken over by a male employee, who was younger than Nicole was, and who had less **seniority.**

After working in the clean room for a few weeks, Nicole informed her supervisor at Cartone that she had a problem working in there because she was losing her hair and that she could not work in the clean room where the workers had to wear nylon caps. Nicole asked to be reassigned to another department. She was seeking a lateral transfer. Although there were seven openings in the package department, Cartone refused to consider her for one of the openings. Nicole's supervisors told her that if she could not work in the clean room, she could quit. The following day, Nicole obtained another note from her doctor, which explicitly stated that there was no weight restriction on her ability to lift, and that because of her sensitivity that she should not work in the clean room.

In spite of this, Cartone refused to return her to expediter position and refused to remove her from the clean room. During the period of time she was under this so-called weight restriction, Cartone made very little effort to accommodate her impairment.

Interestingly enough, the male employee who replaced Nicole as expediter on the second shift, had a back problem too. He was not required to lift any of the containers. One of the day-shift expediters had a back problem as well, but he did not have the work overload that Nicole had.

As a result of all of the stress and harassment, Nicole met with Dr. Erma, a psychologist, on numerous occasions. She told Dr. Erma that she had been experiencing serious physical and mental problems because of all of the stressful actions by Cartone, the demotion, and Cartone's failure to allow Nicole to return to work. Nicole by this time was suffering from ulcers, hypertension, depression, hair loss, headaches, light-headedness, fatigue, the feeling of being overwhelmed, insomnia, interrupted sleep, difficulty concentrating, and memory problems.

Dr. Erma diagnosed Nicole's condition as psychological factors influencing physical condition, including hair loss, and adjustment disorder with depressed mood. On February 27, 1989, and again on May 16, 1989, Dr. Erma stated that Nicole was able to return to work without any work restrictions, except working in the clean room. Even the psychologist that Nicole saw at Cartone's request, said, as early as January 16, 1989, that Nicole could return to work, but not in the clean room. Another doctor stated in his report on September 8, 1989, that Nicole was capable of performing her customary work activities as an expediter without restriction, as there was no objective evidence of any on-going disability. On September 11, 1989, another doctor, a neurosurgeon, stated that Nicole could return to work as an expediter without restrictions. However, on June 27, 1989, the company doctor, Dr. Crane, wrote to Dr. Erma that because of Nicole's depression and work-related stress, Cartone considered "finding a satisfactory slot for her becomes nearly, if not totally impossible."

Nicole was never informed by either her union or Cartone, of any discussions of decisions regarding her return to work in 1989, or early 1990. Although Nicole was ready, willing, and able to return to work, Cartone refused to allow her to return to work in any position.

Since her income had stopped, Nicole fell way behind on her mortgage. To prevent the bank from foreclosing on her home, Nicole sold it for a substantial loss and was forced into subsidized housing.

Having no other choice, Nicole filed suit against Cartone claiming that she was discriminated against because she complained to the federal government about the defective gyroscopes, and that Cartone discriminated against her because of her disabilities. This was nothing more than blatant retaliation, and when all of the facts came out, she would get her job back. Nicole had applied for a promotion to get away from her supervisor, but instead of giving her the promotion, they gave the promotion to a younger male who was clearly not as well qualified. Nicole claimed that was sex discrimination.

Cartone retained one of the largest and most prestigious law firms in Massachusetts. After extensive discovery, Cartone filed a motion for summary judgment. A motion for summary judgment is typical in employment discrimination cases. Even though the facts are almost always disputed, courts are very willing to accept the explanations manufactured by employers, consider the explanations as reasonable business decisions, and then grant summary judgment in favor of employers, thus ending the case for the employee.

One of the favorite tactics of the lawyer representing employers is to comb the employment history of the employee for any problems that occurred throughout her entire history, even if those problems had nothing to do with the current situation. If Nicole's employment history was compared to the employment history of all of the other employees who were in similar positions, you would probably find that her employment history was better than most of the other employees who were not discharged or treated differently. However, for purposes a summary judgment motion, an employer will take an employee's employment history and cast it in the most negative light.

Many employment discrimination cases are dismissed by this summary judgment device, thereby depriving employees of their day in court. In theory, the judge considering a motion for summary judgment is supposed to take all facts in favor of the employee, including all reasonable inferences. In theory, all doubts are supposed to be resolved in favor of the employee. However, in practice, some judges find a way of granting summary judgment in favor of the employer, and keeping the cases away from juries, who are much more likely to be sympathetic to the plight of the average worker.

Summary judgment should rarely be granted in employment cases because the motive or intent of the employer is always a disputed issue of fact. Fortunately, most competent, knowledgeable, and conscientious judges deny motions for summary judgment.

The law firms representing Cartone earned in excess of $100,000 in legal fees.

In the meantime, because of her lack of income, the bank foreclosed on Nicole's home, her marriage broke up, and she was eventually forced into bankruptcy. The appellate court eventually affirmed the judgment of the superior court dismissing all of her claims.

Nicole, who blew the whistle on Cartone over safety issues, has still been unable to find a permanent job. Meanwhile, Cartone still makes gyroscopes for the federal government.

THE LESSON TO BE LEARNED

A court can disregard facts and find what it wants to find.

ADAM

"It's not what you know, but who you know"

Adam had worked for the West Chelsea Housing Authority for more than eighteen years. He had continuous service receiving short-term contracts of employment. Adam always performed his work in a fully satisfactory manner. In 1987, John Candor became his immediate supervisor and was responsible for hiring supervisors to work at various housing projects in West Chelsea. Soon after he came on board, Candor hired his relatives to perform these short-term contracts and as the contracts expired of the other supervisors, he would only renew those he liked. When Candor came on board there were several black supervisors. Candor did not renew any of the short-term contracts for any of the black supervisors, including Adam.

When the West Chelsea Housing Authority failed to renew Adam's short-term employment contract, Adam brought a claim against the West Chelsea Housing Authority for race and age discrimination and retaliation, since by this time, Adam was fifty years old. Adam also brought a claim against the Candor for intentional interference with his contract. The case was first tried on August 30, 1988, before a judge and a jury. The jury deliberated for more than two days and was unable to reach a verdict on race discrimination. The jury did find that there was no age discrimination. The jury also found in favor of Adam and against Candor on a claim that Candor intentionally interfered with Adam's employment contract and awarded Adam $175,000 in damages. Candor's lawyer filed a motion for judgment notwithstanding the verdict as to the $175,000 verdict. The judge granted that motion and gave no reason or explanation on the record, but in chambers, stated to counsel that he never discussed the issue of mitigation of damages with the jury, and that an award of $175,000 was excessive. The judge said that if Adam (who was a fifty-year-old black man in the city of West Chelsea) made a reasonable effort, he could easily have found another job. The trial judge had never had to work a day in his life, since he came from a very wealthy family.

The case was tried again before a different judge on the issue of race discrimination. The second trial judge gave incorrect jury instructions, and after deliberating for more than two days, the second jury found there was no race discrimination in spite of the fact that the West Chelsea Housing Authority never provided a reasonable explanation for the decision not to renew Adam's employment contract.

Although there were many valid grounds to appeal the decisions, Adam was unable to afford the cost of the appeal, and as a result, Adam was out on the street after almost twenty years. He has still been unable to find a comparable job.

THE LESSON TO BE LEARNED

A court can disregard facts and find what it wants to find.

STACEY
"One tainted juror can ruin your whole day"

Stacey began working for the Stone Bank in 1982, as a part-time teller. Although she had a young child at home, she was forced to go to work because her husband was disabled and was only able to work part time. In 1990, his heart condition became so severe that he was no longer able to work even part time. As a result, Stacey requested to be put on full-time duty at the Stone Bank for the extra income and for the medical benefits, which included substantial coverage for prescription medications. By 1990, Stacey's husband required medicines that cost approximately $900 each month. With the medical benefits, Stacey only had to pay $15 each month.

During the course of her employment with the Stone Bank, Stacey performed a variety of jobs, including bank teller, bank teller trainer, loan processor, customer service representative, telephone switchboard operator, safety deposit box attendant, and was even considered for a branch manager's position. In the twelve years of her employment, her evaluations were always good, if not better than good. The Stone Bank also had a stock ownership plan, and Staccy participated in that plan and had acquired 500 shares of stock.

On January 4, 1992, her immediate supervisor gave her a proxy statement all filled out and told her to sign it. Stacey was reluctant to sign it because it had been filled out. However, her supervisor insisted that she sign it, and so Stacey signed the proxy statement reluctantly.

She went home and talked to her husband about it, and he called the Securities and Exchange Commission. He was told that nothing could be done unless they put it in writing. They decided that it would be best if they did nothing. They were concerned that if they made waves, that the bank might try to fire Stacey. Things went pretty smoothly the next several months, but being asked to sign the proxy statement kept grating on Stacey's mind. She finally decided that she would write a letter to the president of the bank, expressing her concern and asking the president to change the practice.

Stacey wrote the letter to the president of Stone Bank, questioning the practice. The bank president called in Stacey's supervisor and the next day, Stacey's supervisor brought Stacey to an isolated, closed area of the bank and yelled at her for almost two hours, complaining to her that she had gone over his head and gotten him into some trouble with the president. Stacey left the bank in tears and went home to her husband. Her husband, seeing her in this state, was incensed and called up the Securities and Exchange Commission. He found out whom to send the letter to, and then had Stacey write a letter to the Securities and Exchange Commission complaining about signing a proxy statement that had already been filled out.

The Securities and Exchange Commission initiated some inquiries at the Stone Bank. Several of the management personnel at the Stone Bank fabricated information and put it in Stacey's personnel folder, without Stacey's knowledge. The president of Stone Bank then filed a response to the letter he received from the Securities and Exchange Commission.

About one week later, Stacey's supervisor said to Stacey, "I can't believe you did that to the bank!" Stacey's supervisor then undertook a campaign of harassment, creating a severe and hostile work environment for Stacey. In July 1993, Stacey told her supervisor that no matter how miserable he made her working conditions, that he could not force her to quit because she needed the money to support her family and she needed the medical benefits, and the payment of the prescription drugs that her husband needed to live.

Shortly after that conversation, Stacey's supervisor started to develop a paper trail to justify discharging Stacey for cause. However, since there was no cause, the supervisor was unable to fire Stacey.

By January 1994, the Stone Bank did need to lay off some of their workers for economic reasons. The bank had 200 employees in eight branches. Management decided to terminate one employee per branch in this lay off. There were no standards, and it was left to the discretion of each branch manager who would be laid off. Although Stacey had more seniority then any other employee at her branch, and although she had performed more different jobs than any other employee, and even though Stacey had better evaluations than many of the employees in the branch, Stacey was selected as the employee to be laid off.

Stacey brought a lawsuit against the Stone Bank for discharging her in violation of public policy and brought a claim against her former supervisor for intentional interference with advantageous contractual relations.

The Stone Bank filed a motion to dismiss, which was denied. The Stone Bank filed a motion for summary judgment, which was denied. Stacey was able to overcome those initial hurdles. Her case was called for trial eight times, and finally the ninth time it was called, it actually went forward to trial.

At the trial, the principal defendants were caught making contradictory statements under oath. Things were going very well at the trial, but then an unanticipated event occurred. About six days into the trial, one of the jurors came forward to talk to the trial judge and the lawyers in chambers. The juror told them that the night before he had met an old friend of his, and although the judge had told the jurors not to discuss the case with anyone, this juror had told his friend that he was a juror in the trial against the bank. The juror identified the bank, and his friend then told the juror that the bank was his father-in-law's bank. At which point, the juror left and reported all of this to the judge. The juror also told them that he had known the son-in-law of the bank's president for about ten to fifteen years and that he even worked for the son-in-law for about five years in the past.

The trial judge then asked the juror if given those circumstances, the juror could render a fair and impartial verdict based on the evidence, and keep an open mind. The juror stated that he could, and the trial judge refused to strike the juror, even though there would have been thirteen jurors left to deliberate, and the usual jury in a civil case has only twelve jurors. In spite of vehement protest by Stacey's attorney, the juror was allowed to sit and participate in the jury deliberations. The jury was out for almost two full days, and then reached a verdict against Stacey and for the bank. After the jury verdict it was learned that the tainted juror knew the son-in-law better than he said he did. The son-in-law was on the board of directors of an institution that hired the juror to work on a part-time basis, had obtained a full-time job for the juror's brother, and the juror had attended the wedding of the son-in-law, where the father-in-law was present.

As a result of losing her job, Stacey lost her medical benefits. She could no longer afford to pay for her husband's expensive prescription drugs. She had three children to feed. She had a mortgage she could not afford. While the case was pending, Stacey's husband died of a heart attack brought on because he had stopped taking his medicines.

THE LESSON TO BE LEARNED

One biased juror can affect the outcome of a case, regardless of the facts and evidence.

PAUL
"Take your pick—protect your life or your job. You can't protect both!"

In 1988, Paul went to work for the Newtown Container Company as a drill press operator. The drill press operation required an extensive amount of lifting and bending. While the job caused him some pain in his legs, shoulders, neck, and back, he was able to tolerate the job and worked in pain. By 1990 the pain had grown sufficiently severe that he sought medical treatment. In 1991, the company purchased a new drill in order to accommodate the larger container. These containers were much heavier than the containers Paul was used to working on. Paul would make suggestions from time to time on how the drill could be modified to make it easier to operate and cause less pain to the operators. Although he continued to make suggestions, no one from the company did anything to improve the drill. In 1992, a Japanese conglomerate bought out the company.

In desperation, Paul went to the Department of Labor and made out a safety complaint with the Occupational Safety and Health Act (OSHA). This law is designed to protect workers and to require employers to provide safe working places. Whenever a worker feels that there is a hazard at the work place, they have a right to complain, and·an inspector or agent from the Department of Labor has a duty to inspect and to make sure whatever health or safety risk exists is eliminated. After the complaint was made, an OSHA inspector arrived at the plant and looked at a drill press and indicated that there were serious problems with the drill that had to be fixed. Only after that inspection, did the company start to make any changes to the drill press.

Unfortunately, the changes were not sufficient to fix the problem and the drill press continued to cause substantial physical problems for Paul. By April 1, 1993, the problems had become so severe that Paul could no longer continue to work at the drill press. He asked his supervisor if there was any other job he could do or if they could fix the drill press so that he could operate it without causing him injury. His supervisor said that there was nothing he could do and so Paul took a medical leave of absence from April 1, 1993, until April 10, 1993. On April 10, 1993, he returned to his supervisor and asked again if something could be done so he could return to work. Paul brought a note from his doctor indicating that he had certain restrictions regarding lifting and bending. His supervisor told him that until he could return to work without any restrictions that there was nothing available.

In the meantime, because he had no savings, he went to a friend who was painting his house and the friend agreed to let Paul help him paint the house. Unknown to Paul, the company hired a private investigator to follow Paul. The private investigator took a video of Paul buying cans of paint and a video of Paul painting a room in the house. When the company refused to let him come back to work on June 10, 1993, Paul filed a charge of discrimination alleging that the company failed to provide a reasonable accommodation for his impairment. After the company refused to provide a reasonable accommodation, they hired a private investigator to watch Paul's activities.

On July 1, Paul agreed to come back to work without restrictions. Paul brought a note from his doctor asking that he be placed on some job other than working on the drill press. The company failed to follow Paul's doctor's recommendations and put Paul back on the drill press. As a result of working on the drill press, Paul started developing severe pain in his shoulders, legs, and back and had to undergo physical therapy. The only time he could get an appointment was late in the afternoon, and as a result, Paul had to leave work four hours early to get this treatment. The company had an attendance policy that stated if an employee had ten or more absences; he or she could be terminated. Every time Paul went for physical therapy, he was given a half-day absence. By August 1, he had accumulated 9.5 days of absence and he was told that if he had one more half-day of absence he would be discharged.

The pain in his neck, back, and legs and the stress of possibly losing his job caused him to seek another medical leave of absence. He also filed a claim for worker's compensation on September 2, 1994. By October 5, 1994, Paul came back to work without any restrictions and requested that he not be put back to work on the drill press. By this time, the company was in the process of closing the Massachusetts plant and they offered Paul a job in their Maine plant. On October 15, 1994, Paul was reassigned to the Maine plant and was put to work painting the new factory. Even though he was doing some bending and climbing of ladders, his condition improved and he was feeling less pain in his legs, neck, back, and shoulders, although he was still getting physical therapy. The improvement allowed him to decrease the physical therapy appointments and he was now down to one appointment a week and was able to get this appointment on a Saturday when he was not at work. Unfortunately for Paul, on December 15, 1994, the company moved the drill press from the Massachusetts plant to the Maine plant and put Paul back working on the drill press in spite of Paul's protests and in spite of the fact that all of the doctors who treated Paul, said that working on the drill press was dangerous to Paul's health. Again, Paul was given the choice of his job or his health. Paul did what he was told and went back to work on the drill press.

The pain in his legs, back, shoulders, and neck became so great that he asked the plant nurse to send him for treatment. The plant nurse recommended a clinic and Paul went there for treatment. Paul explained all his problems to the doctor and told him that on a scale of 0 to 10, his pain was about a 6 or 7. Paul also told the doctor that the pain would come on gradually as he would work on the drill press. The pain is aggravated if he stands for long periods of time. He told the doctor that he liked his job, got along well with his supervisor, but that given his medical condition, he could not go back to work on the drill press. The doctor found that he had severe muscle spasm and strain to his lower back, legs, neck, and shoulders. He also broke down while talking to the doctor and told him it was very difficult to cope with his job at the present time because of the pain.

The doctor contacted the nurse at the company and the doctor was invited to visit the plant to look at the drill press. The purpose of the visit was to evaluate the work tasks, which Paul had described to the doctor, and to attempt to determine whether Paul's symptoms and findings at the present time could be related to the way in which Paul performed his job. The doctor was shown the operation of the drill press. Based upon his observations, the doctor stated that Paul should not return to work on the drill press until he was pain free and his symptoms improved, and they should find a different position for him.

The doctor also suggested that the drill press be evaluated to determine the optimal position for the operator to work in so that the bending of the spine at the waist did not have to be constantly maintained, the arms did not have to be held outstretched for any lengthy period of time, and the hand and wrist motions required to do the job were minimized.

The day following the plant visit, the doctor again had an opportunity to examine Paul. The doctor determined that Paul's problems were job related. Paul described the pain, the intensity of the pain, and physical symptoms. Paul also told the doctor that he could not continue to work because there was no available work for him. He also made it very clear that he wanted to return to work very much. The doctor then told the company that Paul should not be put back on the drill press, that Paul should not be lifting anything weighing more than 10 pounds, that Paul should avoid bending, kneeling, squatting, climbing, and repetitive motion using his shoulders. The doctor also spoke with the company nurse and discussed ways the drill press could be fixed to benefit Paul as well as the other workers. The nurse told the doctor that the company would not be able to accommodate Paul back on light duty until the doctor had discharged Paul.

The doctor also noted that Paul was very depressed, angry with the company, and that Paul wanted to get back to work as quickly as possible. The doctor discussed with Paul's physical therapist that it was important that Paul get back to work as soon as possible. The doctor called the company nurse and told her that every effort should be made to get Paul back to work and allow him to work within the restrictions the doctor recommended. The doctor also told the company nurse that the failure to return Paul to the workplace as soon as possible might result in a prolonged recovery and have possible implications with regard to worker's compensation. The doctor also suggested that it might be helpful to arrange a conference with Paul, herself, the doctor, the physical therapist, and a number of the company's management to attempt to develop a return-to-work plan for Paul.

About two weeks later, the doctor received a call from the company nurse to visit the plant and to evaluate a proposed job to accommodate Paul within the restrictions the doctor recommended. The job being considered was to work on a smaller drill press. When the doctor watched the job being performed, he decided it would not be suitable for Paul as the operator still had to stand up in a forward stooping position with the arms outstretched in order to work the drill press. While the doctor was observing the operation of the drill press, the person operating it spontaneously complained that working the job all day caused him pain in his back and shoulders. The doctor then told the company nurse that the job would not be appropriate for Paul.

Although Paul's physical condition was improving, the company still had no available jobs given Paul's medical restrictions. The doctor also found that Paul was suffering from chronic back pain and that further active physical therapy should be undertaken to help resolve his problems.

The doctor also recommended that Paul be placed on another job so that his medical problems would not return. The company followed the recommendation of the doctor and put Paul on a different job and at that point Paul no longer had any further medical problems in connection with his back, neck, shoulders, and legs. The doctor followed up about one month later and found that Paul had improved significantly and was restored to his normal functioning and was able to work full time without any further restrictions.

Prior to being put back to work, Paul retained an attorney who notified the company that unless they put Paul on a job that would not cause him to have a relapse, that a lawsuit would be brought against them for violating his rights. When they put him on this new job, Paul was thrilled and called his lawyer up a few weeks later and thanked her profusely for having helped him out of this dilemma. He now had a job he enjoyed doing, he was being paid, and he was no longer suffering any pain. It appeared that the case was closed with a positive outcome.

About 8 months later, Paul saw some of the workers dumping hazardous waste into the public drainage system. He asked the workers whether that was legal and they told him to keep his mouth shut, mind his own business, and keep doing his job. Paul was very concerned so he went to his supervisor. His supervisor told him that if he were smart he would keep his mouth shut and just do his job. From time to time, Paul would continue to see some of the workers dumping the chemicals into the public drains. He started reading up about how polluting the area might cause water contamination. He went to people higher up in the company, and they assured him that they weren't doing anything illegal. Paul continued to do his job but saw the workers dumping more and more chemicals. Some of the chemicals they were dumping were into empty lots of land and not just into the public drain system. Paul continued to be concerned and continued to complain to his supervisor who kept telling Paul not to worry about it and mind his own business and that they had permission to do what they were doing. Being concerned about this, Paul finally went to the Department of Labor in Maine to find out whether or not the company was doing anything illegally.

Within a week after his complaint was filed with the Department of Labor, someone from the state came to the plant and Paul showed him where they were dumping the chemicals. Paul also complained to the Federal Department of Labor. About a week after the state agent made the inspection from the Department of Labor, Paul's employment was terminated. This came without any oral or written warning of any kind. The termination notice simply stated "It is apparent that the employment relationship between you and this company is not acceptable to either party. Therefore effective immediately, your employment is terminated." Paul immediately filed a second charge of discrimination with the state fair employment agency, alleging, in addition to disability discrimination for failure to provide a reasonable accommodation, retaliation discrimination for discharging him. The lawsuit was filed in two parts. The first part was for the failure to provide Paul a reasonable accommodation. The second part of the lawsuit was the discharge that occurred on September 1, 1995.

The company's lawyer filed a motion to dismiss the second part of the lawsuit since the discharge occurred in Maine, not Massachusetts and that if Paul had any claim, he should bring the claim in Maine. The company lawyer was able to convince the judge to dismiss the second part of the lawsuit leaving as the only issues to be decided in the Massachusetts lawsuit, the failure of the company to provide Paul a reasonable accommodation when he requested it.

The failure to provide Paul that accommodation for that short period of time amounted to a monetary loss of less than $5,000. Knowing that there was very little left of the Massachusetts case, Paul's lawyer urged the company lawyer to settle the Massachusetts case by paying Paul a small sum of money.

Instead of settling the case, the company's lawyer engaged in extensive discovery, seeking information going back to the beginning of Paul's life and filing motions to uncover every facet of Paul's life. The company conducted over 40 depositions and requested thousands of pages of documents. The company lawyer also deposed Paul for more than 20 hours and also deposed Paul's wife on two separate occasions, even though Paul's wife had no information. The company spent over $350,000 in legal fees over a claim that could have been settled for less than $10,000.

The company refused to settle the case, and Paul did not want the case dismissed. The company's lawyers did everything to prevent the case from being tried. They filed several motions for summary judgment as well as everything else to delay and postpone the trial. The case dragged on for years. Finally, a judge ordered that the case be tried. A trial date was picked and the company filed an appeal to the appellate court seeking to again delay and postpone the trial.

When the appeal was denied, the case was set for a trial date. Unfortunately for Paul, the day set for the trial; Paul's wife was scheduled to go into the hospital for surgery. Paul's lawyer requested a postponement, which the company refused to grant. An emergency motion had to be filed with an affidavit showing that Paul's wife was indeed in the hospital. The Court did grant a brief continuance and finally after hundreds of wasted hours and five years of agony, the case was tried.

Unfortunately, the case was assigned to a judge who had no trial experience and had only been on the bench for a short time. The trial judge allowed irrelevant and highly prejudicial evidence to be introduced and excluded highly relevant information. After five days of trial, the judge directed the verdict against Paul. In other words, the judge took the case away from the jury and told the jury that the case was over. These fourteen jurors had wasted five days and were sent home. The trial judge directed the verdict because he said that Paul failed to prove that he had a handicap, even though it was very clear under the law that Paul did have a handicap. Well over 1,000 hours of legal time were spent on a case that was worth less than $10,000 of out-of-pocket damages and Paul never did get his day in court.

Paul is now with a new company who values the safety of their employees. Paul is a model employee, continues to receive merit pay increases, and continues to earn the respect of his supervisors and co-workers for his concerns for safety issues.

THE LESSON TO BE LEARNED

A court can disregard facts and find what it wants to find.

PART V

Peaceful Solutions

CHAPTER 16

"It is difficult to overstate the importance of the employment relationship as a focus of security and standing in our society. Empirical studies indicate that discharge from employment affects the self-esteem of employees no less severely than it affects their economic well-being. Work plays a crucial role in the individual's psychological identity and sense of order. The growing recognition of the centrality of work in a person's life, together with an awareness of the severe economic consequences resulting from arbitrary treatment in the employment relationship supports the assertion that employer control over the job means that the substance of life is in another person's hands."

Justice Liacos,

Foley v. Polaroid, 400 Mass. 82 (1987).

RESOLVING CONFLICTS AT WORK

The stories you have read are all based on true facts, although the names have been changed and some of the factual background has been altered to protect the privacy of the parties involved. I have selected these stories to point out some egregious examples of miscarriages of justices that can occur in our courts.

Fortunately, more than 75 percent of employment cases are settled without a trial and many cases result in substantial verdicts for workers. It is vital to have an effective jury system in place to resolve employment disputes. An impartial, intelligent, conscientious, and courageous jury will help accomplish the goal of providing workers a fair and just working environment.

The risk of large verdicts will encourage employers to find creative ways to resolve workplace disputes. Employers that are sued are forced to retain counsel and can expect to pay in excess of $100,000 to defend a lawsuit. Furthermore, employers gathering information to defend the lawsuit spend many non-productive hours doing so. Lawsuits often affect employee morale, and some valued employees may leave, causing further problems for employers.

Even when employers win the lawsuit, they often come out the real loser. First, the employer has to pay legal fees. Second, the lawsuit affects worker morale. Third, the lawsuit may cause adverse publicity that may effect the employer's viability. Many companies have gone out of business because of lawsuits that have caused negative publicity. Fourth, there is always the real risk that a jury may render a substantial verdict against the employer. Many companies have been forced into bankruptcy by substantial verdicts against them.

Since we all see things through our own unique filtering system, there will always be differences of opinion regarding issues at work, and very often, differences of opinion result in workplace conflicts or disputes.

As you have seen, there are many ways of resolving workplace disputes. It is important for employers and employees to realize that they share mutual interests. All employers should foster an environment that respects and values their employees. The cooperation between the employer and its employees benefits the organization. Employees are generally the most important part of any organization. Employees who are valued and respected in the organization are more likely to exert a positive effort that can only benefit the organization.

Providing a framework where both the employer and the employee win is a higher form of dispute resolution than the lawsuit where one side wins and one side loses. The reality is that both sides usually lose in a lawsuit in terms of wasted time and money and the emotional trauma associated with the loss of a job. Even when the employer wins the lawsuit, in addition to the high cost of litigation, key personnel are taken away from their normal jobs to deal with the preparation and defense of the lawsuit. This time away is wasted time.

Even when the employee wins, it is often a costly victory. Although I have won millions of dollars in settlements and verdicts for my clients, almost all of them would have preferred to keep their jobs without going through the trauma of a lawsuit. Typical of the feelings of these workers is a case where a 55-year-old man won more than $500,000 for in an age discrimination suit that took five years to resolve after a trial and an appeal. Although he was grateful for the result, he said he would have preferred to keep his job instead of receiving all that money. To him, his job was more important than the money.

For a fraction of the money that it costs employers to defend lawsuits by aggrieved employees, a better result can be achieved through the resolution of these disputes through mediation.

Since conflict is inevitable in the workplace, the question to ask yourself is do you want to have your conflict resolved in court at the highest cost, or do you want to resolve your differences through mediation at a far lower emotional and financial cost?

USING MEDIATION AT WORK

Mediation is a process where disputing parties agree to meet with a neutral third party who will listen to their dispute, assist the parties in understanding the issues, and help the parties resolve their differences through a mutually acceptable agreement.

It is essential to the mediation process that the parties enter into mediation voluntarily, that the mediator be impartial, and that what is discussed at the mediation session is kept confidential, that is, that nothing discussed during the mediation can be used by either of the parties if the matter is not resolved. Mediation is not binding on either party. The process is voluntary, and the parties find their own resolution to the dispute.

Every employer should have a mechanism in place for resolving workplace conflicts. To be successful, it is essential that the mediator be truly neutral and impartial. The mediator should not be someone employed either by the employer or the employee. It is also essential that anything discussed at the mediation be kept confidential from everyone in the organization, other than those who are directly involved in the conflict.

Mediation may not solve all workplace conflicts or disputes. As you have read in the previous case studies, there will be situations where the parties' positions are so fixed that they cannot reconcile their differences. There will also be situations where the supervisor in the situation has conscious, subconscious, or unconscious biases against the particular employee, and the only solution may be separating the parties. We all have different styles and personalities. The employer may have an extremely talented and gifted employee, but that employee has just been placed in the wrong job or under the wrong supervisor. That employee may thrive under different supervision. Since the workers are the most valuable resource for any employer, it is incumbent upon the employer to maximize the potential of each employee. In other words, the employer should always be trying to find the best place for each employee in the organization. If the employee does not fit into that particular organization, it is a mutual benefit to both the employer and employee to learn that information early and help the employee find an organization where the employee will thrive.

Not every dispute can be resolved through mediation, but if mediation can save employers even fifty billion dollars, not to mention the hidden cost, and save the workers and their families from unnecessary grief and trauma, isn't it worth doing?

Mediation gives the parties involved in the conflict an opportunity to express themselves, to identify their dispute, and to find ways of resolving their dispute. Mediation provides an opportunity to discover the underlying basis for the dispute or conflict. It seeks to get at the root of the problem. Mediation is a process that seeks to resolve the dispute, not place blame or fault on either party. Many conflicts and disputes arise because of miscommunication and misunderstandings. Mediation is a process that allows the parties an opportunity to communicate in a way that can clear up many misunderstandings.

A successful mediation process will generally move through five stages:

1. Setting the stage;
2. Defining the issues;
3. Processing the issues;
4. Resolving the issues;
5. Making an agreement.

Setting the stage starts the process. The parties select the mediator and the time and place for the mediation.

Defining the issues by the parties is done at the beginning of the mediation session where the parties state what the conflict is all about and what caused the parties to come to mediation.

Processing the issues means learning about the real needs and interests of the parties and discussing possible solutions.

Resolving the issues is coming up with the solution that meets the needs and interests of the parties.

Making an agreement means that the parties are legally committed to the agreed-upon solution, and this agreement is usually put in writing.

If you like your job and want to keep it, you can be reactive or proactive. When a conflict arises at work, and you are unable to negotiate a resolution, suggest mediation. There are numerous community programs that provide mediation services at minimal cost.

Find a community mediation service near you and suggest mediation to your supervisor as a way of working out your differences. If you cannot find a community mediation service in the yellow pages or on the Internet, you can contact the bar association in your state that will provide names of community mediation services. A listing of bar associations can be found in Appendix C.

The mediator should be someone knowledgeable in labor and employment matters and should be independent of both the employer and the employee.

The mediator will usually meet with both sides in a joint session to hear both sides of the controversy. The mediator will then meet each individually to get more in depth information. The mediator will not disclose any information to the other side that you provide in confidence without permission from you. While many mediations can be resolved in three hours or less, some mediations can take days, weeks, months, or years.

Workers who are wrongfully discharged file lawsuits to vindicate important public policies. Workers need easy access to courts and fast, fair, and just determinations of these conflicts. While mediation may be a useful method of resolving disputes, the resolution should be fair and just.

Think of the lawsuit as war, and the mediation process as making peace. An employer that has a conflict-resolution system in place has a peace treaty. However, peace can never be at the expense of justice. Any peace must be a just peace.

Just as preventative medicine is better than surgery, conflict-resolution systems are better than lawsuits. Making peace in the workplace is a sign of maturity and intelligence, not weakness.

In order to encourage this peace process, the workers must have an effective alternative, the lawsuit. If the lawsuit continues to be a powerful and effective remedy for workers, this will provide the incentive for employers to resolve conflicts in a fair and just way.

A SURVIVOR'S GUIDE TO LEGAL TERMS

After-Acquired Evidence: Anything learned by an employer after a suit is brought that would justify firing the employee and is used by the employer to limit damages.

Affidavit: A statement signed under oath as a true and accurate statement.

Age Discrimination in Employment Act (ADEA):   A federal law that prohibits employers from discriminating against employees who are 40 years of age or older.

Americans with Disabilities Act (ADA) of 1990:   A federal law that prohibits employers from discriminating against employees with handicaps.

Appeal: A claim to a higher court to review a decision made by a lower court to determine if the decision made by the lower court was legally correct.

Appellate Court: A court that reviews decisions by lower courts to determine if the decision made by the lower court was legally correct.

Application of Costs: Court expenses assessed against the losing party in a lawsuit.

Arbitration: A method of resolving a dispute in which the issues are submitted to a third party whose decision is binding on the parties.

Back Pay: The money awarded to a plaintiff in a lawsuit that represents lost wages or salary.

Brief: A legal document filed in an appellate court that formally states the legal arguments of the party.

Charging the Jury: The act in which a judge gives instructions to the jury before the jury is sent to the jury room to decide the case. *See* jury instructions.

Circumstantial Evidence: Evidence that is determined from other facts. For example, if you hear thunder, but did not see the lightning, you can infer that there was lightning that preceded the thunder.

Civil Rights Act of 1964, Title VII: A federal law that prohibits employers from discriminating against employees because of their race, color, sex, national, origin, or religion.

Claimant: A person who brings a claim.

Closing Arguments: At the end of the trial after all the evidence has been submitted and both sides rest, each attorney gets an opportunity to speak to the jury to persuade them to find for his or her client.

Collective Bargaining: The method used by employers and labor unions to agree to terms and conditions of employment.

Collective Bargaining Agreement: The written document setting forth the terms and conditions of employment between an employer and a labor union.

Common Law: Law developed by custom through court decisions.

Compensatory Damages: Money awarded to pay a plaintiff what he or she lost as a result of a wrongful act committed by a defendant.

Consideration: The cause, motive, price, or impelling influence that induces a party to enter into a contract.

Constitution: The written instrument of the union or of a particular state setting forth the fundamental and basic principles of law, the functions of the government, and the rights of the governed.

Contingent Fee: A method of paying a lawyer where the client does not pay the lawyer any money until and unless the lawyer is successful in obtaining money for the client.

Contract: An agreement that is legally enforceable. It requires an offer, an acceptance, and consideration.

Counsel: An attorney.

Cross-Examination: The questioning of a witness by the attorney for the other side to discredit the testimony given under oath.

Deceit: A tort claim for making false statements to induce someone to take action or refrain from taking action.

Defamation: A tort claim for making false statements about a person that holds the person up to scorn or ridicule and damages the person's reputation.

Defendant: The person who is sued in a lawsuit and has to defend the claim.

Demand for Admission of Facts: A legal pleading used in a lawsuit to get a party to the lawsuit to either admit or deny specific facts.

Deposition: The testimony of a witness taken under oath not in court and usually transcribed by a reporter.

Directed Verdict: A procedure used by a judge to take the decision away from the jury and to decide the case for one side.

Discovery Process: The method used to obtain information to be used at a trial. There are several different discovery procedures, such as interrogatories, production of documents, and depositions.

Discrimination: Treating persons differently.

Dispute: A claim or controversy between two or more persons.

Diversity Jurisdiction: A form of jurisdiction that allows cases to be brought in a federal district court if the plaintiffs and defendants are from different states.

Duty of Fair Representation: The union's legal duty, as the exclusive bargaining representative of the union members, to represent each member fairly, impartially, and without discrimination of any kind.

Employee Polygraph Protection Act: A federal law that restricts the use of lie detectors by employers.

Employee Retirement Income Security Act (ERISA):   A federal law designed to protect employees' pension, welfare, and health benefits.

Employment at Will: A legal principle established by common law that allows employers to fire employees for good reason, bad reason, or no reason at all without legal liability.

Equal Employment Opportunity Commission: The federal agency established to receive and investigate claims for employment discrimination in violation of federal law, such as Title VII, ADEA, and ADA.

Equal Pay Act: A federal law that requires employers to pay men and women equal wages or salary for doing the same work.

Equitable Relief: A non-monetary decision requiring action by the losing party to a lawsuit, such as reinstating the employee to a position with the employer.

Evidence: Proof presented at a trial, either through the testimony of witnesses or documents or other exhibits.

Fair Labor Standards Act: A federal law that requires employers to pay nonexempt employees the current minimum wage and to pay employees time and a half for every hour worked in a workweek in excess of forty hours.

Family and Medical Leave Act of 1993:   A federal law that requires employers who have fifty or more employees to give employees up to twelve weeks of unpaid leave for medical reasons or to care for children.

Federal Question Jurisdiction: A form of jurisdiction that allows cases to be brought in a federal district court where claims involve federal law.

Front Pay: Money awarded to compensate an employee for money he or she will lose in the future as a result of being fired.

Grievance Process: A method for resolving a dispute out of court.

Hearsay: Evidence that does not come from the personal knowledge of the witness.

Immigration Reform and Control Act of 1986:   A federal law that protects non-citizens from discrimination by employers.

Implied Covenant of Good Faith and Fair Dealing: A legal principle established by the common law that states that in any contract the parties are legally bound to do everything in their power to make sure the contract agreed to is performed.

Implied Promises of Long-Term Employment: A promise that is not made expressly, but a promise the law will enforce because of the conduct of the parties or the nature of the relationship.

Inference: A process of reasoning by which a fact or proposition sought to be established is deduced as a logical consequence from other facts, or a state of facts, already proved or admitted.

Intentional Infliction of Emotional Distress: A tort in which a person has caused another person to suffer severe emotional injury by some outrageous act.

Intentional Interference with Contractual Relations: A tort in which a person interferes with someone else's contract, such as when a supervisor lies to get an employee fired.

Interrogatories: A form of discovery that asks questions of the other side, and the other side has to provide answers to the questions under oath.

Jurisdiction: The authority or power of a court to decide a claim or controversy.

Jury Instructions: A statement about the law given to the jury by a judge setting forth all the elements of the claims brought that must be found by the jury in order for the plaintiff to win the lawsuit.

Just Cause: A decision based upon fair, reasonable, and adequate grounds.

Key Witness: The most important witness in the case.

Lawsuit: A claim brought in a court.

Libel: Defamation in writing.

Liquidated Damages: An additional amount of money added as a penalty to the actual amount awarded.

Loss of Consortium: A tort claim for the loss of the care, companionship, and intimate relationship of husband and wife caused by a tort injury to one of the parties to the marital relationship.

Loss of Nurture: A tort claim for the loss of the care, companionship, and nurture of minor children caused by the injury to their parent.

Malice: The intentional doing of a wrongful act without just cause or excuse, with intent to inflict an injury or under circumstances that the law will imply an evil motive or purpose.

Mediation: Resolving a dispute through a disinterested third party who acts as a facilitator. Mediation is not binding on either party; is generally confidential, and is usually voluntary.

Misrepresentation: A tort claim for making false statements to induce someone to take action or refrain from taking action.

Motion: A pleading filed in court that asks the judge to take some action regarding the case.

Motion for Judgment Notwithstanding the Verdict: A written request by an attorney that asks the judge to find in your favor even though the verdict was against you. Usually filed by employers.

Motion in Limine: A written request by an attorney that asks the judge to prevent certain evidence from being presented at trial.

Motion to Dismiss: A written request by an attorney that asks the judge to end the case without a trial because you have no legal claim.

Motion for Summary Judgment: A written request by an attorney that asks the judge to end the case without a trial because you do not have enough evidence to prove your case.

Motive: The cause or reason that induces action or inaction.

National Labor Relations Act: A federal law that deals with rights of labor unions, union members, unionized companies, and collective bargaining.

National Labor Relations Board: The federal agency that deals with the rights of labor unions, union members, unionized companies, and collective bargaining.

Negligent Evaluation: A tort action in which you are carelessly evaluated by your supervisor and suffer damages.

Negotiation: A method of resolving a dispute by having the parties talk to each other, make compromises or concessions, and work out a resolution that satisfies their needs or interests.

Occupational Safety and Health Act: A federal law that requires employers to provide a safe working environment.

Opening Statement: Before a trial starts, each lawyer speaks to the jury to tell them what the case is all about.

Perjury: A false statement made under oath.

Plaintiff: The person who brings the lawsuit.

Pleading: A formal legal writing submitted to court.

Prejudicial Evidence: Evidence that leans towards one side in a lawsuit.

Pretext: An excuse usually made by employers to justify their unlawful acts.

Prima Facie Case: Sufficient evidence presented to prove all the elements of a claim.

Privacy: The right to be left alone and to be free from unwarranted interference or publicity.

Production of Documents: A form of discovery that asks the other party to provide written documentation.

Public Policy: What the law requires people to do or refrain from doing for the public good, such as reporting illegal acts or refusing to lie for your employer.

Punitive Damages: Money awarded to punish employers for committing outrageous acts.

Record Appendix: The essential pleadings in a case presented to an appeals court as part of an appeal.

Rehabilitation Act of 1973:   A federal law that prohibits discrimination against handicapped employees by employers who receive federal financial assistance or have federal contracts.

Reinstatement: An order by a judge putting the employee back to work.

Removal: If a case is brought in a state court and either involves federal law claims or parties from different states, it can be taken from the state court and brought in to a federal court. Employers try to remove cases from state courts whenever they can because federal courts are generally more favorable to employers.

Res Judicata: A legal defense to a claim that states the issues or claims in the present lawsuit have been previously decided by another court, agency, or tribunal, and the present court has to dismiss the case.

Respondent: *See* defendant. The person who is defending the claim.

Rest: When each side has fully presented the case to the jury, each states that he or she rests or is finished with presenting evidence in the case.

Seniority: The length of time an employee has been employed with the employer.

Sexual Harassment: A form of discrimination in which sexual favors are asked as a condition of employment or an offensive or hostile work environment is created which is sexual in nature.

Slander: A tort claim in which false and defamatory oral statements are made. *See* defamation.

Statute of Limitations: The period of time within which you must file your lawsuit. If you do not file your lawsuit within the specified period of time, your case will be dismissed. The time begins to run on the date when the wrongful act occurs.

Subpoena: A legal document requiring a person to appear at a time and place to give testimony.

Tort: A private or civil wrong for which the law provides a remedy in a court.

Trial Transcript: The testimony taken by the court reporter that is entered into a written account of the trial.

Unemployment Compensation: Payments made to an employee when the employee loses a job without fault for a fixed period of time or until the employee finds a new job.

Verdict: The decision made by the jury.

Veterans' Readjustment Benefits Act: A federal law designed to protect veterans' reemployment rights and prohibit discrimination against veterans.

Whistleblowing: A complaint made to a federal, state, or municipal agency about some unlawful conduct committed by an employer.

Worker Adjustment and Retraining Notification Act: A federal law requiring employers with more than 100 employees to notify their workers, at least 60 calendar days in advance, if there is going to be a plant closing or a layoff of more than 50 employees.

Workers' Compensation: Payments made to workers injured on the job who are unable to work.

NOTES

CHAPTER 1

1 A deposition is conducted at a pre-trial meeting where a witness is asked under oath to answer questions concerning the disputed facts. The testimony is transcribed and sworn to as the truth. It can be used during the trial to support or contradict a witness's testimony.

2 Sexual harassment was determined by the EEOC in 1980 to be a form of discrimination on the basis of gender.

3 Americans with Disabilities Act of 1990 (ADA), 42 U.S.C. § 12101 *et seq.*

4 Jennifer Babson, "Growing Case Backlog Weighs on MCAD," *Boston Globe,* January 11, 1999, pages A1 and B6. Comments attributed to Robert Gordon, a partner in the law firm of Ropes & Gray, Boston, Massachusetts.

5 Meritor Savings Bank v. Vinson, 477 U.S. 57 (1984).

CHAPTER 2

1 See generally Note, Protecting At-Will Employees Against Wrongful Discharge: The Duty To Terminate Only in Good Faith, 93 *Harv L Rev* 1816, 1824-26 (1980) [hereinafter cited as Wrongful Discharge Note] (discussing historical perspective of "at-will" employment doctrine).

2 H. Wood, *A Treatise on the Law of Master and Servant* §134, at 272 (1877). Prior to the development of this presumption, courts generally construed agreements for hiring for an indefinite period to be for one year. See, e.g., *Adams v. Fitzpatrick,* 125 NY 124, 129-30, 26 NE 143, 145 (1891).

See also Feinman, The Development of the Employment At-Will Rule, 20 *Am J Legal Hist* 118, 119-22 (1976).

Before the application of contract law principles, the law of master and servant governed the employment relationship. E.g., Wrongful Discharge Note, 93 *Harv L Rev* at 1824-25.

3 See, e.g., *Forrer v. Sears, Roebuck & Co.,* 36 Wis 2d 388, 393, 153 NW2d 587, 589-90 (1967); *Payne v. Western & A.R. Co.,* 81 Tenn 507, 517-19 (1889).

4 *Payne v. Western & A.R. Co.,* 81 Tenn 507, 519-20 (1889).

Overruled on other grounds *Hutton v. Watters,* 132 Tenn 527, 179 SW 134 (1915). Indeed, at one point in time the employer's rights under the at-will rule were deemed constitutionally protected. *Adair v. United States,* 208 US 161, 52 L Ed 436, 28 S Ct 277 (1908). This rule, subject to the exceptions discussed herein, is still the general rule prevailing in most states.

See, e.g.:

Alabama: *Bender Ship Repair, Inc. v. Stevens,* 379 So 2d 594, 595 (Ala 1980).

Arizona: *Builders Supply Corp. v. Shipley,* 86 Ariz 153, 155, 341 P2d 940 (1959).

Arkansas: *Miller v. Missouri Pacific Trans. Co.,* 225 Ark 475, 480-81, 283 SW2d 158, 161 (1955).

California: *Mallard v. Boring,* 182 Cal App 2d 390, 394, 6 Cal Rptr 171, 174 (1960).

Colorado: *Justice v. Stanley Aviation Corp.,* 35 Colo App 1, 4, 530 P2d 984, 985 (1974).

Connecticut: *Boucher v. Godfrey,* 119 Conn 622, 627, 178 A 655, 657 (1935).

Delaware: *Haney v. Laub,* 312 A2d 330, 332 (Del 1973).

District of Columbia: *J.E. Hanger, Inc. v. Fitzsimmons,* 50 App DC 384, 386, 273 F 348, 350 (1921).

Florida: *Wynne v. Ludman Corp.,* 79 So 2d 690, 691 (Fla 1955).

Georgia: *Wilkinson v. Trust Co. of Georgia Associates,* 128 Ga App 473, 474, 197 SE2d 146, 148 (1973).

Idaho: *Jackson v. Minidoka Irr. Dist.,* 98 Idaho 330, 333, 563 P2d 54, 57 (1977).

Illinois: *Leach v. Lauhoff Grain Co.,* 51 Ill App 3d 1022, 1024, 366 NE2d 1145, 1147 (1977).

Indiana: *Speeder Cycle Co. v. Teeter,* 18 Ind App 474, 477, 48 NE 595, 596 (1897).

Iowa: *Drake v. Block,* 247 Iowa 517, 74 NW2d 577 (1956).

Kansas: *Midfelt v. Lair,* 221 Kan 557, 563, 561 P2d 805, 811 (1977).

Kentucky: *Wilson v. Haughton,* 266 SW2d 115, 119 (Ky 1954).

Louisiana: *Pechon v. National Corp. Service, Inc.,* 234 La 397, 406, 100 So 2d 213, 216 (1958).

Maine: *Blaisdell v. Lewis,* 32 Me 515, 516 (1851).

Maryland: *Vincent v. Palmer,* 179 Md 365, 370-71, 19 A2d 183, 187 (1941).

Massachusetts: *Askinas v. Westinghouse Elec. Corp.,* 330 Mass 103, 106, 111 NE2d 740, 741 (1953).

Michigan: *Hernden v. Consumers Power Co.,* 72 Mich App 349, 356, 249 NW2d 419, 422 (1977).

Minnesota: *Cederstrand v. Lutheran Brotherhood,* 263 Minn 520, 532, 117 NW2d 213, 221 (1962).

Mississippi: *Rape v. Mobile & O.R. Co.,* 136 Miss 38, 50-53, 100 So 585, 587-88 (1924).

Missouri: *Culver v. Kurn,* 354 Mo 1158, 1162, 193 SW2d 602, 603 (1946).

Montana: *Reiter v. Yellowstone County,* 627 P2d 845, 848-49 (Mont 1981).

Nebraska: *Mau v. Omaha Nat. Bank,* 207 Neb 308, 313, 299 NW2d 147, 151 (1980).

New Hampshire: *Cloutier v. Great Atlantic & Pacific Tea Co.,* 121 NH 915, 919-20, 436 A2d 1140 (1981).

New Jersey: *Jorgenson v. Pennsylvania R. Co.,* 25 NJ 541, 554, 138 A2d 24, 32 (1958).

New Mexico: *Gonzales v. United States Southwest Nat. Bank of Santa Fe,* 93 NM 522, 524, 602 P2d 619 (1979).

New York: *Parker v. Borock,* 5 NY2d 156, 159, 182 NYS2d 577, 579, 156 NE2d 297, 298 (1959).

North Carolina: *Presnell v. Pell,* 298 NC 715, 260 SE2d 611, 616 (1979).

North Dakota: *Wood v. Buchanan,* 72 ND 216, 221, 5 NW2d 680, 682 (1942).

Ohio: *Henkel v. Educational Research Council,* 45 Ohio St 2d 249, 251, 344 NE2d 118, 119 (1976).

Oklahoma: *Singh v. Cities Service Oil Co.,* 554 P2d 1367, 1369 (Okla 1976).

Oregon: *Nees v. Hocks,* 272 Or 210, 216, 536 P2d 512, 514 (1975).

Pennsylvania: *Geary v. United States Steel Corp.,* 456 Pa 171, 175, 319 A2d 174, 175-76 (1974).

Rhode Island: *Rotondo v. Seaboard Foundry, Inc.,* 440 A2d 751, 752 (RI 1981).

South Carolina: *Todd v. South Carolina Farm Bureau Mut. Ins. Co.,* 276 SC 284, 278 SE2d 607, 609 (1981).

Tennessee: *Russ v. Southern Ry. Co.,* 334 F2d 224, 228 (CA6 1964), cert den 379 US 991 (1965).

Texas: *Watson v. Zep Mfg. Co.,* 582 SW2d 178, 179 (Tex Civ App 1979).

Utah: *Bihlmaier v. Carson,* 603 P2d 790, 792 (Utah 1979).

Vermont: *Mullaney v. C.H. Goss Co.,* 97 Vt 82, 87, 122 A 430, 432 (1923).

Virginia: *Wards Co., Inc. v. Lewis & Dobrow, Inc.,* 210 Va 751, 173 SE2d 861, 865 (1970).

Washington: *Roberts v. Atlantic Richfield Co.,* 88 Wash 2d 887, 891, 568 P2d 764, 767 (1977).

West Virginia: *Wright v. Standard Ultramarine & Color Co.,* 141 W Va 368, 382, 90 SE2d 459, 467-68 (1955).

Wisconsin: *Kovachick v. American Automobile Ass'n,* 5 Wis 2d 188, 190-92, 92 NW2d 254, 255 (1958).

Wyoming: *Lukens v. Goit,* 430 P2d 607, 611 (Wyo 1967).

5 *Bender Ship Repair, Inc. v. Stevens,* 379 So 2d 594, 595 (Ala 1980).

6 *Daniel v. Magma Copper Co.,* 127 Ariz 320, 324, 620 P2d 699, 703 (Ariz App 1980).

7 *Ivy v. Army Times Pub. Co.,* 428 A2d 831 (DC App 1981) (per curiam).

8 *Pfeffer v. Ernst,* 82 A2d 763, 763-64 (DC Mun App 1951).

9 *Hablas v. Armour & Co.,* 270 F2d 71, 73, 78-79 (CA8 1959).

10 See Golder, *Labor and Emp. Law: Compl. and Lit.* Chapter 4, Section 4:77.80, California (Cal Labor Code §1102.1); Connecticut (Conn Gen Stat §53-303e); District of Columbia (DC Code Ann §§1-2501 to 1-2557); Hawaii (Haw Rev Stat §378-2); Massachusetts (Mass Gen L ch 151B); Minnesota (Minn Stat §363.01 to 363.15, subd 45); New Jersey (NJ Rev Stat §10:5-4); Rhode Island (RI Gen Laws §28-5-7); Vermont (Vt Stat Ann tit 21, §495(a) et seq.); Wisconsin (Wis Stat §111.337).

11 See Golder, *Labor and Emp. Law: Compl. and Lit.* Chapter 1, Section 1:07 - Public policy.

12 See Golder, *Labor and Emp. Law: Compl. and Lit.* Chapter 1, Section 1:09 - Implied covenants of good faith and fair dealing.

13 See Golder, *Labor and Empl. Law: Compl. and Lit.* Chapter 1, Section 1:10 - Implied promise of long-term employment.

14 *Egerton v. Brownlow,* 4 H.L. Cas. 1, 196; *B.B. Chemical Co. v. Ellis,* 314 U.S. 495.

15 *Petermann v. Teamsters Local 396,* 174 Cal App. 2d 184, 188-189, 344 2d 25, 27-28 (1959).

16 *Frampton v. Central Indiana Gas Co.,* 260 Ind 249, 252-253, 297 NE2d 425, 428 (1973).

17 *Hawaiian Airlines, Inc. v. Norris,* 9 IER 929 (S.Ct. 1994).

18 *Agis v. Howard Johnson Co.,* 371 Mass 140, 145, 355 NE2d 315, 319 (1976).

19 *Food Fair Inc. v. Anderson,* 382 So. 2d 150 (Fla. App. 1980); *Pierre v. Printing Developments, Inc.,* 468 F. Supp 1028 (SD NY 1979), affirmed, 615 F.2d 1290 (CA2 1979); *Gates v. Life of Montana Insurance Company,* 668 P.2d 213 (Mont. 1983).

20 *Food Fair Inc. v. Anderson,* 382 So.2d 150, 153-156 (Fla App. 1980).

21 *Pirre v. Printing Development Inc.,* 468 F. Supp. 1028 (D NY 1979), affirmed 615 F.2d 1290 (2d Cir. 1979).

22 *Comey v. Hill,* 387 Mass. 11, 19-21, 438 NE2d 811, 816-817 (1982).

23 *Phillips v. Smalley Maintenance Services,* 711 F.2d 1524 (CA11 1983); *Frat. Order of Police v. Philadelphia,* 1 IER cases (BNA) 574 (ED PA 1986); *O'Brien v. Papa Gino's,* 780 F.2d 1067 (CA1 1986); but see *Barkstale v. IBM,* 620 F. Supp. 1380 (WD NC 1985).

24 See Golder, *Labor and Empl. Law: Compl. and Lit.* Chapter 1, Section 1:09 - Implied covenants of good faith and fair dealing; *Fortune v. National Cash Register Co.,* 373 Mass. 96, 364 NE 2d 1251 (1977).

25 See Golder, *Labor and Empl. Law: Compl. and Lit.* Chapter 1, Section 1:10 - Implied promise of long-term employment.

26 This doctrine, of course, conflicts with the legal principle that courts will not weigh the adequacy of consideration; a fact which has led a number of courts to reject the doctrine.

Not included in the discussion in this section is the use of an estoppel theory to provide a remedy for anticipatory repudiation. See, e.g., *Grouse v. Group Health Plan, Inc.,* 306 NW2d 114, 116 (Minn 1981) (employee terminated prior to commencing work held to have expectation of employment for reasonable period).

27 See Golder, *Labor and Empl. Law: Compl. and Lit.* Chapter 1, Section 1:04. *Chatelier v. Robertson,* 118 So 2d 241, 244 (Fla App 1960). But see *Hope v. National Airlines, Inc.,* 99 So 2d 244, 246-47 (Fla App 1957) (working through strike does not constitute additional consideration).

28 *Brawthen v. H.& R. Block, Inc.,* 28 Cal App 3d 131, 138, 104 Cal Rptr 486, 491 (1972) (move from Minnesota to California). But see *Griffith v. Sollay Foundation Drilling, Inc.,* 373 So 2d 979, 981-82 (La 1979) (long distance move found not to constitute additional consideration).

29 *Bussard v. College of Saint Thomas, Inc.,* 294 Minn 215, 223, 200 NW2d 155, 161 (1972).

30 *McNulty v. Borden, Inc.,* 474 F Supp 1111, 1118-19 (ED Pa 1979). See also *Rabago-Alvarez v. Dart Industries, Inc.,* 55 Cal App 3d 91, 96-97, 127 Cal Rptr 222, 225 (1976).

31 See, e.g., *Morris v. Park Newspapers of Georgia, Inc.,* 149 Ga App 674, 675, 255 SE2d 131 (1979).

32 *Hope v. National Airlines, Inc.,* 99 So 2d 244, 246-47 (Fla App 1957) (working during strike); *Page v. Carolina Coach Co.,* 667 F2d 1156, 1158 (CA4 1982) (relinquishment of position as driver to accept promotion to dispatcher); *An-Ti Chai v. Michigan Technological University,* 493 F Supp 1137, 1153-4 (WD Mich 1980) (relinquishment of prior position and moving); *Roberts v. Atlantic Richfield Co.,* 88 Wash 2d 887, 895-96, 568 P2d 764, 769-70 (1977) (moving and relinquishment of other job opportunities); *Albers v. Wilson & Co., Inc.,* 184 F Supp 812, 813 (D Minn 1960) (acceptance of employment during strike with threats of violence); *Degen v. Investors Diversified Services, Inc.,* 260 Minn 424, 428-30, 110 NW2d 863, 866-67 (1961); *Orsini v. Trojan Steel Co.,* 219 SC 272, 276-77, 64 SE2d 878, 880 (1951) (relinquishing of former position and moving).

33 *Martin v. Capital Cities Media, Inc.,* 354 Pa Super 198, 511 A2d 830 (1986) (handbook containing standards of conduct the employer expected of its employees did not show an intent to make the employee dischargeable only for "just cause").

Enis v. Continental Illinois Nat. Bank & Trust Co. of Illinois, 795 F2d 39 (CA7 1986) (no violation of conditions in Bank's employee manual when it discharged an employee who violated a provision recognized by manual as grounds for "immediate dismissal").

An at-will employment relationship was not converted into a contract of employment, which could only be terminated for "just or good cause" because of the employer's personnel policy manual. It was not established that the employee ever read or relied on the manual, and the employer was free to change the manual at any time, and certain executives could disregard or modify the manual at their pleasure. *Spero v. Lockwood, Inc.,* 122 LRRM (BNA) 2543 (Idaho 1986).

Action for wrongful discharge and breach of implied covenant of good faith and fair dealing where employee summarily discharged in violation of written policies not barred by California statute of frauds, since oral employment contracts without termination dates can be performed in less than a year. *Steward v. Mercy Hospital,* 1 IER Cases (BNA) 1694 (Cal 1987).

Lewis v. Equitable Life Assur. Society, 389 NW2d 876 (Minn 1986) (personnel handbook that states except for misconduct serious enough to warrant dismissal all employees are entitled to warning and probationary period prior to discharge definite enough to constitute valid contract).

Renny v. Port Huron Hospital, 1 IER Cases (BNA) 1560 (Mich 1987) (whether employee handbook constitutes a binding contract is jury question).

Jury permitted to determine that employee handbook constituted binding contract. *Small v. Springs Industries, Inc.,* 2 IER Cases (BNA) 267 (SC 1987).

Aiello v. United Airlines, Inc., 2 IER Cases (BNA) 345 (CA5 1987) (jury verdict upheld finding employee handbook binding on company).

Statements that salesman could have job "as long as he wanted" or for "as long as he desired" sufficient to uphold finding of lifetime contract. *Schneider v. Russell Corp.,* 2 IER Cases (BNA) 521 (CA11 1987).

Oral contracts for life are valid in Massachusetts. *Sereni v. Star Sportswear Mfg. Corp.,* 24 Mass App 428, 509 NE2d 1203 (1987).

$154,000 verdict upheld for breach of oral employment contract. *Mayo v. Schooner Capital Corp.,* 2 IER Cases (BNA) 663 (CA1 1987).

34 *Rabago-Alvarez v. Dart Industries, Inc.,* 55 Cal App 3d at 96-97, 127 Cal Rptr at 225.

Accord *Terrio v. Millinocket Community Hospital,* 379 A2d 135, 137-38 (Me 1977).

Contra *Hollowell v. Career Decision, Inc.,* 100 Mich App 561, 567-69, 298 NW2d 915, 918-20 (1980) (employee received assurances only of at-will employment); *Land v. Delta Airlines, Inc.,* 130 Ga App 231, 232, 203 SE2d 316, 317-18 (1973) (alleged promises of lifetime employment).

35 *Hepp v. Lockheed-California Co.,* 86 Cal App 3d 714, 718-20, 150 Cal Rptr 408, 410-11 (1978).

36 *Grouse v. Group Health Plan, Inc.,* 306 NW2d 114 (Minn 1981).

37 *Small v. Springs Industries, Inc.,* 292 SC 481, 357 SE2d 452 (1987).

38 *Woolley v. Hoffmann-LaRoche, Inc.,* 99 NJ 284, 491 A2d 1257 (1985), mod on other grounds, 101 NJ 10, 491 A2d 1257 (1985). See also *Toussaint v. Blue Cross & Blue Shield of Michigan,* 408 Mich 579, 292 NW2d 880 (1980).

39 See, e.g., *Toussaint v. Blue Cross & Blue Shield of Michigan,* 408 Mich 579, 292 NW2d 880 (1980); *Pine River State Bank v. Mettile,* 333 NW2d 622 (Minn 1988). Compare *Cederstrand v.*

Lutheran Brotherhood, 117 NW2d 213 (Minn 1962); *Simpson v. Western Graphics Corp.,* 293 Or 96, 643 P2d 1276 (1982).

40 See, e.g., *Weiner v. McGraw-Hill, Inc.,* 57 NY2d 462, 457 NYS2d 193, 443 NE2d 441 (1982). Compare *Rynar v. Ciba-Geigy Corp.,* 560 F Supp 619 (ND Ill 1983).

41 See, e.g., *White v. Chelsea Industries, Inc.,* 425 So 2d 1090 (Ala 1983); *Reynolds Mfg. Co. v. Mendoza,* 644 SW2d 536 (Tex App 1982); *Richardson v. Charles Cole Memorial Hospital,* 320 Pa Super 106, 466 A2d 1084 (1983).

42 *Towns v. Emery Air Freight, Inc.,* 1988 WL 156258, 3 IER Cases (BNA) 911 (SD Ohio 1988).

43 *Pine River State Bank v. Mettile,* 333 NW2d 622 (Minn 1983).

44 Restatement (2d) Contracts 24.

45 *Brodie v. General Chemical Corp.,* 934 P2d 1263 (Wyo 1996).

46 *Doyle v. Holy Cross Hospital,* 289 Ill App 3d 75, 682 NE2d 68 (1997).

47 *Toussaint v. Blue Cross & Blue Shield of Michigan,* 408 Mich 579, 614-619, 292 NW 2d 880, 892-895 (1980).

49 *Weiner v. McGraw-Hill, Inc.,* 57 NY 2d 458, 465-466, 457 NYS 2d at 197, 443 NE 2d at 445.

50 See *Berry v. Doctor's Health Facilities,* 715 SW 2d 60 (Tex. App. 1986) (no contract where handbook states it is not a contract); *Bailey v. Perkins Restaurants Inc.,* 1 IER Cases (BNA) 1327 (ND 1986); *Thebner v. Xerox Corp.,* 480 So.2d 454 (La. App. 1985); *Crain v. Burroughs Corp.,* 560 F. Supp. 849 (SD 1983); *Woolley v. Hoffman-LaRouche,* 491 A2d 1257 (NJ 1985) (handbook can become employment contract, but employers' disclaimers will be honored); *McCluskey v. Unicare Health Facility,* 484 So.2d 389 (Ala. 1986); *Leikvold v. Valley View Community Hospital,* 688 P.2d 170 (Ariz. 1984); *Thompson v. St. Regis Paper Co.,* 685 P.2d 1081, 1088 (Wash. 1984); *Martin v. Capital Cities Media Inc.,* 511 A.2d 830 (Pa. Supr. 1986); *Langley v. Blue Cross & Blue Shield of Michigan,* 136 Mich. App. 336, 356 ND2d 20 (1984) (no contract where a handbook states employee can be terminated for any reason); *Reid v. Sears, Roebuck & Co.,* 790 F.2d 413 (6 Cir. 1986) (no contract where employment application contains disclaimer); *Granculas v. Trans World Airlines,* 761 F.2d 1391 (9th Cir. 1985); *Shelby v. Zayre Corp.,* 474 So.2d 1065 (Ala. 1985); *Batchelor v. Sears, Roebuck & Co.,* 574 F. Supp. 1480 (ED Mich. 1983); *Summers v. Sears, Roebuck & Co.,* 549 F. Supp. 1157 (ED Mich. 1982); *Novosel v. Sears, Roebuck & Co.,* 495 F. Supp. 344 (ED Mich. 1980).

51 *Row v. Noren Pattern Foundry Co.,* 91 Mich App 254, 258-262, 283 NW 2d 713, 715-718 (1971).

52 *Ryan v. J.C. Penney Co. Inc.,* 627 F.2d 836, 838 (7) Cir. (1980).

53 *Chamberlain v. Bissell Inc.,* 547 F. Supp. 1067 (WD Mich 1982).

54 See Golder, *Labor and Empl. Law: Compl. and Lit.* Chapter 1, Section 1:145.

55 See Golder, *Labor and Empl. Law: Compl. and Lit.* Chapter 1, Section 1:08.50.

56 *Hunt v. Weatherbee,* 39 FEP Cases (BNA) 1469 (D. Mass. 1986).

57 *Gram v. Liberty Mutual Insurance Co.,* 384 Mass. 659, 429 NE2d 21 (1981); *Fortune v. National Cash Register Co.,* 373 Mass. 96, 364 NE2d 1251 (1977).

58 *Maddaloni v. Western Mass. Bus Lines Inc.,* 383 Mass. 877, 438 NE2d 351 (1982).

59 *Maddaloni v. Western Mass. Bus Lines Inc.,* 383 Mass. 877, 438 NE2d 351 (1982); *Gram v. Liberty Mutual Insurance Co.,* 384 Mass. 659, 429 NE2d 21 (1981); *Toussaint v. Blue Cross & Blue Shield of Michigan,* 408 Mich 579, 614-619, 292 NW2d 880, 892-895 (1980).

60 *Cancellier v. Federated Department Stores,* 672 F.2d 1312 (9th Cir. 1982).

61 *Holmes v. Oxford Chemicals Inc.,* 510 F. Supp. 915 (MD Ala. 1981); *Cleary v. American Airlines Inc.,* 111 Cal. App.

62 E.g., *Cancellier v. Federated Dept. Stores,* 672 F2d 1312, 1318 (CA9 1982); *Cleary v. American Airlines, Inc.,* 111 Cal App 3d 443, 456, 168 Cal Rptr 722 (1980); *Harris v. Jones,* 281 Md 560, 380 A2d 611 (Md App 1977).

CHAPTER 3

1 *McKennon v. Nashville Banner Publishing Co.,* 513 US 352, 115 S Ct 879, 130 LEd2d 852, 66 FEP Cases (BNA) 1192 (1995).

CHAPTERS 4–7

No notes.

CHAPTER 8

1 *Dred Scott v. Sanford,* 19 How, 393, 404 (1857).

2 *Bradwell v. State of Illinois,* 83 U.S. 130 (1873).

3 *Plessey v. Ferguson,* 163 U.S. 256, 261 (1896).

CHAPTERS 9–16

No notes.

APPENDIX A

STATE AND FEDERAL AGENCIES THAT DEAL WITH EMPLOYMENT DISCRIMINATION

For race, color, national origin, religion, sex, age, and handicap discrimination in employment under federal law.

FEDERAL AGENCIES

Equal Employment Opportunity Commission (EEOC) located at 1801 L Street, N.W., Washington, DC 20507.
Phone: (800) 669-4000.

EEOC also has field offices at the following locations:

Albuquerque, New Mexico District Office located at 505 Marquette, N.W., Suite 900, Albuquerque, NM 87102.
Phone: (505) 248-5201.

Atlanta, Georgia Office located at 100 Alabama Street, Suite 4R30, Atlanta, GA 30303.
Phone: (404) 562-6800.

Baltimore, Maryland District Office located at 10 South Howard Street, Third Floor, Baltimore, MD 20201.
Phone: (410) 962-3932.

Birmingham, Alabama District Office located at 1900 Third Avenue, North, Suite 101, Birmingham, AL 35203-2397.
Phone: (205) 731-1359.

Boston, Massachusetts area office located at 1 Congress Street, Tenth Floor, Room 1001, Boston, MA 02114.
Phone: (617) 565-3200.

Buffalo, New York office located at 6 Fountain Plaza, Suite 350, Buffalo, NY 14202.
Phone: (716) 846-4441.

Charlotte, North Carolina Office located at 129 West Trade Street, Suite 400, Charlotte, NC 28202.
Phone: (703) 344-6682.

Chicago, Illinois Office located at 500 West Madison Street, Suite 2800, Chicago, IL 60661.
Phone: (312) 353-2713.

Cincinnati, Ohio Office located at 525 Vine Street, Suite 810, Cincinnati, OH 45202-3122.
Phone: (513) 684-2851.

Cleveland, Ohio Office located at 1660 West Second Street, Suite 850, Cleveland, OH 44113-1454.
Phone: (216) 522-2001.

Dallas, Texas Office located at 207 South Houston Street, Third Floor, Dallas, TX 75202-4726.
Phone: (214) 655-3355.

Denver, Colorado Office located at 303 East 17th Avenue, Suite 510, Denver, CO 80203.
Phone: (303) 866-1300.

Detroit, Michigan Office located at 477 Michigan Avenue, Room 865, Detroit MI, 48226-9704.
Phone: (313) 226-7636.

El Paso, Texas area office located at The Commons, Building C, Suite 100, 4171 North Mesa Street, El Paso, TX 79902.
Phone: (915) 534-6550.

Fresno, California Office located at 1265 West Shaw Avenue, Suite 103, Fresno, CA 93711.
Phone: (209) 487-5793.

Greensboro, North Carolina Office located at 801 Summit Avenue, Greensboro, NC 27405-7813.
Phone: (910) 333-5174.

Greenville, South Carolina Office located at Wachovia Building, Suite 530, 15 South Main Street, Greenville, SC, 29601.
Phone: (803) 241-4400.

Honolulu, Hawaii Office located at 300 Ala Moana Blvd, Room 7123-A, Post Office Box 50082, Honolulu, HI 96850-0051.
Phone: (808) 541-3120.

Houston District Office located at 1919 Smith Street, 7th Floor, Houston, TX 77002.
Phone: (713) 209-3320.

Indianapolis, Indiana Office located at 101 West Ohio Street, Suite 1900, Indianapolis, IN 46204-4203.
Phone: (317) 226-7212.

Jackson, Mississippi Office located at 207 West Amite Street, Jackson, MI 39201.
Phone: (601) 965-4537.

Kansas City, Kansas Office located at 400 State Avenue, Suite 905, Kansas City, KS 66101.
Phone: (913) 551-5655.

Little Rock, Arkansas Office located at 425 West Capital Avenue, Suite 625, Little Rock, AK 72201.
Phone: (501) 324-5060.

Los Angeles, California Office located at 255 East Temple Street, 4th Floor, Los Angeles, CA 90012.
Phone: (213) 894-1000.

Louisville, Kentucky Office located at 600 Dr. Martin Luther King Jr. Place, Suite 268, Louisville, KY 40202.
Phone: (502) 582-6082.

Memphis, Tennessee Office located at 1407 Union Avenue, Suite 521, Memphis, TN 38104.
Phone: (901) 544-0115.

Miami, Florida Office located at 1 Biscayne Tower, Suite 2700, Miami, FL 33131.
Phone: (305) 536-4491.

Milwaukee, Wisconsin Office located at 310 West Wisconsin Avenue, Suite 800, Milwaukee, WI 53203-2292.
Phone: (414) 297-1111.

Minneapolis, Minnesota Office located at 330 South Second Avenue, Suite 430, Minneapolis, MN 55401-2224.
Phone: (612) 335-4040.

Nashville, Tennessee Office located at 50 Vantage Way, Suite 202, Nashville, TN 37228.
Phone: (615) 736-5820.

Newark, New Jersey Office located at 1 Newark Center, 21st Floor, Newark, NJ 07102-5233.
Phone: (201) 645-6383.

New Orleans, Louisiana Office located at 701 Loyola Avenue, Suite 600, New Orleans, LA 70113-9936.
Phone: (504) 589-2329.

New York, New York Office located at 7 World Trade Center, 18th Floor, New York, NY 10048-0948.
Phone: (212) 748-8500.

Norfolk, Virginia Office located at World Trade Center, 101 West Main Street, Suite 4300, Norfolk, VA 23510.
Phone: (804) 441-3470.

Oakland, California Office located at 1301 Clay Street, Suite 1170-N, Oakland, CA 94612-5217.
Phone: (510) 637-3230.

Oklahoma City, Oklahoma Office located at 210 Park Avenue, Oklahoma City, OK 73102.
Phone: (405) 231-4911.

Philadelphia, Pennsylvania Office located at 21 South 5th Street, 4th Floor, Philadelphia, PA 19102.
Phone: (215) 451-5800.

Phoenix, Arizona Office located at 3300 North Central Avenue, Suite 300, Phoenix, AZ 85012-1848.
Phone: (602) 640-5000.

Pittsburgh, Pennsylvania Office located at 1001 Liberty Avenue, Suite 300, Pittsburgh, PA 15222-4187.
Phone: (412) 644-3444.

Raleigh, North Carolina Office, located at 1309 Annapolis Drive, Raleigh, NC 27608-2129.
Phone: (919) 856-4064.

Richmond, Virginia Office located at 3600 West Broad Street, Room 229, Richmond, VA 23230.
Phone: (804) 278-4651.

San Antonio, Texas Office located at 5410 Fredericksburg Road, Suite 200, San Antonio, TX 78229-3555.
Phone: (210) 229-4810.

San Diego, California Office located at 401 B Street, Suite 1550, San Diego, CA 92101.
Phone: (619) 557-7235.

San Francisco Office, located at 901 Market Street, Suite 500, San Francisco, CA 94103.
Phone: (415) 356-5100.

San Jose, California Office located at 96 North Third Street, Suite 200, San Jose, CA 95112.
Phone: (408) 291-7352.

Savannah, Georgia Office located at 410 Mall Blvd., Suite G, Savannah, GA 31406-4821.
Phone: (912) 652-4234.

Seattle, Washington Office located at 909 First Avenue, Suite 400, Seattle, WA 98104-1061.
Phone: (206) 220-6883.

St. Louis, Missouri Office located at 122 Spruce Street, Room 8-100, St. Louis, MS 63103.
Phone: (314) 539-7800.

Tampa, Florida Office located at 501 East Polk Street, 10th Floor, Tampa, FL 33602.
Phone: (813) 228-2310.

Washington, D.C. Field Office located at 1400 L Street, N.W., Suite 200, Washington, DC 20005.
Phone: (202) 275-7377.

For handicap discrimination under federal law:

U.S. Department of Justice, Civil Rights Division, Office on the Americans with Disabilities Act, P.O. Box 66118, Washington, D.C. 20023-6118.
Phone: (202) 514-0301 (voice).
Phone: (202) 514-0383 (TDD).

President's Committee on Employment of People with Disabilities, 1331 F Street, NW, Third Floor, Washington, D.C. 20004.
Phone: (202) 376-6200 (voice).
Phone: (202) 376-6205 (TDD).

National Institute on Disability and Rehabilitation Research, U.S. Department of Education, 400 Maryland Avenue, SW, Washington, DC 20202-2572.
Phone: (202) 732-1134 (voice).
Phone: (202) 732-5079 (TDD).

For race, color, national origin, religion, sex, age, handicap, and sexual orientation discrimination in employment under state law:

Almost every state prohibits employment discrimination. Many of these states have agencies that investigate charges of discrimination. Almost all of these state laws prohibit discrimination on the basis of race, religion, national origin, sex, age, and disability. Some of the state laws prohibit discrimination on the basis of marital status, and a few of the states prohibit discrimination based on sexual orientation. The following state agencies are listed.

Alaska

State Commission for Human Rights Administrative and Central Investigative Units, 800 A Street, Suite 204, Anchorage, AK 99501-3669.
Phone: 907-274-4692.

Anchorage Equal Rights Commission, 620 E Tenth Avenue, Suite 204, Anchorage, AK, 99501.
Phone: 907-343-4342.

Arizona

Civil Rights Division, Attorney General's Office, 1275 West Washington Street, Phoenix, AZ 85007.
Phone: 602-542-5263.

Southern Arizona Office, 402 Congress Street, W., Suite 314, Tucson, AZ 85701.
Phone: 520-628-6500.

Governor's Office of Equal Opportunity, 1700 West Washington Street, Room 156, State Capital, Phoenix, AZ 85007.
Phone: 602-542-3711.

California

Department of Fair Employment and Housing Headquarters, 2014 T Street, Suite 210, Sacramento, CA 95814.
Phone: 916-227-2883.

Colorado

Civil Rights Commission, 1560 Broadway, Suite 1050, Denver, CO 80202-5143.
Phone: 303-894-2997.

Connecticut

Commission on Human Rights and Opportunities, Central Office, 90 Washington Street, Hartford, CT 06106.
Phone: 203-566-3350.

Delaware

Department of Labor, Office of Labor Law Enforcement, 820 North French Street, 6th Floor, Wilmington, DE 19801.
Phone: 302-577-2882.

District of Columbia

Office of Human Rights, 441 4th Street, N.W., Suite 970, Washington, D.C. 20001.
Phone: 202-724-1385.

Florida

Commission on Human Relations, 325 John Knox Road, Bldg. F, Suite 240, Tallahassee, FL 32303-4149.
Phone: 904-488-7082.

Georgia

Commission on Equal Opportunity, 710 Cain Tower, 229 Peachtree Street, Atlanta, GA 30303.
Phone: 404-656-1736.

Hawaii

Civil Rights Commission, 888 Mililani Street, 2nd Floor, Honolulu, HI 96813.
Phone: 808-856-8692.

Idaho

Human Rights Commission, 1109 Main Street, P.O. Box 83720, Boise, ID 83720-0040.
Phone: 208-334-2873.

Illinois

Department of Human Rights, James R. Thompson Center, 100 W. Randolph Street, Suite 10-100, Chicago, IL 60601.
Phone: 312-814-6200.

Indiana

Civil Rights Commission, Indiana Government Center North, 100 N. Senate Avenue, Room N-103, Indianapolis, IN 46204.
Phone: 317-232-2600.

Iowa

Civil Rights Commission, 211 East Maple Street, Second Floor, Des Moines, Iowa 50309.
Phone: 800-457-4416.

Kansas

Human Rights Commission, Landon State Office Bldg., 900 S.W. Jackson Street, Suite 851S, Topeka, KS 66612-1258.
Phone: 913-296-3206.

Kentucky

Commission on Human Rights, 332 West Broadway, 7th Floor, Heyburn Building, Louisville, KY 40202.
Phone: 800-292-5566.

Louisiana

Department of Labor, 1001 N. 23rd Street, P.O. Box 94094, Capitol Station, Baton Rouge, LA 70804.
Phone: 504-342-3075.

Maine

Human Rights Commission, 51 Station, State House, Augusta, ME 04333.
Phone: 207-624-6050.

Maryland

Commission on Human Relations, 6 Saint Paul Street, 9th Floor, Suite 900, Baltimore, MD 21202.
Phone: 410-767-8600.

Massachusetts

Massachusetts Commission Against Discrimination, McCormack State Office Bldg., 1 Ashburton Place, Room 601, Boston, MA 02108.
Phone: 617-727-3990.

Michigan

Department of Civil Rights, 303 West Kalamazoo, 4th Floor, Lansing, MI 48913.
Phone: 517-335-3165.

Minnesota

Department of Human Rights, 500 Bremer Tower, 7th Place and Minnesota Street, St. Paul, MN 55101.
Phone: 612-296-5663.

Missouri

Commission on Human Rights, 3315 W. Truman Blvd., Suite 212, P.O. Box 1129, Jefferson City, MS 65102.
Phone: 314-751-3325.

Montana

Human Rights Commission, 616 Helena Avenue, P.O. Box 1728, Helena, MT 59624.
Phone: 406-444-2884.

Nebraska

Nebraska Equal Opportunity Commission, 301 Centennial Mall, South, State Office Building, 5th Floor, P.O. Box 94934, Lincoln, NB 68509-4934.
Phone: 402-471-2024.

Nevada

Equal Rights Commission, 1515 E. Tropicana Avenue, Suite 590, Las Vegas, NV 89119.

New Hampshire

Commission for Human Rights, 162 Louden Road, Concord, NH 03301.
Phone: 603-271-2767.

New Jersey

Division on Civil Rights, Department of Law and Public Safety, P.O. Box 46001, 31 Clinton Street, 3rd Floor, Newark, NJ 07102.
Phone: 201-648-2700.

New Mexico

Human Rights Division, 1596 Pacheco Street, Santa Fe, NM 87502.
Phone: 505-827-6838.

New York

State Division of Human Rights, 55 West 125th Street, New York, NY 10027.
Phone: 212-961-8400.

North Carolina

Human Relations Commission, 217 W. Jones Street, Raleigh, NC 27603.
Phone: 919-733-7996.

North Dakota

Department of Labor, 600 East Blvd. Avenue, State Capitol Building, 13th Floor, Bismarck, ND 58505.
Phone: 701-328-2660.

Ohio

Civil Rights Commission, 220 Parsons Avenue, Columbus, OH 43215-5385.
Phone: 614-446-2785.

Oklahoma

Human Rights Commission, Room 480, 2101 N. Lincoln Blvd., Oklahoma City, OK 73105.
Phone: 405-521-2360.

Oregon

Bureau of Labor and Industries, Civil Rights Division, Suite 1070, 800 N.E. Oregon Street, No. 32, Portland, OR 97232.
Phone: 503-731-4075.

Pennsylvania

Human Rights Commission, 101 South Second Street, Suite 300, Harrisburg, PA 17101.
Phone: 717-787-4410.

Puerto Rico

Department of Labor and Human Resources, Anti-Discrimination Unit, 505 Munoz Rivera Avenue, Hato Rey 00918.
Phone: 809-754-5353.

Rhode Island

Commission for Human Rights, 10 Abbott Park Place, Providence, RI 02903.
Phone: 401-277-2661.

South Carolina

Human Affairs Commission, 2611 Forest Drive, Columbia, SC 29204.
Phone: 803-253-6336.

South Dakota

Division on Human Rights, 222 East Capitol, Suite 11, 500 East Capitol Avenue,
Pierre, SD 57501.
Phone: 605-773-4493.

Tennessee

Human Rights Commission, 530 Church Street, Suite 400, Nashville, TN 37243-0745.
Phone: 615-741-5825.

Texas

Commission on Human Rights, 8100 Cameron Road, Suite 525, P.O. Box 13493,
Austin, TX 78754.
Phone: 512-837-8534.

Utah

Industrial Commission Anti-Discrimination Division, 160 East 300 Street, South, 3rd Floor,
Salt Lake City, UT 84111.
Phone: 801-530-6801.

Vermont

Human Rights Commission, 135 State Street, 2nd Floor, Drawer 33, Montpelier, VT
05633-6301.
Phone: 802-828-2480.

Virginia

Council on Human Rights, Commonwealth of Virginia, Washington Building, 1100 Bank
Street, 12th Floor, Richmond, VA 23219.
Phone: 804-225-2292.

Washington

Washington State Human Rights Commission, 711 South Capitol Way, Suite 402, Post
Office Box 42490, Olympia, WA 98504-2490.
Phone: 360-753-6770.

West Virginia

Human Rights Commission, 1321 Plaza East, Room 104/106, Charleston, WV 25301-1400.
Phone: 304-558-2616.

Wisconsin

Department of Industry, Labor and Human Relations, Equal Rights Division, 201 E. Washington Avenue, P.O. Box 8928, Madison, WI 53708.
Phone: 608-266-6860.

Wyoming

Department of Employment, Labor Standards Division, U.S. West Bldg., 6101 Yellowstone
Road, Room 259C, Cheyenne, WY 82002.
Phone: 307-777-7261.

For discrimination or denials of equal protection of the laws, or in the administration of justice in the area of voting rights, enforcement of federal civil rights law, and equality of opportunity in education, employment, and housing:

United States Commission on Civil Rights is located at 624 Ninth Street, N.W., Washington, D.C. 20425.
Phone: (202) 376-7700.

There are regional offices located throughout the country:

Central Regional Division is located at Old Federal Office Building, 911 Walnut Street, Room 3103, Kansas City, MS 64106.
Phone: (816) 426-5253.

Eastern Regional Division is located at 624 Ninth Street, N.W., Suite 500, Washington, D.C. 20425.
Phone: (202) 376-7539.

Midwestern Regional Division is located at 55 West Monroe, Chicago, IL 60604.
Phone: (312) 353-8311.

Rocky Mountain Regional Division is located at 1961 Stout Street, Denver, CO 80294.
Phone: (303) 844-6716.

Southern Regional Division is located at 101 Marietta Street, Suite 2821, Atlanta, GA 30303.
Phone: (404) 730-2476.

Western Regional Division is located at 3660 Wilshire Blvd., Room 810, Los Angeles, CA 90010.
Phone: (213) 894-3437.

For race, color, sex, and handicap discrimination in employment by employers who have contracts with the federal government or receive federal financial assistance:

Office of Federal Contract Compliance Programs Employment Standards Administration is located at OFCCP/ESA, U.S. Department of Labor, 200 Constitution Avenue, N.W., Washington, D.C. 20210.
Phone: (202) 219-0368.

There are regional and area offices located throughout the country:

Region I is located at 1 Congress Street, 11th Floor, Boston, MA 02114.
Phone: (617) 565-2055.

Region II is located at 201 Varick Street, Room 750, New York, NY 10014.
Phone: (212) 337-2007.

Region III is located at Gateway Building, Room 15340, 3535 Market Street, Philadelphia, PA 19104.
Phone: (215) 596-6168.

Region IV is located at 1375 Peachtree Street, N.E., Suite 678, Atlanta, GA 30367.
Phone: (404) 347-3200.

Region V is located at Kluczynski Federal Bldg., Room 570, 230 South Dearborn Street, Chicago, IL 60604.
Phone: (312) 353-0335.

Region VI is located at Federal Office Bldg., Room 840, 525 S. Griffin Street, Dallas, TX 75202.
Phone: (214) 767-75202.

Region VII is located at Federal Office Bldg., Room 2011, 911 Walnut Street, Kansas City, MS 64106.
Phone: (816) 426-5384.

Region VIII is located at Federal Office Bldg., 1801 California Street, Suite 935, Denver, CO 80202.
Phone: (303) 391-6082.

Region IX is located at Stevenson Street, Suite 1700, San Francisco, CA 94105.
Phone: (415) 744-6640.

Region X is located at 1111 Third Avenue, Suite 610, Seattle, WA 98101-3212.
Phone: (206) 553-4508.

The Secretary of Labor also has a **Women's Bureau,** dealing with female issues, located at Women's Bureau, U.S. Department of Labor, 200 Constitution Avenue, N.W., Washington, D.C. 20210.
Phone: (202) 219-6611.

There are also regional offices of the Women's Bureau located throughout the country:

Region I is located at 1 Congress Street, 11th Floor, Boston, MA 02114.
Phone: (617) 565-1988.

Region II is located at 201 Varick Street, Room 601, New York, NY 10014.
Phone: (212) 337-2389.

Region III is located at 3535 Market Street, Gateway Bldg., Room 13280, Philadelphia, PA 19104.
Phone: (215) 596-1183.

Region IV is located at 1371 Peachtree Street, N.E., Atlanta, GA 30367.
Phone: (404) 347-4461.

Region V is located at 230 South Dearborn Street, Tenth Floor, Chicago, IL 60604.
Phone: (312) 353-6985.

Region VI is located at Federal Building, Room 731, 525 Griffin Street, Dallas, TX 75202.
Phone: (214) 767-6985.

Region VII is located at Federal Building, Room 2511, 911 Walnut Street, Kansas City, MS 64106.
Phone: (816) 426-6108.

Region VIII is located at Federal Building, Room 1452, 1961 Stout Street, Denver, CO 80294. Phone: (303) 844-4138.

Region IX is located at 71 Stevenson Street, Suite 927, San Francisco, CA 94105. Phone: (415) 995-5431.

Region X is located at 1111 Third Avenue, Room 885, Seattle, WA 98101-3211. Phone: (206) 442-1534.

For handicap discrimination:

See **Equal Employment Opportunity Commission (EEOC)** located at 1801 L Street, NW, Washington, DC 20507 and field offices in the first part of Appendix A.
Phone: Technical Assistance: (800) 669-4000 or (800) 669-6820 (TDD).
Web site: http://www.eeoc.gov

See state agencies in the second part of Appendix A to determine if a particular state offers protection against handicap discrimination.

Clearinghouse on the Handicapped, Office of Special Education and Rehabilitation Services, U.S. Department of Education, Room 3106, Switzer Building, Washington, D.C. 20202. Phone: (202) 732-1241.

President's Committee on Employment of People with Disabilities, The Job Accommodation Network, 1331 F Street, NW, Washington, D.C. 20004-1107.
Web site: http://www.pcepd.gov
Phone: 1-800-ADA-WORK (1-800-232-9675).

National Institute on Disability and Rehabilitation Research (NIDRR).
Phone: (202) 205-5633.

Web site: http:///www.infouse.com/disabilitydata/workdisability.html
Regional Disability and Business Technical Assistance Centers.
Phone: (800) 949-4232 (V/TDD).

For sexual orientation discrimination:

See state agencies in the second part of Appendix A to determine if a particular state offers protection against sexual orientation discrimination.

For veterans' rights:

Veterans Administration Department of Veterans Benefits, 810 Vermont Avenue, Washington, D.C. 20420.
Phone: 202-872-1151.

APPENDIX B

NON-PROFIT INSTITUTIONS THAT DEAL WITH WORKER'S RIGHTS

For Age Discrimination:

American Association of Retired Persons (AARP), 601 E Street, NW, Washington, D.C. 20049

Branch Offices:

Midwest Regional Office
8750 W. Bryn Mawr Avenue, Suite 600
Chicago, IL 60631
Phone: 773-714-9800
Fax: 773-714-9927

Northeast Regional Office
One Boston Place, Suite 1900
Boston, MA 02108
Phone: 617-723-7600
Fax: 617-305-0444

West Regional Office
9750 Third Avenue, NE
Suite 400
Seattle, WA 98115
Phone: 206-526-7918
Fax: 206-523-8138

Southwest Regional Office
8144 Walnut Hill Lane, Suite 700 LB-39,
Dallas, TX 75321
Phone: 214-265-4060
Fax: 214-265-4061

Southeast Regional Office
999 Peachtree Street NE, Suite 1650,
Atlanta, GA 30309
Phone: 404-888-0077
Fax: 404-888-0902

American Civil Liberties Union
125 Broad Street, New York, NY 10004
Phone: (212) 549-2500.
Web site: http://www.aclu.org

Branch Offices:

Alabama
207 Montgomery Street, Suite 825, Montgomery, AL 36101
Phone: 334-262-0304

Alaska
P.O. Box 201844, Anchorage, AK 99520
Phone: 907-276-2258; Fax: 907-258-0288
E-mail: akclu@alaska.net

Arkansas
Boyle Building
103 W. Capitol, #1120
Little Rock, AR 72201
Phone: 501-374-2660

Arizona
77 E. Columbus, Suite 205, Phoenix, AZ 85012
Phone: 602-650-1967

California
ACLU of Northern California
Web site: http://www.aclunc.org
1663 Mission Street, Suite 460, San Francisco, CA 94103
Phone: 415-621-2493

Chapters:

San Francisco Chapter Web site: http://www.aclusf.org
Sonoma County Chapter Web site: http://users.ap.net/-aclu
ACLU of Southern California Web site: http://www.aclu-sc.org
1616 Beverly Blvd., Los Angeles, CA 90026
Phone: 213-977-9500

ACLU of San Diego Web site: http://www.aclusandiego.org,
P.O. Box 87131
San Diego, CA 92138-7131
Phone: 619-232-2121

Colorado
400 Corona Street, Denver, CO 80218
Phone: 303-777-5482

Connecticut
32 Grand Street, Hartford, CT 06106
Phone: 860-247-9823

District of Columbia, Washington, D.C.
1400 20th St., NW, Suite 119, Washington, D.C. 20036
Phone: 202-457-0800

Delaware
100 West 10th Street, Suite 309, Wilmington, DE 19801
Phone: 302-654-3966
Email: aclu@del.net

Florida
3000 Biscayne Blvd., Suite 215, Miami, FL 33137
Phone: 305-576-2336; Fax: 305-576-1106
Email: ACLUFL@aol.com

Georgia
142 Mitchell Street, SW Suite 301, Atlanta, GA 30303
Phone: 404-523-5398

Hawaii
P.O. Box 3410, Honolulu, HI 96801
Phone: 808-522-5900
Email: office@acluhawaii.org

Iowa
446 Insurance Exchange Bldg. Des Moines, IA 50309
Phone: 515-243-3576
Email: iclu@radiks.net

Idaho
P.O. Box 1897, Boise, ID 83701
Phone: 208-344-5243

Illinois
180 N. Michigan Ave., Suite 2300, Chicago, IL 60601
Phone: 312-201-9740
Email: acluil@aol.com

Indiana
1031 E. Washington St., Indianapolis, IN 46202
Phone: 317-635-4056

Kansas
1010 W. 39th St., Suite 103, Kansas City, MO 64111
Phone: 816-756-3113
Email: aclu@kctera.net

Kentucky
425 W. Muhammad Ali Blvd., Suite 230, Louisville, KY 40202
Phone: 502-581-1181

Louisiana
PO Box 70496, New Orleans, LA 70172
Phone: 504-522-0617

Maine
233 Oxford St., Suite 32K, Portland, ME 04101
Phone: 207-774-5444

Maryland
2219 St. Paul St., Baltimore, MD 21218
Phone: 410-889-8555
Email: aclu@aclu-md.org

Massachusetts
99 Chauncy St., Suite 310, Boston, MA 02111
Phone: 617-482-3170

Michigan
1249 Washington Blvd., Suite 2910, Detroit, MI 48226-1822
Phone: 313-961-4662

Minnesota
1021 W. Broadway, Minneapolis, MN 55411
Phone: 612-522-2423

Missouri
4557 Laclede Avenue St. Louis, MO 63108
Phone: 314-361-2111
http://www.aclu-em.org

Mississippi
P.O. Box 2242, Jackson, MS 39225
Phone: 601-355-6464

Montana
P.O. Box 3012, Billings, MT 59103
Phone: 406-248-1086
Email: aclu@mcn.net

North Carolina
P.O. Box 28004, Raleigh, NC 27611
Phone: 919-834-3390

North Dakota
418 E. Broadway, Suite 20, Bismarck, ND 58501
Phone: 701-255-4727

Nebraska
941 0 Street, Suite 1020 Lincoln, NE 68508
Phone: 402-476-8091

New Hampshire
18 Low Ave., Concord, NH 03301
Phone: 603-225-3080

New Jersey
35 Halsey St., Suite 4B, Newark, NJ 07102
Phone: 973-642-2084

New Mexico
PO Box 80915, Albuquerque, NM 87198
Phone: 505-266-5915

Nevada
325 S. Third St., Suite 25, Las Vegas, NV 89101
Phone: 702-366-1226

New York
http://www.nyclu.org/
125 Broad St., 17th Floor, New York, NY 10004
Phone: 212-344-3005

Ohio
1266 W. 6th St., Suite 200, Cleveland, OH 44113
Phone: 216-781-6276

Oklahoma
3012 N. Lee Suite A, Oklahoma City, OK 73103
Phone: 405-524-8511

Oregon
P.O. Box 40585, Portland, OR 97240-0585
Phone: 503-227-3186
Email: info@aclu-or.org

Pennsylvania
www.aclupa.org
P.O. Box 1161, Philadelphia, PA 19105
Phone: 215-923-4357

Rhode Island
10 Abbot Park Place, 3rd Floor, Providence, RI 02903
Phone: 401-831-7171

South Carolina
1338 Main St., Suite 800, Columbia, SC 29201
Phone 803-799-5151
Email: aclusc@aot.com

South Dakota
418 E. Broadway, Suite 20, Bismarck, ND 58501
Phone: 701-255-4727

Tennessee
P.O. Box 120160, Nashville, TN 37212
Phone: 615-320-7142

Texas
PO Box 3629, Austin, TX 78764
Phone: 512-441-0077

Utah
355 N. 30OW, Suite 1, Salt Lake City, UT 84103
Phone: 801-521-9289

Virginia
6 N. 6th St., Suite 400, Richmond, VA 23219
Phone: 804-644-8022

Vermont
110 E. State St., Montpelier, VT 05602
Phone/Fax: 802-223-6304
Email: acluvt@aol.com

Washington
705 Second Ave., Suite 300, Seattle, WA 98104
Phone: 206-624-2184   Legal complaint line: 206-624-2180

West Virginia
P.O. Box 3952, Charleston, WV 25339
Phone: 304-345-9246

Wisconsin
207 E. Buffalo St., Suite 325, Milwaukee, WI 53202
Phone: 414-272-4032

Wyoming
514 Majestic Building, 1603 Capitol Avenue, Cheyenne, WY 82001
Phone: 307-637-4565

The Gray Panthers
733 15th Street, NW, Suite 437, Washington, D.C. 20005.
Phone: (800)-280-5362.

Branch Offices:

Arizona
Tucson/Southern Arizona
Rachel Zane, 832 N. Jefferson Avenue, Tucson, AZ 85711-1430.
T/F: 520-745-3660.

Arkansas
John N. Sutcliffe
Kingston, AR 72742
501-783-3395

California
Berkeley
Irv Rautenberg, 1403 Addison Street, Berkeley, CA 94702.
510-548-9696.
F: 510-548-9697.
E: Gerda@sirius

Central Contra Costa
Doris Copperman & Monica Larson, P.O. Box 2335, Walnut Creek, CA 94595.
Doris: 925-937-8321.
F: 925-937-5396, call 1st
E: Dcopperman@earthlink.net
Monica: 925-229-0813.

Hayward
Betsy Cawn
Hayward, CA 94544
510-783-3395

LA West
Eva Bluestein, 11344 Berwick St #U, Los Angeles, CA 90049.
310-472-9365.
E: EvaBlue@aol.com

Long Beach
Al Dawson, 2235 Mira Mar Ave, Long Beach, CA 90815.
562-597-6062.

Marin County
Louise Aldrich & Ann Garfield, P.O. Box 2874, San Rafael, CA 94912.
415-491-0113.
E: Aldrich@igc.org

Mendocino Coast
Anne Deirup & Linda Leahy, P.O. Box 276, Ft. Bragg, CA 95437.
707-937-4310.
E: graypanthers@hotmail.com

North Orange County
Shirley Cohen, P.O. Box 10101, Santa Ana, CA 92711.
714-220-0224.

Oakland-Emeryville
Jane Jackson, 275 E. 12th St., #201, Oakland, CA 94606.
510-444-7555.
F: 510-444-7554.

Orange County
Maxine Quirk, 331 N. Olive St., Orange, CA 92866.
714-639-0565.
F: 714-532-4163.

Sacramento
Joan Lee, P.O. Box 19438, Sacramento, CA 95819.
916-332-5980.
Betty:916-739-1540.
E: JoanBLee@iuno.com

San Diego
Jim Wahl, 1295 University Avenue, San Diego, CA 92103.
619-448-1151.

San Fernando Valley
Sigrid Hawkes, 10825 Woodward, Sunland, CA 91040.
818-353-1162.
F: 818-951-8875.
E: shawkesAturn.org

San Francisco
Karen Talbot & Aroza Simpson, 1182 Market St., Rm 203, San Francisco, CA 94102.
F: 415-552-8801.
Karen: 415-759-9774.
Aroza:415-567-5348.
E: graypanthersfaction@juno.com

Santa Barbara
Selma Rubin, P.O. Box 92209, Santa Barbara, CA 93190.
805-964-3757.
E: SOSRubin@aol.com

Southern Alameda County
Betty Moose, 1328 Via El Monte, San Lorenzo, CA 94580.
510-278-2094.

South Bay
Georgia Petrie, P.O. Box 9054, Torrance, CA 90504.
310-540-6736.

West Contra Costa
Art Schroeder, 706 Sea View, El Cerrioto, CA 94530.
510-525-0177.

Colorado
Denver
Robert Danknich, 1420 Ogden St., Denver, CO 80218.
Office: 303-861-2524.
Bob: 303-343-7701.
F: 303-365-1129.
E: Rdanknich@aol.com

District of Columbia
Metro D.C.
Bernice Fonteneau, 711 8th St., NW, Washington, DC 20001.
T/F: 202-347-9541.
E: gpanther@capaccess.org

Florida
North Dade
Rebecca Rosen & Irma Rochlin, 3 Island Avenue, 12H,
Miami, FL 33139.
Reb: T/F 305-531-2552.
Irma: 954-456-2879.

South Dade
Norman Saxe & Gail Neumann, 10725 SW 82nd Ave, Miami, FL 33156.
Norman: T/F: 305-595-0594.
Gail: 305-233-8013.

Sarasota/Manatee
Carol Burman-Jahn, PO Box 3492, Sarasota, FL 34320.
941-922-4691.
F: 941-923-6664.
E: seebeejay@aol.com

Illinois
Chicago
Agnes Ranseen, 1020 Grove St., Evanston, IL 60201.
Agnes: 847-869-0481.
Giudi Weiss: 773-955-1224.
E: giudi@sprynet.com

Indiana
Monroe County/Bloomington
Gal Shifton & Karen Groom, c/o Center for Behavioral Health, 645 S. Rogerst St., Bloomington, IN 47403.
Karen: 812-855-1162.
Gal: 812-337-2340.
E: kgrooms@indiana.edu

Maryland
Montgomery County
Abraham Bloom, P.O. Box 164, Kensington, MD 20895.
T/F: 301-942-4254.

Prince George's Co./Greenbelt
Janet Parker, 6 N. Ridge Rd., Greenbelt, MD 20770.
301-474-6668.

Massachusetts
Boston
Art Mazer, c/o Cambridge YWCA, 7 Temple St., Cambridge, MA 02139.
office: 617-876-3400.
F: 617-876-3410.
E: KMazer7086@aol.com

Pioneer Valley
Rhoda Dizard, P.O. Box 771, Amherst, MA 01004.
413-253-2844.

Michigan
Huron Valley
Arthur Parris, 1803 Cayuga Pl, Ann Arbor, MI 48104.
734-663-1053.
E: Arthurpar@aol.com

Metro Detroit
Randy Block & Ethel Schwartz, P.O. Box 37033, Oak Park, MI 48237.
Randy: 248-549-5170.
F: 248-549-5331.
Ethel: 248-669-6343.
E: BeeLock4@aol.com

Minnesota
Twin Cities
Sally Brown & Jo Lowery, 3249 Hennepin Avenue, Minneapolis, MN 55408.
Office: T/F 612-822-1011.

New Jersey
Northern New Jersey
Dr. May Hollinshead & Ed Purtill, 2 Winthrop Pl., Leonia, NJ 07605.
May: 201-944-0676.
Ed: 201-768-4557.

Southern New Jersey
Irene DiRenza, 210 W. Crystal Lake Ave., Apt. 119-D,
Haddonfield, NJ 08033.
609-858-6535.
E: Eugene1000@aol.com

New Mexico
Greater Albuquerque
Teri Selcoe, 12304 Haines Ave., NE, Albuquerque, NM 87112.
505-271-4983.
E: JMBC@aol.com

New York
New York City
Lillian Sarno, 165 W. 86th St., New York, NY 10024.
Office: 212-799-7572.

Suffolk County
Beverly Carpenter & George Reilly, P.O. Box 373, Sayville, NY 11782.
Beverly: 516-589-6480.
George: 516-665-6383.

Westchester County
Edwin Levine, 465 E. Lincoln Ave., Mt. Vernon, NY 10552.
914-668-3248.

Ohio
Greater Columbus
Marianne Husten, 1084 Loring Rd., Columbus, OH 43224.
T/F: 614-263-7385.

Oregon
Portland
Bill Gordon & Bobbi Gary, 1819 NW Everett, Portland, OR 97305.
Bill: 503-224-5190.
T: Bobbi: 503-231-7509.
F: Bobbi: 503-335/8211.

Pennsylvania
Crawford County
Contact Gray Panthers Natl., 800-280-5362,

Graterford
T. J. Moore & C. E. Morrison, #CN1103, STEP Program, Box 244, Graterford, PA 19426.
610-489-4151.

Rhode Island
Richard Bidwell, 32 D. Avenue, Pawtucket, RI 02860.
401-725-1122.
F: 401-725-1020.

Texas
Austin
Charlotte Flynn, 3710 Cedar St., Rm. 235, Austin, TX 78705.
Office: 512-458-3738.
F: 512-458-9727.

Houston
Contact Gray Panthers Natl., 800-780-5362.

Virginia
New River Valley
Henry & Patricia Smoot, 1407 Crestview Dr., Blacksburg, VA 24060.
D: 540-951-7225.

Washington
Seattle
Marge Lueders, 4649 Sunnyside Ave. N., Seattle, WA 98103.
Office: 206-675-8859.
Marge: 206-523-6865.
F: 206-527-4847.
E: LKALUBA@aol.com

Wisconsin
Clemens Blaine, 614 S. Dickinson, Madison, WI 53703.
608-255-6096.

For Disability and Handicap Issues:

American Amputee Foundation, P.O. Box 250218, Hillcrest Station, Little Rock, Arkansas 72225.
Phone: (501) 666-2523.

American Association on Mental Retardation, 1719 Kalorama Road, NW, Washington, D.C. 20009.
Phone: (202) 386-1068.
http://www.aamr.org

See American Civil Liberties Union, 125 Broad Street, New York, NY 10004.
Phone: (212) 549-2500 (*See* Age Discrimination Section on page 198 for branch offices).

American Council of the Blind, 1115 15th Street, NW, Suite 720, Washington, D.C. 20005.
Phone: (202) 467-5081 (voice only).
Phone: (800) 424-8666 (Monday through Friday 3-5:30 P.M. EST only).

American Foundation for the Blind, Inc., 15 West 16th Street, New York, NY 10011.
Phone: (212) 620-2000.

American Heart Association, 7230 Greenville Avenue, Dallas, TX 75231.
Phone: (214) 373-6300.

American Lung Association, 1740 Broadway, New York, NY 10019
Phone: (212) 315-8700.

American Psychiatric Association, 1400 K Street, NW, Washington, D.C. 20005.
Phone: (202) 628-6000.

American Red Cross, 2025 E Street, NW, Washington, D.C. 20006.
Phone: (212) 728-6530.

American Speech-Language Hearing Association, 10801 Rockville Pike, Rockville, MD 20852.
Phone: (301) 897-5700.

Associated Services for the Blind, 919 Walnut Street, Philadelphia, PA 19107.
Phone: (215) 627-0600.

Association of Persons in Supported Employment, 5001 W. Broad Street, Suite 34, Richmond, Virginia 23230.
Phone: (804) 282-3655 (voice only).

Association for Retarded Citizens, 500 East Border Street, Arlington, TX 76010.
Phone: (817) 261-6003.

Center for Mental Health Services, Parklawn Building, 5600 Fishers Lane, Room 15-C-26, Rockville, MD 20857.
Phone: (301) 443-3667.

Council of State Administrators of Vocational Rehabilitation, 1213 29th Street, NW, Washington, D.C. 20007.
Phone: (202) 638-4634.

Disability Rights Education and Defense Fund, 2212 Sixth Street, Berkeley, CA 94710.
Phone: (510) 644-2555 (voice).
Phone: (510) 644-2629 (TDD).
Phone: (800) 466-4232 (voice and TDD).

Dole Foundation for Employment of People with Disabilities, 1819 H Street, NW, Suite 850, Washington, D.C. 2006.
Phone: (202) 457-0318 (voice and TDD).

Employment Law Center, 1663 Mission Street, Suite 400, San Francisco, CA 94103.
Phone: (415) 864-8848 (voice).

Epilepsy Foundation of America, 4351 Garden City Drive, Landover, MD 20785.
Phone: (301) 459-3700.

Federation of the Handicapped, 211 West 14th Street, New York, NY 10011.
Phone: (212) 206-651-5000.

Guild for the Blind, 180 North Michigan Avenue, Chicago, IL 60601.
Phone: (312) 236-8569.

Independent Living Research Utilization Project, TIRR—The Institute for Rehabilitation and Research, 133 Moursund Avenue, Houston, TX 77030.
Phone: (713) 799-5000.

Industry-Labor Council of National Center for Disability Services, 201 I. U. Willets Road, Albertson, NY 11507.
Phone: (516) 747-6323 (voice).
Phone: (516) 747-5355 (TDD).

International Association of Business, Industry and Rehabilitation, P.O. Box 15242, Washington, D.C. 20003.
Phone: (202) 543-6353 (voice).

Institute of Rehabilitation Medicine, New York University Medical Center, 400 East 34th Street, New York, NY 10016.
Phone: (212) 340-7300.

Legal Action Center, 153 Waverly Place, New York, NY 10014.
Phone: (212) 944-9800 (voice).

Legal Action Center, 236 Massachusetts Avenue, NE, Washington, D.C. 20002.
Phone: (202) 544-5478 (voice only).

Minneapolis Society for the Blind, Inc., 1936 Lyndale Avenue, South, Minneapolis, MN 55403.
Phone: (612) 871-2222.

Minnesota State Services for the Blind Communication Center, 1745 University Avenue, St. Paul, MN 55104.
Phone: (612) 642-0500.

National Association for Protection and Advocacy Systems, 900 Second Street, NE, Suite 211, Washington, D.C. 20002.
Phone: (202) 408-9514. TDD (202) 408-9521.
Email: HN4537@handsnet.org

Branches:

Alabama
Alabama Disabilities Advocacy Program
The University of Alabama, P.O. Box 870395, Tuscaloosa, AL 35487-0395
Phone: (205) 348-4928; 205-348-9484 TDD; (800) 826-1675

Alaska

Disability Law Center of Alaska, 615 East 82d Avenue, Suite 101, Anchorage, AK 99518
Phone: 907-344-1002 Voice/TDD; 800-478-1234

American Samoa

Protection & Advocacy, P.O. Box 3937, Pago Pago, American Samoa 96799
Phone: 011-684-633-2441

Arizona

Arizona Center for Disability Law, 3131 North Country Club, Suite 100,
Tucson, AZ 85716
Phone: 520-327-9547 Voice/TDD

Arkansas

Advocacy Services, Inc., Evergreen Place, Suite 201, 1100 North University
Little Rock, AR 72207
Phone: 501-296-1775; Voice/TDD 800-485-1775

California

Protection & Advocacy, Inc., 100 Howe Avenue, Suite 185N, Sacramento, CA 95825
Phone: 916-488-9950; 800-776-5746

Colorado

The Legal Center, 455 Sherman Street, Suite 130, Denver, CO 80203
Phone: 303-722-0300; Voice/TDD 800-288-1376

Connecticut

Office of P&A for Handicapped and Developmentally Disabled Persons
60B Weston Street, Hartford, CT 06120-1551
Phone: 860-297-4300; 860-566-2102/TDD

Delaware

Disabilities Law Program, 913 Washington Street, Wilmington, DE 19801
Phone: 302-575-0660 Voice/TDD

Florida

Advocacy Center for Persons with Disabilities, Webster Building, Suite 100,
2671 Executive Center, Circle West Tallahassee, FL 32301-5024
Phone: 904-488-9071; 800-342-0823; 800-346-4127/TDD

Georgia

Georgia Advocacy Office, 999 Peachtree Street NE., Suite 870, Atlanta, GA 30309-3166
Phone: 404-885-1234 Voice/TDD; 800-282-4538

Guam

Guam Protection and Advocacy Reflection Center, 222 Chalan Santo Papa, Suite 204,
Agana, Guam 96910
Phone: 011-671-472-8985/86/87; 011-671-472-8988/TDD

Hawaii

Protection and Advocacy Agency, 1580 Makaloa Street, Suite 1060, Honolulu, HI 96814
Phone: 808-949-2922 Voice/TDD

Idaho

Co-Ad, Inc., 4477 Emerald, Suite B-100, Boise, ID 83706
Phone: 208-336-5353 Voice/TDD; 800-632-5725

Illinois

Equip for Equality, Inc., 11 East Adams, Suite 1200, Chicago, IL 60603
Phone: 312-341-0022; Voice/TDD 800-537-2632

Indiana

Indiana Protection & Advocacy Services, 850 North Meridian, Suite 2-C,
Indianapolis, IN 46204
Phone: 317-232-1150; Voice/TDD 800-622-4845

Iowa

Iowa P&A Service, Inc., 3015 Merle Hay Road, Suite 6, Des Moines, IA 50310
Phone: 515-278-2502; 515-278-0571ffDD; 800-779-2502

Kansas

Kansas Advocacy & Protection Services, 501 Southwest Jackson, Suite 425,
Topeka, KS 66603
Phone: 913-232-3469

Kentucky

Office for Public Advocacy Division for P&A, 100 Fair Oaks Lane, Third Floor,
Frankfort, KY 40601
Phone: 502-564-2967; 800-372-2988/TDD

Louisiana

Advocacy Center for the Elderly and Disabled, 225 Baronne, Suite 2112, New Orleans, LA
70112-2112
Phone: 504-522-2337; Voice/TDD 800-960-7705

Maine

Maine Advocacy Services, P.O. Box 2007, 32 Winthrop, Augusta, ME 04338
Phone: 207-626-2774; 800-452-1948/TDD

Maryland

Maryland Disability Law Center, Central Maryland Office, The Walbert Building, Suite
204, 1800 North Charles Street, Baltimore, MD 21201
Phone: 410-234-2791; 410-727-6387 Voice/TDD; 800-233-7201

Massachusetts

Disability Law Center, Inc., 11 Beacon Street, Suite 925, Boston, MA 02108
Phone: 617-723-8455 Voice/TDD

Center for Public Representation, 22 Green Street, Northampton, MA 01060
Phone: 413-586-6024 Voice/TDD

Michigan

Michigan P&A Service, 106 West Allegan, Suite 300, Lansing, MI 48933
Phone: 517-487-1755 Voice/TDD

Minnesota

Minnesota Disability Law Center, 430 First Avenue North, Suite 300, Minneapolis, MN
55401-1780
Phone: 612-332-1441; 800-292-4150

Mississippi

Mississippi P&A System for DD, Inc., 5330 Executive Place, Suite A, Jackson, MS 39206
Phone: 601-981-8207 Voice/TDD

Missouri

Missouri P&A Services, 925 South Country Club Drive, Unit B-1, Jefferson City, MO 65109
Phone: 573-893-3333; 800-392-8667

Montana

Montana Advocacy Program, P.O. Box 1680, 316 North Park, Room 211, Helena, MT 59624
Phone: 406-444-3889; Voice/TDD 800-245-4743

Nebraska

Nebraska Advocacy Services, Inc., 522 Lincoln Center Building, 215 Centennial Mall
South, Lincoln, NE 68508
Phone: 402-474-3183 Voice/TDD

Nevada

Nevada Advocacy & Law Center, Inc., 401 South Third Street, Suite 403,
Las Vegas, NV 89101
Phone: 702-383-8150; 702-383-8170/TDD; 800-992-5715

New Hampshire

Disabilities Rights Center, P.O. Box 3660, 18 Low Avenue, Concord, NH 03302-3660
Phone: 603-228-0432 Voice/TDD

New Jersey

New Jersey P&A, Inc., 210 South Broad Street, Third Floor, Trenton, NJ 08608
Phone: 609-292-9742; 800-792-8600

New Mexico

Protection & Advocacy, Inc., 1720 Louisiana Boulevard NE., Suite 204,
Albuquerque, NM 87110
Phone: 505-256-3100 Voice/TDD; 800-432-4682

New York

NY Commission on Quality of Care for the Mentally Disabled, 99 Washington Avenue,
Suite 1002, Albany, NY 12210
Phone: 518-473-7378; 518-473-4057; 800-624-4143/TDD

North Carolina

Governor's Advocacy Council for Persons with Disabilities, 2113 Cameron Street, Suite
218, Raleigh, NC 27605
Phone: 919-733-9250 Voice/TDD; 800-821-6922

North Dakota

The North Dakota Protection & Advocacy Project, 400 East Broadway, Suite 616, Bismarck, ND 58501

Phone: 701-328-2950; 800-472-2670; 800-642-6694; (24-hour line) 800-366-6888/TDD

Northern Mariana Islands

Northern Marianas Protection & Advocacy System, Inc., P.O. Box 3529, C. K. Saipan, MP 96950

Phone: 011-670-235-7274/3

Ohio

Ohio Legal Rights Service, 8 East Long Street, Fifth Floor, Columbus, OH 43215

Phone: 614-466-7264 Voice/TDD 800-282-9181

Oklahoma

Oklahoma Disability Law Center, Inc., 2915 Classen Boulevard, Suite 300, Oklahoma City, OK 73106

Phone: 405-525-7755; 800-880-7755

Oregon

Oregon Advocacy Center, 620 SW Fifth Avenue, Fifth Floor, Portland, OR 97204-1428

Phone: 503-243-2081; 800-452-1694; 800-556-5351/TDD

Pennsylvania

Pennsylvania P&A, Inc., 116 Pine Street, Harrisburg, PA 17101

Phone: 717-236-8110 Voice/TDD; 800-692-7443

Puerto Rico

Office of the Governor, Ombudsman for the Disabled, P.O. Box 4234

San Juan, PR 00902-4234

Phone: 787-721-4299; 800-981-4125

Rhode Island

Rhode Island P&A System, Inc., 151 Broadway, Third Floor, Providence, RI 02903

Phone: 401-831-3150; 401-831-5335 TDD; 800-733-5332

South Carolina

Protection & Advocacy for People with Disabilities, Inc., 3710 Landmark Drive, Suite 208, Columbia, SC 29204

Phone: 803-782-0639 Voice/TDD; 800-922-5225

South Dakota

South Dakota Advocacy Services, 221 South Central Avenue, Pierre, SD 57501

Phone: 605-224-8294 Voice/TDD; 800-658-4782

Tennessee

Tennessee P&A, Inc., P.O. Box 121257, Nashville, TN 37212

Phone: 615-298-1080 Voice/TDD; 800-342-1660

Texas
Advocacy, Inc., 7800 Shoal Creek Boulevard, Suite 171-E, Austin, TX 78757
Phone: 512-454-4816 Voice/TDD; 800-252-9108

Utah
Legal Center for People with Disabilities, 455 East 400 South, Suite 410,
Salt Lake City, UT 84111
Phone: 801-363-1347 Voice / TDD; 800-662-9080

Vermont
Vermont Protection & Advocacy, 21 East State Street, Suite 101,
Montpelier, VT 05602
Phone: 802-229-1355

Virginia
Department for Rights of Virginians with Disabilities, Ninth Street Office Building, 202
North Ninth Street, Ninth Floor, Richmond, VA 23219
Phone: 804-225-2042 Voice/TDD 800-552-3962

Virgin Islands
Virgin Islands Advocacy Agency, 7A Whim Street, Suite 2, Frederiksted, VI 00840
Phone: 809-772-1200; 809-776-4303; 809-772-4641/TDD

Washington
Washington P&A System, 1401 East Jefferson, Suite 506, Seattle, WA 98122
Phone: 206-324-1521 Voice / TDD 2

West Virginia
West Virginia Advocates, Inc. Litton Building, Fourth Floor, 1207 Quarrier Street,
Charleston, WV 25301
Phone: 304-346-0847 Voice/TDD; 800-950-5250

Wisconsin
Wisconsin Coalition for Advocacy, 16 North Carroll Street, Suite 400, Madison, WI 53703
Phone: 608-267-0214; 608-267-0214/TTY

Wyoming
Wyoming P&A System, 2424 Pioneer Avenue, Suite 101, Cheyenne, WY 82001
Phone: 307-638-7668; 307-632-3496; 800-821-3091 Voice / TDD; 800-624-7648

Native American
DNA People's Legal Services, Inc., P.O. Box 392, Shiprock, NM 87410
Phone: 505-368-3216

National Association of the Deaf
814 Thayer Avenue, Silver Spring, MD 20910-4500.
Phone: (301) 587-1788 (voice).
Phone: (301) 587-1789 (TDD).

National Association for Retarded Citizens, 1522 K Street, NW, Suite 516, Washington, D.C. 20005.
Phone: (202) 785-3388 (Voice).
Phone: (202) 785-3411 (TDD).

National Association of Veterans' Affairs, 1100 17th Street, NW, Washington, D.C. 20036.
Phone: (202) 233-4000.

National Center on Law and the Deaf, 800 Florida Avenue, NE, Room 326, Ely Center, Washington, D.C. 20002.
Phone: (202) 651-5373 (Voice and TDD).

National Disability Action Center, 1101 15th Street, NW, Washington, D.C. 20005.
Phone: (202) 775-9231 (Voice and TDD).

National Easter Seals Society, 1350 New York Avenue, NW, Washington, D.C. 20005.
Phone: (202) 347-3066 (Voice).
Phone: (202) 347-7385 (TDD).

National Federation of the Blind, 1800 Johnson Street, Baltimore, MD 21230.
Phone: (301) 659-9314.

National Handicap Housing Institute, Inc., 4556 Lake Drive, Robinsdale, MN 55422.
Phone: (612) 535-9771.

National Head Injury Foundation, 1140 Connecticut Avenue, NW, Suite 812, Washington, D.C. 20036.
Phone: (202) 296-6443 (Voice only).
Phone: (800) 444-6443 (families, consumers; voice only).

National Information Center on Deafness, Gallaudet University, 800 Florida Avenue, NE, Washington, D.C. 20002.
Phone: (202) 651-5051 (Voice).
Phone: (202) 651-5052 (TDD).

National Institute of Arthritis, Diabetes, and Digestive and Kidney Diseases, Bldg. 31, Room 9A04, 9000 Rockville Pike, Bethesda, MD 20205.
Phone: (301) 496-4000.

National Mental Health Association, 1021 Prince Street, Alexandria, VA 22314.
Phone: (703) 684-7722.

National Mental Health Law Project, 1101 15th Street, NW, Suite 1212, Washington, D.C. 20002.
Phone: (202) 467-5730 (Voice).
Phone: (202) 467-4232 (TDD).

National Organization for Rare Disorders, P.O. Box 8923, New Fairfield, CT 06812-1783.
Phone: (800) 999-6673 (Voice only).
Phone: (203) 746-6518 (Voice only).

National Rehabilitation Information Center, 4407 8th Street, N.E., Washington, D.C. 20017.
Phone: (202) 877-1000.

National Spinal Cord Injury Association, 600 West Cummings Park, Suite 2000, Woburn, MA 01801.
Phone: (617) 935-2722 (voice only).

N. Neal Pike Institute on Law and Disability, Boston University School of Law, 765 Commonwealth Avenue, Boston, MA 02215.
Phone: (617) 353-294.

PADD Administration on Developmental Disabilities, Hubert H. Humphrey Building 200 Independence Avenue SW, Washington, D.C. 20201.
Phone: 202-690-6905.

Paralyzed Veterans of America, Inc., 801 18th Street, NW, Washington, D.C. 20006.
Phone: (202) 872-1300.

President's Committee on Employment of People with Disabilities, 1111 20th Street, NW, Washington, D.C. 20036.
Phone: (202) 653-5044.

Public Interest Law Center of Philadelphia, 125 South Ninth Street, Seventh Floor, Suite 700, Philadelphia, PA 19107.
Phone: (215) 627-7100 (voice).

Rehabilitation Services Administration, Switzer Building, Room 323, 330 C Street SW. Washington, D.C. 20202-2735.
Phone: 202-205-8719.

Rochester Institute of Technology, National Center on Employment for the Deaf, Lyndon Baines Johnson Building, P.O. Box 9887, Rochester, NY 14623-0887.
Phone: (716) 475-6219 (voice).
Phone: (716) 475-6205 (TDD).

Self Help for Hard-of-Hearing People, 7800 Wisconsin Avenue, NW, Bethesda, MD 20814.
Phone: (301) 657-2248 (voice).
Phone: (301) 657-2249 (TDD).

Stout Vocational Rehabilitation Institute, Materials Development Center, University of Wisconsin-Stout, Menomonie, WI 54751.
Phone: (715) 232-2195.

University Center for International Rehabilitation, College of Education, 513 Erickson Hall, Michigan State University, East Lansing, MI 48824.
Phone: (517) 353-8920.

Vocational Guidance and Rehabilitation Services, 2239 East 55th Street, Cleveland, OH 44103.
Phone: (216) 431-7800.

Western Law Center for the Handicapped, 1441 West Olympic Boulevard, Los Angeles, CA 90015.
Phone: (213) 736-1031 (voice).

For National Origin Discrimination:

American Civil Liberties Union, 125 Broad Street, New York, NY 10004.
Phone: (212) 549-2500 (See age discrimination section on page 198 for branch offices).

American Immigration Lawyers Association, 1400 1st Street, NW, Washington, D.C. 20005.
Phone: (202) 371-9377.

Center for Immigrants' Rights, Inc., 48 St. Marks Place, New York, NY 10003.
Phone: 212- 505-6890; Fax 212- 995-5876.

Immigrant Legal Resource Center, 1663 Mission St., Suite 602, San Francisco, CA 94103-2449.
Phone: 415-255-9499.

National Center of Immigration Rights, 1550 West 6th St. Los Angeles, CA 90017.

National Lawyers' Committee, 1450 G Street, Suite 400, NW, Washington, D.C.
Phone: (202) 662-8300.

Local Independent Affiliates of the Lawyers' Committee:

Los Angeles, California
Public Counsel, 601 South Ardmore Avenue, Los Angeles, CA 90005.
Phone: (213) 385-9089.

San Francisco, California
San Francisco Lawyers' Committee for Urban Affairs, 301 Mission Street, Suite 400, San Francisco, CA 94105.
Phone: (415) 543-9444.

Denver, Colorado
Colorado Lawyers' Committee, 555 17th Street, Suite 2900, Denver, CO 80202.
Phone: (303) 296-8261.

Chicago, Illinois
Chicago Lawyers' Committee for Civil Rights Under Law, Inc., 100 North La Salle Street, Suite 600, Chicago, IL 60602-2403.
Phone: (312) 630-9744.

Boston, Massachusetts
Lawyers' Committee for Civil Rights Under Law of the Boston Bar Association, 294 Washington Street, Suite 940, Boston, MA 02108.
Phone: (617) 482-1145.

Philadelphia, Pennsylvania
Public Interest Law Center of Philadelphia, 125 South 9th Street, Suite 700, Philadelphia, PA 19107.
Phone: (215) 627-7100.

Texas
Lawyers' Committee for Civil Rights of Texas, Immigrant & Refugee Rights Project, 2311 North Flores, San Antonio, TX 78265.

Washington, D.C.
Washington Lawyers' Committee, 1300 19th Street, NW, Suite 500, Washington D.C. 20036
Phone: (202) 682-6900.

For Race or Color Discrimination:

American Civil Liberties Union, 125 Broad Street, New York, NY 10004.
Phone: (212) 549-2500 (See age discrimination section on page 198 for branch offices).

Anti-defamation League of B'Nai B'rith, New York, NY.
Phone: 212-885-7700.

Regional Offices:

Alabama/Georgia/South Carolina/Tennessee
Email: atlanta@adl.org
Phone: 404-262-3470; Fax: 404-262-3548.

Arizona
Email: arizona@adl.org
Phone: 602-274-0990.
Gloria Goldman, Esq. 1575 W. Ina Road, Tucson, AZ 85704
Phone: 520-797-9229; Fax: 520-797-1407.

California
Email: san-francisco@adi.org
Phone: 415-981-3500; Fax: 415-981-8933.
Email: los-angeles@adl.org
Phone: 310-446-8000; Fax: 310-470-8712.
Email: las-vegas@adl.org
Phone: 702-862-8600.
Email: san-fernando-valley@adl.org
Phone: 818-464-3220; Fax: 818-464-3247.
Email: orange-county@adl.org
Phone: 714-979-4733; Fax: 714-979-4138.

San Diego Anti-Defamation League, 7851 Mission Center Court, Suite 320, San Diego, CA 92108.
Phone: 619-293-3770; Fax: 619-293-7010.
Email: san-diego@adl.org

Carolinas
Gerald M. Chapman, Esq. 404-A N. Eugene St., Greensboro, NC 27402.
Phone: 336-334-0034; Fax: 336-334-0036.

Colorado
Marie Lowe, Esq., 1776 S. Jackson St. Suite 1002, Denver, CO 80210.
Phone: 303-757-7100; Fax: 303-757-1771.

Connecticut
Email: connecticut@adi.org
Phone: 203-787-4281; Fax: 203-787-1524.

District of Columbia/Maryland/Virginia/North Carolina
Email: washington-dc@adl.org
Phone: 202-452-8320; Fax: 202-296-2371.

Florida
Email: miami@adi.org
Phone: 305-373-6306; Fax: 305-374-5887.
Email: palm-beach-county@adi.org
Phone: 561-832-7144; 561-265-0515; Fax: 561-832-3071.

Florida—Central
Edward C. Beshara, Esq., 1850 Lee Road, Suite 300 Winter Park, FL 32789.
Phone: 407-629-6455; Fax: 407-629-4569.

Georgia
Charles Kuck, Esq. 5500 Interstate North Parkway Suite 450, River Edge One, Atlanta, GA 30328.
Phone: 770-951-1100; Fax: 770-951-1113.

Illinois/Missouri
Email: st-louis@adi.org
Phone: 314-432-6868; Fax: 314-432-6039.
Email: chicago@adl.org
Phone: 312-782-5080; Fax: 312-782-1142.

Louisiana/Arkansas/Mississippi
Email: new-orleans@adl.org
Phone: 504-522-9534; Fax: 504-525-2576.

Massachusetts
126 High Street, Boston, MA 02110.
Email: boston@adl.org
Phone: 617-457-8800.

Michigan
Email: detroit@adl.org
Phone: 248-355-3730; Fax: 248-355-9534.

Nebraska/Iowa/Kansas
Email: omaha@adl.org
Phone: 402-333-1303; Fax: 402-333-5497.

New Jersey
Email: new-jersey@adl.org
Phone: 201-669-9700; Fax: 201-669-9749.

New Mexico
Email: new-mexico@adi.org
Phone: 505-823-2712; Fax: 505-823-0887.

New York
New York Regional Office Anti-Defamation League, 823 United Nations Plaza,
New York, NY 10017.
Phone: 202-885-7970.
Email: new-york@adl.org

Ohio, Kentucky, and Allegheny Region
Email: cleveland@adl.org
Phone: 206-579-9600; 800-821-4058; Fax: 216-579-9690.

Pennsylvania—Eastern/Delaware
Phone: 215-735-4267; Fax: 215-735-5445.

Texas—North/Oklahoma
Email: dallas@adl.org
Phone: 214-960-0342/43; Fax: 214-960-0591.

Texas
Email: houston@adl.org
Phone: 713-627-3490; Fax: 713-627-2011.

Washington/Idaho/Montana/Oregon/Alaska
Email: seattle@adl.org
Phone: 206-448-5349; Fax: 206-448-5355.

National Association for the Advancement of Colored People (NAACP) Legal Department, Washington Bureau, 1025 Vermont Avenue, NW, Suite 1120, Washington, D.C.
20005.
Phone: 202-638-2269.
http://www.naacp.org

Branches:

Regions I & VI
Covering: Alaska, Arizona, Arkansas, California, Hawaii, Idaho, Louisiana, Nevada, New
Mexico, Oklahoma, Oregon, Texas, Utah, Wyoming, Washington
NAACP, 4929 Wilshire Boulevard, Suite 360, Los Angeles, CA 90010.
Phone: 213-931-6331; 800-622-2799; Fax: 213-931-9036.

Regions III & IV
Covering: Colorado, Illinois, Indiana, Iowa, Kansas, Kentucky, Michigan, Oklahoma,
West Virginia
NAACP, 17 Ford Avenue, Highland Park, MI 48203
Phone: 313-869-3717; Fax: 868-7302.

Regions II & VII
Covering: Connecticut, Delaware, District of Columbia, Maine, Maryland, Massachusetts, New Hampshire, New Jersey, New York, Pennsylvania, Rhode Island, Vermont, Virginia
NAACP, 39 Broadway, 22nd Floor, New York, NY 10006
Phone: 212-344-7474; 800-221-4277; Fax: 212-1212.

Region V
Covering: Alabama, Florida, Georgia, Mississippi, North Carolina, South Carolina, Tennessee
NAACP, 970 Martin Luther King Drive, S.W., Atlanta, GA 30314.
Phone: 404-688-8868; Fax: 524-3633.

Massachusetts
451 Massachusetts Avenue, Boston, MA 02118
Phone: (617) 296-7904.

Lawyers Committee for Civil Rights Under Law, 1450 G Street, NW, Suite 400, Washington, DC 20005.
Phone: (202) 662-8350 (See section on national-origin discrimination on page 217 for branch offices).

For Religious Discrimination:

American Civil Liberties Union, 125 Broad Street, New York, NY 10004.
Phone: (212) 549-2500 (See section on age discrimination on page 198 for branch offices).

Anti-defamation League of B'Nai B'rith, New York, NY.
Phone: (212) 490-2525 (See section on race discrimination on page 218 for branch offices).

For Sex Discrimination:

American Civil Liberties Union, 125 Broad Street, New York, NY 10004.
Phone: (212) 549-2500 (See section on age discrimination on page 198 for branch offices).

Ms. Foundation, 141 Fifth Ave., Suite 65, New York, NY 10010.

National Committee on Working Women, Wider Opportunities for Women (WOW), 11325 G St., NW, Washington, D.C. 20005.
Phone: (202) 737-5764.

9 to 5, National Association of Working Women, 614 Superior Ave., NW, Cleveland, OH 44113-1387.
Phone: 800-522-0925.

National Lawyers Guild, New York, NY.
Phone: (212) 627-2656.

Branch Offices:

Massachusetts
14 Beacon Street, Suite 407, Boston, MA 02108.
Phone: (617) 227-7335.

National Organization for Women (NOW)
NOW Action Center, 1000 16th Street, NW, Suite 700 Washington, DC 20036.
Phone: 202-331-006 Fax: 202-785-8576.
Email: now@now.org

Chapter Contacts:
http://now.org/chapters/states.html

Branch Offices:

Massachusetts
971 Commonwealth Avenue, Boston, MA.
Phone: (617) 782-1056.

For Sexual Orientation Discrimination:

American Civil Liberties Union, 125 Broad Street, New York, NY 10004.
Phone: (212) 549-2500 (See section on age discrimination on page 198 for branch offices).

Gay and Lesbian Advocates and Defenders (GLAD), 294 Washington Street, Room 740, Boston, MA 02108
Phone: (617) 426-1350.

Massachusetts Lesbian and Gay Bar Association, P.O. Box 9072, Boston, MA 02114.
Phone: (617) 277-2101.

National Gay and Lesbian Task Force, 1734 14th St., NW, Washington, D.C. 20009-4309.
Phone: 202-332-6483.

For general workers' rights, particularly gender discrimination, ethnic discrimination, sexual orientation discrimination, immigration issues, occupational safety and health issues, worker benefits, but particularly collective rights:

Jobs with Justice Local Coalitions:

Alabama
Birmingham Jobs with Justice, Frank Paige, 1524 Matt Leonard Drive, Birmingham, AL 35211.
Phone: (205) 942-4143.

Arizona
Tucson Jobs with Justice, Steve Valencia, 443 W. Louisiana, Tucson, AZ 85706.
Phone: (520) 889-1927.

Arkansas
Arkansas Jobs with Justice, EJ Miller-IUE, 8803 Oman Road, Little Rock, AR 72209.
Phone: (501) 565-3488.

California
Orange Country Workers for Justice and Democracy,
c/o UE, 828 North Bristol, Santa Ana, CA 92703.
Phone: (717) 836-4101.

Colorado

Colorado Jobs with Justice, Leslie Moody
2840 South Vallejo, Englewood, CO 80110.
Phone: (303) 806-0818.

Georgia

Georgia Jobs with Justice, Stewart Acuff—Atlanta
CLC, 501 Pulliam Street SW, #517, Atlanta, GA 30312.
Phone: (404) 525-3559.

James Orange—IUD, P.O. Box 476, Riverdale, GA 30312.
Phone: (404) 766-8631.

Illinois

Chicago Area Jobs with Justice, Frank Klein—UNITE
910 West Van Buren 7th Fl., Chicago, IL 60607.
Phone: (312) 738-6060.

Kentucky

Louisville Jobs with Justice, Segal, Isenberg, et al., 2100 Waterfront Plaza, 325 West Main
Street, Louisville, KY 40202.
Phone: (502) 568-5600.

Massachusetts

Massachusetts JwJ, Russ Davis or Heather Gonzales
160 2nd Street, Cambridge, MA 02142.
Phone: (617) 491-2525.

Michigan

Michigan Jobs with Justice, Ron Whittenberg, 11425 Rawsonville Road, Belleville, MI
48111-9373.
Phone: (313) 461-1034.

Missouri

Missouri JwJ, Rita Voorheis—CWA, District 6, 10820 Sunset Office Drive, #302, Sunset
Hills, MO 63127.
Phone: (314) 822-2477.

Mississippi

Mississippi Jobs with Justice, Melbin Horton-A. Philip, Randolph Institute, P.O. Box 9754,
Jackson, MS 39206.
Phone: (601)-834-3699.

Montana

Montana Community/Labor Alliance, Matt Levin, 208 East Main Street, Missoula, MT 59802.
Phone: (406) 728-7265.

New Jersey

New Jersey JwJ, Carol Gray—CWA, District 1, 1030 Saint Georges Street, Avenel, NJ
07001.
Phone: (908) 750-5580.

New York

NYC Jobs with Justice, Rachel Burd, 80 Pine Street, 37th Floor, New York, NY 10001.
Phone: (908) 750-5580.

Coalition for Economic Justice/Jobs with Justice
Joan Malone, 2123 Bailey Avenue, Buffalo, NY 14211-2056.
Phone: (716) 894-2013.

Solidarity Committee of the Capital District, John Funiciello, 55 Grant Avenue, Albany, NY 12206.
Phone: (518) 489-4749.

Ohio

Cleveland Area Jobs with Justice, John Ryan—CWA, Local 4309, 709 Brookpark Road, Cleveland, OH 44109
Phone: (216) 749-0500.

Oregon

Portland Jobs with Justice, Leslie Kochan, 822 NE Shaver Street, Portland, OR 97212.
Phone: (503) 282-2911.

Eugene Springfield Solidarity Network, Dennis Gilbert, P.O. Box 10272, Eugene, OR 97440.
Phone: (503) 343-1572.

Willamette Valley JwJ, Jeannie Berg-Rempel
5016 Riverside South, Salem, OR 97306.
Phone: (503) 364-9127.

Pennsylvania

Pennsylvania JwJ, Marge Krueger—CWA, District 13
230 S. Broad Street, 15th Floor, Philadelphia, PA 19102.
Phone: (215) 546-5574.

Pennsylvania JwJ-APA, Linda Wambaugh—SEIU, Local 585, 237 Sixth Street, Pittsburgh, PA 15238.
Phone: (412) 828-5100.

Tennessee

Tennessee JwJ, Melba Collins—UPIU, 3340 Perimeter Hill Drive, Nashville, TN 37217.
Phone: (615) 834-8590.

Tennessee JwJ, Doug Niehouse, 6116 New Nashville Hwy., Murfeesboro, TN 37129.
Phone: (615) 459-2111.

Texas

Texas JwJ, Travis Donoho—TSEU/CWA, 1412 W. 6th Street, Austin, TX 78703.
Phone: (512) 448-4225.

Texas JwJ, Elaine or Gene Lantz—UAW Local 848,
Box 225822, Dallas, TX 75222.
Phone: (214) 942-4236.

Vermont

Vermont JwJ, Kim Lawson-UE 203, Battell Block Office, #203, Middlebury, VT 05753. Phone: (802) 388-3708.

Washington

Washington State Jobs with Justice, Jonathan Rosenblum, 150 Denny Way, Seattle, WA 98109. Phone: (206) 448-7348.

Wisconsin

Milwaukee Solidarity Committee, Bruce Colburn,
633 South Hawley Road, Milwaukee, WI 53204.
Phone: (414) 771-7070.

National Employment Law Project
55 John Street, 7th Floor, New York, NY 10038.
Phone: (212) 285-3025; FAX (212) 285-3044.
Email: HN0699@handsnet.org

APPENDIX C

SOURCES FOR LAWYERS

National and state bar associations usually have Labor and Employment Law Sections. The lawyers in these special sections generally are more knowledgeable about this area of the law and can provide a resource for finding a lawyer who will represent you.

National Employment Lawyers Association is a national organization of lawyers dedicated to representing workers with labor and employment problems.

National Employment Lawyers Association (NELA), 600 Harrison Street, Suite 535, San Francisco, CA 94107.
Phone: (415) 227-4655.

NELA Affiliate Organizations

Alabama
Edward Still, Esq., 714 South 29th Street, Birmingham, AL 35223.
Phone: (205) 324-9966.

Arizona
N. Douglas Grimwood, Esq., Tritty, Sievwright & Mills, 2702 North Third Street, Suite 4007, Phoenix, AZ 85004.
Phone: (602) 248-9424.

Arkansas
Richard Quiggle, Esq., 904 West Second Street, Little Rock, AR 72201.
Phone: (501) 375-2963.

California
California Employment Lawyers Association
Nancy Bornn, Esq., 1411 Fifth Street, Suite 200, Santa Monica, CA 90401.
Phone: (310) 395-0009.

Bay Area Plaintiffs Employment Lawyers Association
David F. Offen-Brown, Trial Attorney, United States Equal Employment Opportunity Commission, 901 Market Street, Suite 500, San Francisco, CA 94103.
Phone: (415) 356-5114.

Legal Eagle (Los Angeles)
Joseph Posner, Esq., 16311 Ventura Blvd., Suite 555, Encino, CA 91463.
Phone: (818) 990-1340.

Sacramento
Cathy Felch, Esq., 1922 Twenty-First Street, Sacramento, CA 95814.
Phone: (916) 454-9775.

San Diego
Gary M. Laturno, Esq., Laturno & Graves, 9255 Towne Centre Drive, Suite 520, San Diego, CA 92121.
Phone: (619) 455-9499.

San Joaquin Valley
William J. Smith, Esq., Richeel & Smith, 2350 West Shore Avenue, Suite 154, Fresno, CA 93711.
Phone: (209) 432-0986.

Colorado
Colorado Plaintiffs Lawyers Association, Thomas J. Arckey, Esq., Arckey & Reha, LLC, 26 West Dry Creek Circle, Suite 740, Littleton, CO 80120.
Phone: (303) 798-8546.

Connecticut
Connecticut Plaintiffs Employment Lawyers Association, Victoria De Toledo, Esq., Casper & De Toledo, 1111 Summer Street, Stamford, CT 06905.
Phone: (203) 325-8600.

District of Columbia
Metropolitan Washington Employment Lawyers Assn., John F. Karl, Jr., Esq., McDonald & Karl, 2100 Pennsylvania Avenue, NW, Suite 675, Washington, D.C. 20037.
Phone: (202) 293-3200.

Florida
Florida Employment Lawyers Association, William R. Amlong, Esq., Amlong & Amlong, 500 Northeast Fourth Street, Second Floor, Ft. Lauderdale, FL 33301.

Georgia
Georgia Employment Lawyers Association, Janet E. Hill, Esq., Neslon & Hill, P.A., P.O. Box 307, Athens, GA 30603.
Phone: (706) 353-7272.

Hawaii
Hawaii Employment Lawyers Association, Michael F. Nauyokas, Esq., Choy & Nauyokas, 733 Bishop Street, Suite 2300, Honolulu, HI 96813.
Phone: (808) 538-0553.

Illinois
Illinois Employment Lawyers Association, Robin B. Potter, Esq., Potter & Schaffner, 30 North LaSalle Street, Suite 1724, Chicago, IL 60602.
Phone: (312) 759-2500.

Indiana

Indiana Employment Lawyers Association, Cynthia Rockwell, Esq., Haller & Colvin, 444 East Main Street, Fort Wayne, IN 46802.
Phone: (219) 426-0444.

Iowa

Iowa Employment Layers Association, John O. Haraldson, Esq., Law Offices of Robert J. Kuhle, 1501 42nd Street, Suite 390, West Des Moines, IA 50266.
Phone: (515) 224-6686.

Kansas

Kansas Employment Lawyers Association, John P. Gage, II, Esq., The Gage Law Firm, P.C., 10901 Lowell, Suite 120, Overland Park, KS 66213.
Phone: (913) 451-8660.

Kentucky

Barbara Bonar, Esq., Wolnitzek, Rowekamp, Bender & Bonar, P.O. Box 352, Covington, KY 41012.
Phone: (606) 491-4444.

Louisiana

Louisiana Employment Lawyers Association, Glenn C. McGovern, Esq., Glenn C. McGovern Law Offices, 10555 Lake Forest Blvd., Bldg. 5 E, New Orleans, LA 70127.
Phone: (504) 241-9150.

Maine

Maine Employment Lawyers Association, Alan J. Levenson, Esq., Levenson, Vickerson & Beneman, 183 Middle Street, Portland, ME 04101.
Phone: (207) 775-5200.

Maryland

Maryland Employment Lawyers Association, Kathleen M. Cahil, Esq., Law Offices of Kathleen M. Cahil, 210 North Charles Street, Suite 1415, Baltimore, MD 21201.
Phone: (410) 332-1610.

Massachusetts

Plaintiff Employment Lawyers Association of Massachusetts, Kevin C. Powers, Esq., Law Offices of Kevin C. Powers, 1 Fanueil Hall Marketplace, Boston, MA 02109.
Phone: (617) 723-8727.

Michigan

Michigan Employment Lawyers Association, Lyn Schecter, Esq., Roy, Schecter & Vocht, 1400 Woodward Avenue, Suite 205, Bloomfield Hills, MI 48304.
Phone: (810) 540-7660.

Minnesota

Minnesota Employment Lawyers Association, Charles L. Friedman, Esq., Friedman Law Office, 4840 IDS Center, 80 South Eighth Street, Minneapolis, MN 55402.
Phone: (612) 341-8020.

Missouri

Missouri NELA (MO NELA), Majorie B. Tarcow, Esq., Tarcow Law Offices, 609 Redbud Lane, Columbia, MO 65203.
Phone: (573) 874-4185.

Kansas City-Denis E. Ejan, Esq., The Popham Law Firm, P.C., 922 Walnut Street, Suite 1300, Kansas City, MO 64106.
Phone: (816) 221-2288.

St. Louis-Kenneth M. Chackes, Esq., Van Amburg, Chackes, Carlson & Spritzer, L.L.P., 8420 Delmar Blvd., Suite 406, St. Louis, MO 63124.
Phone: (314) 872-8420.

Nevada

Nevada Employment Lawyers Association, Daniel Marks, Esq., Law Offices of Daniel Marks, 302 Carson, Suite 702, Las Vegas, NV 89101.
Phone: (702) 386-0536.

New Hampshire

New Hampshire Employment Lawyers Association, Brian T. Stern, Esq., Law Offices of Brian T. Stern, 86 Boca Street, Dover, NH 03820.
Phone: (603) 742-7789.

New Jersey

New Jersey Employment Lawyers Association, Patricia Breuninger, Esq., Breuninger, Hansen & Fellman, P.O. Box 485, 313 South Avenue, Fanwood, NJ 07030.
Phone: (908) 889-8900.

New Mexico

New Mexico Employment Lawyers Association, Steven K. Sanders, Esq., Law Offices of Steven Sanders, 8 Twenty-Second Street, N.W., Albuquerque, NM 87102.
Phone: (505) 243-7170.

New York

NELA New York—Wayne N. Outten, Esq., Lantkenau, Kovner, Kurtz & Outten, LLP, 1740 Broadway
New York, NY 10019.
Phone: (212) 489-8230.

Rochester
Lonnie H. Dolin, Esq., Lonnie H. Dolin & Associates, 135 Corporate Woods, Second Floor, Rochester, NY 14623.
Phone: (716) 272-0540.

Ohio

Ohio Employment Lawyers Association, Frederick M. Gittes, Esq., Spater, Gittes, Schulte & Kolman, 723 Oak Street, Columbus, OH 43205.
Phone: (614) 221-1160.

Akron
Akron NELA, Denis R. Thompson, Esq., Thompson Law Offices, 120 East Mill Street, Suite 406, Akron, OH 44308.
Phone: (330) 374-0200.

Cincinnati
Randolph H. Freking, Esq., Freking & Betz, 215 East Ninth Street, 5th Floor, Cincinnati, OH 45202.
Phone: (513) 721-1975.

Cleveland
Denise J. Knecht, Esq., Denise J. Knecht & Associates, Co., LPA, 75 Public Square, Suite 1300, Cleveland, OH 44113.
Phone: (216) 621-4882.

Toledo
Harold M. Britz, Esq., Britz & Zemmelman, 414 North Erie Street, Suite 100, Toledo, OH 43624.
Phone: (419) 242-7415.

Oklahoma
Oklahoma City
Mark Hammons, Esq., Hammons & Associates, 401 North Hutson, Lower Level, Oklahoma City, OK 73102.
Phone: (405) 235-6100.

Tulsa
Steven A. Novick, Esq., Steven A. Novick, P.P., 1717 South Cheyenne Council Oak Center, Tulsa, OK 74119.
Phone: (918) 582-4411.

Oregon
Oregon Employment Lawyers Association, Charles J. Merten, Esq., 1905 NW 169th Place, Suite A, Beaverton, OR 97006.
Phone: (503) 690-0501.

Pennsylvania
PELA of Pittsburgh
David F. Wiener, Esq., Carlin & Wiener, USX Tower, 600 Grant Street, Suite 660, Pittsburgh, PA 15219.
Phone: (412) 391-2857.

Eastern Pennsylvania Chapter NELA
Doris J. Dabrowski, Esq., Dabrowski Law Offices, 1308 Spruce Street, Philadelphia, PA 19107.
Phone: (215) 790-1115.

Rhode Island
Rhode Island Employment Lawyers Association, Robert E. Savage, Esq., Savage & Savage, 75 Lambert Lind Highway, Rt. 5, Warwick, RI 02886.
Phone: (401) 732-9500.

South Carolina
Terry Ann Rickson, Esq. Rickson Law Firm, 116 Church Street, 3rd Floor, P.O. Box 1065, Charleston, SC 29402.
Phone: (803) 722-1500.

Tennessee
Robert Belton, Professor of Law, Vanderbilt University School of Law, Nashville, TN 37240.
Phone: (615) 322-2856.

Texas

Texas Statewide
Margaret A. Harris, Esq., Butler & Harris, 3223 Smith Street, Suite 308, Houston, TX 77006.
Phone: (713) 526-5677.

Austin
Virginia J. Vekassy, Esq., Virginia J. Vekassy, P.C., 7122 Woodhollow, Suite 25, Austin, TX
78731.
Phone: (512) 346-0644.

Dallas/Ft. Worth
Genice A.G. Rabe, Esq., Law Offices of Genice Rabe, 3301 Elm Street, Dallas, TX 75226.
Phone: (214) 939-9228.

Houston
Martin Adam Shellist, Esq., Valetutto, Shellist, Lore & Lazarz, 1990 Post Oak Blvd., Rt.
910, Houston, TX. 77056.

San Antonio
Russell G. Amsberry, Esq., Law Offices of Russell G. Amsberry, 115 East Travis, Suite
1108, San Antonio, TX 78205.
Phone: (210) 354-2244.

West Texas
David L. Kern, Esq., Gage, Gage & Kern, L.L.P., 6044 Gateway East, Suite 800, El
Paso, TX 79905.
Phone: (915) 532-4357.

Utah

Utah Employment Lawyers Association, Roger H. Hoole, Esq., Hoole & King, L.C., 4276
Highland Drive, Salt Lake City, UT 84124.
Phone: (801) 227-1989.

Vermont

Vermont Employment Lawyers Association, Eileen M. Blackwood, Esq., Blackwood and
Kraynak, 131 Main Street, Burlington, VT 05002.
Phone: (802) 863-2517.

Virginia

Harris D. Butler, III, Esq., Butler, Macon, Williams
1309 East Cary Street, 2nd Floor, Richmond, VA 23219.
Phone: (804) 648-4848.

Washington

Washington Employment Lawyers Association, Marilyn J. Endriss, Esq., Marilyn J.
Endriss, P.S., 705 Second Avenue, Suite 1200, Hoge Building, Seattle, WA 98104.
Phone: (206) 624-3313.

Herman L. Wacker, Esq., Wacker Law Offices, 217 Pine Street, Suite 620, Seattle, WA 98101.
Phone: (206) 467-5090.

West Virginia

West Virginia Employment Lawyers Association, Walt Auvil, Esq., Pyles & Auvil, 1208 Market Street, Parkersburg, WV 26101.
Phone: (304) 485-3058.

Wisconsin

Wisconsin Employment Lawyers Association, Tom Olson, Esq., Hall, Patterson & Charne, S.C., 324 East Wisconsin Avenue, Suite 1200, Milwaukee, WI 53202.
Phone: (414) 271-2001.

American Bar Association, 750 North Lake Shore Drive, Chicago, IL 60611.
Phone: (312) 988-5000.

State Bar Associations

Alabama

Alabama State Bar, P.O. Box 671, Montgomory, AL 36101.
Phone: (334) 269-1515.

Alaska

Alaska Bar Association, P.O. Box 100279, Anchorage, AK 99510.
Phone: (907) 272-7469.

Arizona

Arizona State Bar, 111 West Monroe, Suite 1800, Phoenix, AZ 85003.
Phone: (602) 252-4804

Arkansas

Arkansas Bar Association, 400 West Markham, 4th Floor, Little Rock, AR 72201.
Phone: (501) 375-4606

California

California Bar Association, 555 Franklin Street, San Francisco, CA 94102.
Phone: (415) 561-8200.

Colorado

Colorado Bar Association, 1900 Grant Street, Suite 950, Denver, CA 80203.
Phone: (303) 860-1115.

Connecticut

Connecticut Bar Association, 101 Corporate Place, Rocky Hill, CT 06067.
Phone: (203) 721-0025.

Delaware

Delaware State Bar Association, 1225 North King Street, 10th Floor, Wilmington, DE 19801.
Phone: (302) 658-5279.

Florida

Florida Bar, 650 Apalachee Parkway, Tallahassee, FL 32399.
Phone: (904) 561-5600.

Georgia

Georgia State Bar, 800 Hurt Building, 50 Hurt Plaza, Atlanta, GA 30303.
Phone: (404) 527-8700.

Hawaii
Hawaii State Bar Association, 1136 Union Mall, Penthouse 1, Honolulu, HI 96813.
Phone: (808) 537-1868.

Idaho
Idaho State Bar, P.O. Box 895, Boise, ID 83701.
Phone: (208) 334-4500.

Illinois
Illinois State Bar Association, Illinois Bar Center, 424 South Second Street, Spring-
field, IL 62701.
Phone: (217) 525-1760.

Indiana
Indiana State Bar Association, 230 East Ohio Street, 4th Floor, Indianapolis, IN 46204.
Phone: (317) 639-5465.

Iowa
Iowa State Bar Association, 521 East Locust Street, Third Floor, Des Moines, IA 50309.
Phone: (515) 243-3179.

Kansas
Kansas Bar Association, 1200 South West Harrison Street, P.O. Box 1037, Topeka, KS 66601.
Phone: (913) 234-5696.

Kentucky
Kentucky Bar Association, 514 West Main Street, Frankfort, KY 40601.
Phone: (502) 564-3795.

Louisiana
Louisiana State Bar Association, 601 St. Charles Avenue, New Orleans, LA 70130.
Phone: (504) 566-1600.

Maine
Maine State Bar Association, P.O. Box 788, Augusta, ME 04332.
Phone: (207) 622-7523.

Maryland
Maryland State Bar Association, Inc., 520 West Fayette Street, Baltimore, MD 21201.
Phone: (410) 685-7878.

Massachusetts
Massachusetts Bar Association
20 West Street
Boston, MA 02111
Phone: (617) 338-0500

Michigan
Michigan State Bar, 306 Townsend Street, Lansing, MI 48933.
Phone: (517) 372-9030.

Minnesota
Minnesota State Bar Association, 514 Nicolet Mall, Suite 300, Minneapolis, MN 55402.
Phone: (612) 333-1183.

Mississippi

Mississippi Bar, P.O. Box 2168, Jackson, MS 39225.
Phone: (601) 948-4471.

Missouri

Missouri Bar, P.O. Box 119, Jefferson City, MO 65102.
Phone: (314) 635-4128.

Montana

Montana State Bar, 46 North Main Street, Box 577, Helena, MT 59624.
Phone: (406) 442-7660.

Nebraska

Nebraska State Bar Association, 635 South 14th Street, Lincoln, NE 68508.
Phone: (402) 475-7091.

Nevada

Nevada State Bar, 201 Las Vegas Blvd. S, Suite 200, Las Vegas, NV 89101.
Phone: (702) 382-2200.

New Hampshire

New Hampshire Bar Association, 112 Pleasant Street, Concord, NH 03301.
Phone: (603) 224-6942.

New Jersey

New Jersey State Bar Association, 1 Constitution Square, New Brunswick, NJ 08901.
Phone: (908) 249-5000.

New Mexico

New Mexico State Bar, P.O. Box 25883, Albuquerque, NM 87125.
Phone: (800) 876-6227.

New York

New York State Bar Association, 1 Elk Street, Albany, NY 12207.
Phone: (518) 463-3200.

North Carolina

North Carolina State Bar, P.O. Box 25908, Raleigh, NC 27611.
Phone: (919) 828-4620.

North Dakota

North Dakota State Bar Association, P.O. Box 2163, Bismark, ND 58502.
Phone: (701) 255-1404.

Ohio

Ohio State Bar Association, P.O. Box 16562, Columbus, OH 43216.
Phone: (614) 487-2050.

Oklahoma

Oklahoma Bar Association, 1901 Lincoln Blvd, P.O. Box 53036, Oklahoma City, OK 73105.
Phone: (404) 524-2365.

Oregon

Oregon State Bar, 5200 Southwest Meadows Road, P.O. Box 1689, Lake Oswego, OR 97035. Phone: (503) 620-0222.

Pennsylvania

Pennsylvania Bar Association, 100 South Street, P.O. Box 186, Harrisburg, PA 17108. Phone: (717) 238-6715.

Rhode Island

Rhode Island Bar Association, 115 Cedar Street, Providence, RI 02903. Phone: (401) 421-5740.

South Carolina

South Carolina Bar, P.O. Box 2138, Columbia, SC 29202. Phone: (803) 799-6653.

South Dakota

South Dakota State Bar, 222 East Capital, Pierre, SD 57501. Phone: (605) 224-7554.

Tennessee

Tennessee Bar Association, 3622 West End Avenue, Nashville, TN 37205. Phone: (615) 383-7421.

Texas

Texas State Bar, P.O. Box 12487, Austin, TX 78711. Phone: (512) 463-1463.

Utah

Utah State Bar, 645 South 2200 East, Room 310, Salt Lake City, UT 84111. Phone: (801) 531-9077.

Vermont

Vermont Bar Association, P.O. Box 100, Montpelier, VT 05601. Phone: (802) 223-2020.

Virginia

Virginia State Bar, 707 East Main Street, Suite 1500, Richmond, VA 23219. Phone: (804) 775-0500.

Virginia Bar Association, 701 East Franklin Street, Suite 1120, Richmond, VA 23219. Phone: (804) 644-0041.

Washington

Washington Bar Association, 2001 Sixth Avenue, Suite 500, Seattle, WA 98121. Phone: (206) 727-8200.

West Virginia

West Virginia State Bar, 2006 Knawha Boulevard E., Charleston, WV 25311-2204. Phone: (304) 558-9126.

Wisconsin

Wisconsin State Bar, 402 West Wilson, Madison, WI 53703. Phone: (608) 257-3838.

Wyoming
Wyoming State Bar, P.O. Box 109, Cheyenne, WY 82003.
Phone: (307) 632-9061.

Washington D.C.
Washington D.C. Bar, 1250 H Street, NW, 6th Floor, Washington, D.C. 20005.
Phone: (202) 737-4700.

Association of Trial Lawyers of America
1050 31st Street, NW, Washington, D.C. 20007.
Phone: (800) 424-2725.

Affiliated Trial Lawyer Associations

Alabama
Alabama Trial Lawyers Association, 77 Washington Avenue, Suite 170, Montgomery, AL 36104.
Phone: (334) 262-4974

Alaska
Alaska Academy of Trial Lawyers, 540 L Street, Suite 206, Anchorage, AK 99501.
Phone: (907) 258-4040.

Arizona
Arizona Trial Lawyers Association, 1661 East Camelback Road, Suite 204, Phoenix, AZ 85016.
Phone: (602) 235-9356.

Arkansas
Arkansas Trial Lawyers Association, 225 East Markham, Suite 200, Little Rock, AR 72201.
Phone: (501) 376-2852.

California
Consumer Attorneys of California, 980 Ninth Street, Suite 200, Sacramento, CA 95814.
Phone: (916) 442-6902.

Consumer Attorneys Association of Los Angeles, 3435 Wilshire Boulevard, Suite 2870, Los Angeles, CA 90010.
Phone: (213) 487-1212.

Consumer Attorneys of San Diego, 1305 Seventh Avenue, Suite 110, San Diego, CA 92101.
Phone: (619) 696-1166.

Orange County Trial Lawyers Association, 5 Hutton Centre Drive, #950, Santa Ana, CA 92711.
Phone: (714) 558-0677.

San Francisco Trial Lawyers Association, 207 World Trade Center, San Francisco, CA 94111.
Phone: (415) 956-6401.

Colorado
Colorado Trial Lawyers Association, 1888 Sherman Street, Suite 370, Denver, CO 80203.
Phone: (303) 831-1192.

Connecticut
Connecticut Trial Lawyers Association, 96 Oak Street, Hartford, CT 06106.
Phone: (860) 522-4345.

Delaware
Delaware Trial Lawyers Association, 715 King Street, Second Floor, Wilmington, DE 19801.
Phone: (302) 421-2800.

Washington, D.C.
Trial Lawyers Association of Metropolitan D.C., 1100 Connecticut Avenue, NW,
Washington, D.C. 20036.
Phone: (202) 659-3532.

Florida
Academy of Florida Trial Lawyers, 218 South Monroe Street, Tallahassee, FL 32301.
Phone: (904) 224-9403.

Georgia
Georgia Trial Lawyers Association, 1250 The Hurt Building, 50 Hurt Plaza, S.E.,
Atlanta, GA 30303.
Phone: (404) 522-8487.

Hawaii
Consumer Lawyers of Hawaii, 1088 Bishop Street, Suite 1111, Honolulu, HI 96813.
Phone: (808) 599-2769.

Idaho
Idaho Trial Lawyers Association, 1517 West Hays Avenue, Boise, ID 83702.
Phone: (208) 345-1890.

Illinois
Illinois Trial Lawyers Association, 110 West Edwards Street, P.O. Box 5000, Spring-
field, IL 62704.
Phone: (217) 789-0755.

Indiana
Indiana Trial Lawyers Association, 150 West Market Street, Suite 210, Indianapolis, IN 42604.
Phone: (317) 634-8841.

Iowa
Iowa Trial Lawyers Association, 526 Fleming Building, 218 Sixth Avenue, Des Moines, IA
50309.
Phone: (515) 280-7366.

Kansas
Kansas Trial Lawyers Association, 700 S.W. Jackson, Suite 706, Topeka, KS 66603.
Phone: (913) 232-7756.

Kentucky
Kentucky Academy of Trial Attorneys, 4101 Danville Building, 12700 Shelbyville Road,
Louisville, KY 40243.
Phone: (502) 244-1320.

Louisiana

Louisiana Trial Lawyers Association, 442 Europe Street, Baton Rouge, LA 70802.
Phone: (504) 383-5554.

Maine

Maine Trial Lawyers Association, 160 Capitol Street, P.O. Box 428, Augusta, ME 04332.
Phone: (207) 623-2661.

Maryland

Maryland Trial Lawyers Association, 1018 North Charles Street, Baltimore, MD 21201.
Phone: (410) 539-4336.

Massachusetts

Massachusetts Academy of Trial Attorneys, 15 Broad Street, Suite 415, Boston, MA 02109.
Phone: (617) 248-5858.

Michigan

Michigan Trial Lawyers Association, 501 South Capitol, Suite 405, Lansing, MI 48933.
Phone: (517) 482-7740.

Minnesota

Minnesota Trial Lawyers Association, 140 Baker Building, 706 Second Avenue, South,
Minneapolis, MN 55402.
Phone: (612) 375-1707.

Mississippi

Mississippi Trial Lawyers Association, P.O. Box 1992, Jackson, MS 39205.
Phone: (601) 948-8631.

Missouri

Missouri Association of Trial Attorneys, 240 East High Street, Suite 300, P.O. Box 1792,
Jefferson City, MO 65102.
Phone: (573) 635-5215.

Montana

Montana Trial Lawyers Association, P.O. Box 838, Helena, MT 59624.
Phone: (406) 443-3124.

Nebraska

Nebraska Association of Trial Attorneys, 605 South 14th Street, Suite 450A, Lincoln, NE 68508.
Phone: (402) 435-5526.

Nevada

Nevada Trial Lawyers Association, 406 North Nevada, Carson City, NV 89703.
Phone: (702) 883-3577.

New Hampshire

New Hampshire Trial Lawyers Association, 280 Pleasant Street, P.O. Box 447,
Concord, NH 03302.
Phone: (603) 224-7077.

New Jersey

ATLA—New Jersey, 150 West State Street, Trenton, NJ 08608.
Phone: (609) 396-0096.

New Mexico

New Mexico Trial Lawyers Association, 301 Edith NE, Suite 110, P.O. Box 301, Albuquerque, NM 87103.
Phone: (505) 243-6003.

New York

New York State Trial Lawyers Association, 132 Nassau Street, New York, NY 10038.
Phone: (212) 349-5890.

North Carolina

North Carolina Academy of Trial Lawyers, 1312 Annapolis Drive, P.O. Box 100918, Raleigh, NC 27608.
Phone: (919) 832-1413.

North Dakota

North Dakota Trial Lawyers Association, 105 Third Avenue, N.W., P.O. Box 1176, Mandan, ND 58554.
Phone: (701) 663-4285.

Ohio

Ohio Academy of Trial Lawyers, 395 East Broad Street, Suite 200, Columbus, OH 43215.
Phone: (614) 341-6800.

Vermont

Vermont Trial Lawyers Association, 64 Main Street, Montpelier, VT 05602.
Phone: (802) 223-0501.

Virginia

Virginia Trial Lawyers Association, 700 East Main Street, Suite 1512, Richmond, VA 23219.
Phone: (804) 343-1143.

Washington

Washington State Trial Lawyers Association, 1809 Seventh Avenue, Suite 909, Seattle, WA 98101.
Phone: (206) 464-1011.

West Virginia

West Virginia Trial Lawyers Association, 1018 Kanawha Boulevard, #207, P.O. Box 3968, Charleston, WV 25309.
Phone: (304) 344-0692.

Wisconsin

Wisconsin Academy of Trial Lawyers, 44 East Mifflin Street, Suite 103, Madison, WI 53703.
Phone: (608) 257-5741.

Wyoming

Wyoming Trial Lawyers Association, 2601 Central Avenue, Suite 100, Cheyenne, WY 82001.
Phone: (307) 635-0820.

For age discrimination:

National Academy of Elder Law Attorneys
1604 North Country Road, Tucson, AZ 85716.
Phone: (520) 881-4005.

ACKNOWLEDGMENTS

I am grateful for this opportunity to thank and acknowledge the people in my life.

To my first and best teachers my mother Ida, sweeter than apple cider, and my father Mickey, better known as Large Mike or L.M., who taught me to be a mensch.

To all my relatives who helped me along the way. To my grandparents Lena and Jacob Gropman. To my grandparents Julia and Sam Golder. To Uncle Al and Aunt Millie. To Aunt Minnie and Uncle Red. To Uncle Myer and Aunt Pauline. To Aunt Marion and Uncle Mike. To Aunt Polly and Uncle Ben. To Uncle Ben and Aunt Rose.

To my sister Carole and her husband Lou and their children-my nephews Jason, Craig, and Adam, and my niece Nicole. And to Lou's mother Esther Smith.

To my brother Joel and his wife Harriet and their children—my nephew Paul and my niece Stacey.

To Esther and Lennie Cohen, my in-laws, and the special relatives that came with them: Fannie and Harry Engel; Bessie Cohen; Uncle Sam; Aunt Rona; Aunt Edie and Aunt Simi; Beverly and Alan Kaplan and their children—my nephews Jonathan (my first) and Daniel (my godson); Mark and Wanda Cohen and their children—my nephews Jessie and Ben.

To all my cousins, especially Bobby and Peter Matloff; Dick, Jay, and Billy Shapiro; Gary and Lorraine Gropman; Linda Golder; and to Brooklyn Stanley Rauch, who took me to see the 1955 Brooklyn Dodgers and to his wonderful wife Selma and his mother Mary.

To my best friends growing up Jimmy Miller and Ronnie Goldberg, and the others.

To my Chelsea contingency, Roberta, Steve, Roz, Jerry, Ralph, Bruce, Sheila, Arthur, Diane, Barbara, Adrienne, Billy, Eddie, Earl, Bev, Annette, Howard, and the rest of the gang.

To my Revere contingency, Bobby, Steve, Sheldon, Roz, Barbara, Carol, Phyllis, Russell, Newtie, Mosey, Nancy, and the rest of the gang.

To my best friend in high school Jimmy Feldbau, and to all the rest.

To my high school English teacher, Jack McCarron, who inspired me to read, think, and write in a new way, and to the others at Revere High School.

To my best friends in college Joe Auciello, Tony Pasciuto, and Sheila Cooper, and to all the others.

To my best friends in law school Alan Eizman, Barry Faber, Sheldon Fine, Don Glazer, Larry Hirsh, and Nelson Lovins, and to all the others.

To my law professors, particularly Professors Baldes, Elias, Nolan, Sargent, and Horovitz, who not only provided me a great legal education, but also helped shape my love of the law.

To Professor Alfred Maleson, who taught me the importance of being ethical and moral, particularly in the practice of law.

An extra special thank you to Professor John E. Fenton, Jr., a great law professor, who taught me that the law is more than a set of rules, it is an honorable profession, and that as a lawyer each of us has a great opportunity and sacred responsibility to help others in need.

To Al Ross who encouraged me to attend New York University Law School for my master's degree in labor law.

To my law professors, who encouraged and nurtured my interest in labor and employment law, particularly Professors Christianson, Kroner, Trotta, Vladeck, and Kaynard.

To Ralph Nader who taught me, when I was a law student, that the law is a noble profession and that the highest calling is to help those in need of protection from unfair, arbitrary, and abusive actions, and to have the courage to speak out against injustice, and to find ways to see that justice is done and also for his insightful suggestions to my book.

To my very dear friend and colleague Paul Tobias, who has done so much for the cause of protecting the rights of workers and in trying to create a fair and just working environment and to all his help and support with my book.

To Professor Laura Nader who provided excellent input for the final draft.

To my other colleagues of the National Employment Lawyers Association, Teri Chaw, Naida Axford, Joe Garrison, Joe Golden, Janice Goodman, Steve Heikens, Penny Kahan, Mary Ann Oakley, Wayne Outten, Cliff Palesky, Joe Posner, Barry Roseman, Vicki Abrahamson, Len Flamm, Fred Gittes, Doug Heiden, Larry Lapidus, Mary Ann Sedey, Kent Spriggs, Carla Barbosa, John Weiss, Craig Cornish, Gary Phelan, Robin Potter, Alan Levenson, Howard Reben, Kathy Bogas, Fred Gross, Nancy Smith, Peter van Schaick, Janette Johnson,

Janet Vecchia, Hal Gillespie, Roxanne Conlin, Alfred Blumrosen, Fritz Barnett, Robert Belton, Liz Glidden, Richard Seymour, Cathy Ventrell-Monsees, Judge Mark Bennett, Alice Ballard, Roxanne Conlin, Dennis Egan, Steve Platt, Jim Kaster, and all the others.

To my clients who have given me the privilege and opportunity of representing them in their struggle for dignity and respect in the workplace. To Jack, Eunice, Richard, Arthur, Frank, Paula, Lillie, Nina, Anthony, Phil, Argirios, Rona, Alice, Mike, Claire, Melody, Madeline, Tom, Bruce, Marilyn, Alan, Jay, Bob, Tammy, Mark, Francine, Catherine, Steve, George, John, Dan, Patricia, Nancy, Jim, Solange, Harry, Leo, David, Amy, Marjorie, Rebecca, Bill, Walter, Doug, Dennis, Mimi, Stephanie, Stuart, Dianne, Peter, Stanley, Kim, Paul, Don, Ann, Savina, Lisa, Francis, Theresa, Dom, Edric, Brian, Liana, Louanne, Katherine, Len, Valerie, Howard, Mary Ann, Barbara, Sheri, Elaine, Debbie, Roslyn, Mary, Joe, Maureen, Sharon, Gary, Claude, Janet, Leslie, Kevin, Kimbra, Roberta, Margaret, Jessica, Ed, Norma, Selma, Abdel, Karen, Francisco, Colleen, Linda, Joan, Ina, Grover, Loretta, Linn, Abraham, Aaron, Ilene, Sumner, Sid, Roger, Charles, Paula, Andrea, Ethel, Sanrda, Rebecca, Louis, Carol, Pamela, Ava, Merville, Tani, Martin, Wanda, Heather, Al, Cletus, Ted, Ginger, Jane, Gladys, David, Amar, Agatha, Chet, Jerry, Harry, Ralph, Henry, Karen, Rosetta, Earl, Andrew, Seraphin, Donna, Gail, Roy, Glenn, Camille, Jean, Lillie. If I have forgotten anyone I apologize.

To all the outstanding lawyers I worked with over the years. To Max Fixman, who gave me my first job in a law firm while I was a still law student.

To Sumner D. Goldberg, a first-rate trial lawyer and my first mentor.

To Gerry Shulman, Lennie Liberman, Stanley Glickman, Joel Cherwin, Morris Shubow, Richard Costa, Harley Gordon, Alan Berman, Burton Penn, Norman "Mickey" Lazarus, Dan Featherston, Barry Field, and Max Rubin.

To Judge Nancy Gertner, the best federal judge ever, a unique person whom I will always cherish, and my dear friend forever.

To leaders in the labor and employment law field that I have had the honor and privilege of working with over the years. To Larry Humphrey, Lester Slate, Loretta Attardo, S. Beville May, Ellen Messing, Dahlia Rudavsky, Ned Perry, Nancy Shilepsky, Joan Ackerstein, Jason Berger, Cathy Reuben, Harvey Schwartz, Ron Glover, Ann Leibowitz, Jeff Binder, Bob Johnson, Betty Gittes, Jim Paulson, Stuart Graham, Ken Kolpan, Cherie Gaines, Burt Rosenthal, Barry Guryan, Anne Taylor, Joel Finger, Wayne Soini, Liz Rodgers, Judge Sandra Lynch, John Mason, Marc Greenbaum, Bob Gordon, Kay Hodge, Paul Stanzler,

Ed Englander, Mark Schreiber, Joan Dolan, Emilie Athanasoulis, Bob Joy, Richard Ward, Wendy Kaplan, George Napolitano, Kevin Powers, Jeff Hirsch, Michael Avery, Margaret Burnham, Justine Brousseau, Frank V. McDermott, Jr., Rosemary Pye, John Martin, Marjorie O'Reilly, Jerry Levinsky, Charles Walker, David Rapaport, Maria Campagna, Nan Evans, Sally Fleschner, Sharon Litwin, Rob Mantell, Jon Margolis, Paul Merry, Lynn Weissberg, Jane Alper, Ann Clarke, Nadine Cohen, Sam Berk, Diane Saunders, Mark Irvings, Peter Berry, Tom Birmingham, Arthur Flamm, Warren Pyle, Nina Joan Kimball, Norman Holtz, Michael Gilman, Arnold Marrow, Bob Fuchs, Sandy Kowal, Susan Katz Hoffman, Marcia Wagner, Larry Katz, John Sikorski, Bill Benoit, Rick Reilly, Christina Newhall, Judge Margaret Marshall, Ilene Robinson Sunshine, Sarah Garraty, Joe Sandulli, Sal Salini, Monica Halas, Lynn Girton, Richard Alfred, Diane Drapeau, Maria Walsh, Diane Zarr Cochran, and all the others.

To other lawyers I have worked with over the years, Henry Owens, Terry Segal, Paul Sugarman, Howard Alperin, Judge William Young, Judge Howard Whitehead, Judge Walter Skinner, Judge Robert Keaton, Roland Orlandi, Mike Paris, Joel Pierce, Wendy Kaminer, Laurie Riccio, Leslie Gainer, Judge Elizabeth Butler, Joe Balliro, Judge Edith Fine, Dwight Allison, Bob Bouley, Alan Pierce, Lennie Glazer, Bill Dailey, Barbara Steadman, Willie Davis, Arthur Brecher, Doug Schwartz, Steve Zeidman, Mel Norris, Harold Brown, Charlie Demakis, Greg Demakis, Magistrate Robert Collings, Judge Patti Saris, Judge Michael Ponsor, Dick Gelinas, Judge Bonnie MacLeod, Judge Jonathan Brant, Judge Paul Chernoff, Judge John Cratsley, Judge Gordon Doerfer, Paul Demakis, Jeff Kitaeff, Ken Halperin, Dante Mummolo, Jordan Shapiro, Henry Friedman, Tom Trimarco, Harvey Peters, Leslie Bloomenthal, Jack Backman, Mike Dukakis, Neil Chayet, Jim Dilday, Phil Foley, Camille Sarrouf, Walter Costello, Jr., Leo Boyle, Jim Meehan, Jack Herlihy, Martin Aronson, Paul Goodale, Al Zabin, Alan Miller, Al Cullen, Jim Krasnoo, Jeff Stern, Fred Halstrom, Judy Wong, Jim Samels, J. Alden Lincoln, F. Lee Bailey, Alex Moschella, Steve Coren, Max Volterra, Carol Kenner, Geoffrey Wilson, Judge Constance Sweeney, Ray Kenney, Mary Ann Driscoll, Bernard Whalen, Mark Antine, Allan Rodgers, Tom Reilly, Dore Hunter, Paul Garrity, Nat Pitnof, Mike Angelini, Lennie Lewin, Tom Lebach, Judith Bernstein Tracy, Bob Hughes, and all the others.

To Harry McKenna and all the other court reporters that play such an essential role in the administration of justice.

To George McGrath, Austin Jones, Peter Skarmeas, Frank Tirrell and all the other caring clerks that provide the necessary support in running the courts.

To Judge John J. McNaught and all the other judges that are fair, kind, compassionate, caring, intelligent, competent, and strive to do justice.

To my colleagues at the Massachusetts School of Law at Andover, Larry Velvel, Louise Rose, Larry Beeferman, Tim Cagle, Tony Copani, Phil Coppola, Mike Coyne, Joe Devlin, Paula Dickinson, Peter Malaguti, Tom Martin, Connie Rudnick, Diane Sullivan, Judy Wolfe, and all the others.

To my colleagues at Northeastern University.

To my colleagues at Suffolk University Law School, Bernard Ortwein, Bill Corbett, Jim Whitters, Marc Perlin, Lorraine Cove, Carole Wagon, and all the others.

To my colleagues at Emory Law School, Professor Molly O'Brien, Amy Misner, Judge Susan Block, Judge Patti Broderick, Judge Diane Cannon, Myron Bromberg, Big Houston, Leila D'Aquin, Arthur Mallory, Judge Booker T. Shaw, Richard Rubin, and all the others.

To my friends Judy and Eddie, David, Michael, and Danny, Sam and Linda, Scott and Michael, Alan and Sue, Daniel, Jessica, and Joshua, Carol and Lennie, Pamela and Lennie, Roz and George, Todd, Nancy and John, Eric and Lauren, Mickey and Joyce, Mark, Jack and Marcia, Paul and Harriet, David and Barbara, Eddie and Maureen, Sue and Paul, Wayne, Jim "the hammer," Buddy, Don, and all the others.

To my accountants Pat and Peter and their staff who know.

To my barber Maureen who really knows for sure.

To the best neighbors, Martin and Jacqueline Horowitz and their children Rachel and Robert. Even they helped me with my book.

To my dearest friends, the Kerbers, Albee, Cynthia, Liz, and Jen.

To the wonderful people at the Cambridge Dispute Settlement Center, Gail Packer, Mimi Grosser, Jeanne Cleary, Art, and Mark Cohen who showed me another way to look at conflicts and provided the impetus for Chapter 16, The Better Way.

To my present colleagues George "The Burger" Bernstein and Marc Miller, two extraordinary people who make practicing law so much better.

To the staff who put up with me each day, Karen, Barbara, Anne, and Caron. To the other lawyers in the office Elisabeth LeBrun, Jim Tewhey, and John Romano. Thanks for all your help.

To my law students, who inspire me to teach them, not only the law, but also what the law can be if we respect each other as individuals, to seek the truth, and do justice.

Special thanks to my former law students Ed Becker for providing information included in the Appendices and Jeff Mazer for helping with some of the research.

To the wonderful, talented, and professional people who provided so much help in crafting this book. Anyone writing a book should have the good fortune to work with Rita Ferrandino, Leigh Melander, Ron Hampton, Gina Hagen, and Sue Carsten.

To my children, Rachel, David, and Naomi, who inspire me to want to help make the world a better place to live for them and for everyone else.

And most especially to my wife Caron, who is my best friend and has put up with my craziness all these wonderful years.

Quick Order Form

Telephone orders: To order additional copies of *Uncivil Rights,* call In Motion toll-free at 1 (888) 235-7947. Please have your credit card ready.

Please send more FREE information on:

❏ Other books   ❏ Speaking/seminars   ❏ Consulting

Name: _____

Organization: _____

Address: _____

City: _____ State: _____ Zip: _____

Telephone: _____

Fax: _____

E-mail address: _____

Lyra Enterprises, Ltd.
205 Pleasant Street
Marblehead, Massachusetts 01945